'What an incredible balance of education, definitions, frameworks, and industry updates combined with real-world examples and practical advice from years in the field. Combine a seasoned, award-winning content marketing professional and an established leader in higher education, and you'll get a book students will absorb in class and keep post-graduation.'

Cathy McPhillips – *Chief Growth Officer,*
Marketing Artificial Intelligence Institute

'With overly simplistic idioms like "content is king" and the rapid growth in generative AI technology, many think that content marketing is easy ("everyone's a marketer"). Quite the contrary, truly excellent content marketing requires strategic thinking, journalistic storytelling and, most importantly, a passion and curiosity to understand your customer and the challenges they face. With this first-ever content marketing textbook written by two authors with decades of experience in the trenches, instructors, students, and practitioners are now armed with an invaluable guide to plan and execute effective content marketing programs.'

John Graff – *Chief Marketing Officer and Lecturer,*
McCombs School of Business, The University of Texas at Austin

'Dan and Rebecca created a book that connects established theory with modern practice. Students who reviewed this book valued the ideas and said the content was unlike anything they had seen in their previous marketing and communication courses.'

Craig Davis – *Professor of Strategic Communication at*
Ohio University and former advertising agency executive

'I've known Dan for more than a decade and hired around a dozen of his former students. He has an uncanny ability to connect communication theory to real-world situations in a way that empowers students to apply what they learn and immediately jump-start their careers.'

Heather Whaling – *Founder and President,*
Geben Communication

Strategic Content Marketing

Strategic Content Marketing offers a comprehensive guide to planning, creating, implementing, and analyzing an effective content marketing strategy in practice.

Each chapter marries established theory with modern practice, illustrating concepts with real-world case studies and examples alongside interviews with prominent content marketers, including a foreword by Joe Pulizzi, founder of the Content Marketing Institute and often referred to as the Father of Content Marketing. Chapter objectives and summaries structure learning, while reflective questions and activities aid comprehension. On reading, students will understand:

- The definition, purpose, and practical implementation of a content marketing program
- The relationship between content marketing and broader marketing, strategic positioning, buyer personas, and research initiatives
- The most effective and valued forms of content marketing and how they are structured and used, including a special focus on digital and B2B content marketing
- How to create persuasive content and measure the effectiveness of content marketing
- The careers, associated competencies, and software technologies in the burgeoning field of content marketing.

This comprehensive text is perfect core and recommended reading for advanced undergraduate and postgraduate students studying content marketing, inbound marketing, marketing communications, digital and social media marketing, and public relations. In practice, the book is also highly valuable for practicing professionals studying for professional qualifications and looking to develop their skills. Online resources include instructor teaching slides, four-color images and templates, and chapter test bank questions.

Dan Farkas is a Lecturer in Strategic Communication at Ohio State University, US. Dan has taught courses on research methods, strategy, content creation, crisis communication, analytics, and measurement. Dan also advises chapters of the Public Relations Student Society of America. In Dan's 12 years of advising, his chapters have earned national recognition including Chapter of the Year, Student-Run Firm of the Year, Pacesetter, and Star Chapter. For this mentorship, Dan is one of only 20 people to have earned the Walt Seifert Award for Outstanding Service to PRSA. A nationally sought keynote speaker on emerging marketing,

Dan is also a business owner who helped clients receive media coverage from ESPN, the *New York Times*, the *Washington Post*, the BBC, NPR, and the Associated Press. Dan has earned more than 20 awards for his work in television news, which appeared on CNN, MSNBC, and SI.com. He currently hosts the *Strategic Communicator* podcast through the Marketing Podcast Network.

Rebecca Geier has worked for over 30 years with technical professionals to develop their brands and tell their company's stories to target audiences. She has worked in corporate marketing settings, founded and served as CEO of her own inbound and content B2B marketing agency, and has served as Chief Marketing Officer of two SaaS startups in the chemical and AI software industries. She has uniquely worked alongside engineers and scientists to develop specific, measurable content strategies and persuaded those who previously believed content marketing doesn't work for skeptical, technical audiences. Named by *The Wall Street Journal* editors among America's Most Innovative Entrepreneurs, Rebecca has dedicated her time to researching the modern, digital buying journey and published annual reports that are read by tens of thousands of B2B business leaders around the world. Based on her research and decades of practice, in 2016, she published her first book, *Smart Marketing for Engineers: An Inbound Marketing Guide to Reaching Technical Audiences*. She has served as the keynote speaker on the topic of inbound and content marketing globally, including serving for many years as a featured speaker at the premier annual event for content marketers, Content Marketing World.

Strategic Content Marketing

Creating Effective Content in Practice

Dan Farkas and Rebecca Geier

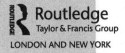
Routledge
Taylor & Francis Group

LONDON AND NEW YORK

Designed cover image: © MicroStockHub

First published 2024
by Routledge
4 Park Square, Milton Park, Abingdon, Oxon OX14 4RN

and by Routledge
605 Third Avenue, New York, NY 10158

Routledge is an imprint of the Taylor & Francis Group, an informa business

British Library Cataloguing-in-Publication Data
A catalogue record for this book is available from the British Library

ISBN: 978-1-032-43849-8 (hbk)
ISBN: 978-1-032-43848-1 (pbk)
ISBN: 978-1-003-36910-3 (ebk)

DOI: 10.4324/9781003369103

Typeset in Bembo
by Apex CoVantage, LLC

Access the Support Material: www.routledge.com/9781032438481

Contents

SECTION 2
Content Delivery

6   Earned Media and Its Role in Content Marketing

7   Owned Media (Part 1) – Websites, Blogs, and
Branded Publications

Foreword by Joe Pulizzi
The Father of Content Marketing

When I discovered that Rebecca and Dan were working on a textbook for the practice of content marketing, I simply had to get involved. Let me tell you why.

When I first began in marketing over 20 years ago, everything was about interruption. Put more simply, every company I worked with wanted to distract people from the content they were engaged in to tell consumers about the amazing products and services the company had.

The internet, in its infancy, actually made the problem worse. Marketing professionals thought that more channels meant more ways to spam consumers about why they were so incredible. The entire ordeal left me disgusted.

Then I found content marketing (then called many things, like custom publishing, custom media, and branded content). Content marketing was the idea that a brand could send valuable and compelling information to a targeted group of people consistently over time, building a loyal and trusted audience in the process. Once we earn that trust, then we gain the privilege of selling them our products and services. Because they trust us and love our content, they buy (and do they ever).

I thought this was too good to be true . . . an actual marketing practice that worked by first delivering value to customers (not pushing product)? I found my religion, and I went out to tell the world.

Only it didn't work. Every chief marketing officer I talked to wanted immediate results, and were totally enamored with ads of every kind (from 30-second spots to pay per click).

But slowly, things started to change. Google's importance in how buyers made decisions was a critical start. To make it to number one on Google for a keyword result, you had to have amazing content, and Google preferred content from credible sites that delivered valuable and regular information (think media sites).

Then social media came around. When a brand pitched a product on any social media channel, it only hurt the brand. Brand marketers began to realize that to make any kind of impact on social, they had to create valuable and consistent content.

Without fail, every new channel that developed and grew needed the same formula, from e-newsletters to videos to podcasts. In order to get any kind of attention, the brand had to create compelling content on a regular basis about something that was truly unique and valuable . . . and . . . do so over a long period of time (just like a media company).

Marketers began to learn that quick fixes and blasts of content were useless. They finally realized that they lost whatever control they thought they had. Buyers were now in complete control of their own buyers' journey.

The name of the game in gathering attention is now about building audiences . . . and audience building cannot happen without a long-term content marketing strategy.

As so, here we are, with this book in your hands or in your ears. Content marketing, as a discipline and a practice, won the battle because it is the correct way to market. Now, don't get me wrong; advertising is still the biggest game in town. Advertising is the sun while content marketing is barely Pluto (not even a planet).

But the Truth is out there. Content marketing provides a better, more human way to market. This book holds the key to the difference you can make, not only in your company but in yourself.

If content marketing hadn't come around, I would never have stayed in marketing. Thankfully, you have a choice . . . and you have chosen wisely.

Joe Pulizzi

5x content marketing author, including *Killing Marketing*,
Content Inc., and *Epic Content Marketing*
Find out about Joe at JoePulizzi.com

CHAPTER 1

Content Marketing Myths

Content is king.

It's a quote marketers and strategic communicators have used for years to describe the digital transformation of how brands communicate with customers in business-to-business (B2B) and business-to-consumer (B2C) marketing.

For centuries, products have been continually invented that completely transform our lives, from the commercial passenger jet that flies us halfway across the world in a matter of hours to Google's search engine that delivers content answers to billions of user questions in a matter of seconds. Our reliance on new medical inventions, for instance, has hardly felt so real or so personal in generations than during the coronavirus pandemic of 2020, when the world was brought to its knees by a molecule invisible to the naked eye called COVID-19. Policymakers could legislate, business leaders could pivot and protect margins, but only new products, from vaccines to new test kits, could save us.

Prospective buyers at thousands of companies work to innovate and invent new products and services to help them do their jobs better, faster, and cheaper. Non-profit organizations work to develop value to potential donors so they can help others. Billions of consumers go online to determine which product or service will help them live better lives.

The way people research and develop preference and consideration for products varies in the level of involvement and the extent to which their decisions are made rationally or emotionally, based on perceived risks and fears of making the wrong decision (Gourville & Norton, 2019). Central to earning a buyer's trust as a supplier is through education and demonstrating in a compelling way how the product or service offers improvement over the status quo in a relevant and compelling way.

A primary way marketers appeal to these prospective buyers is through content marketing (CM). CM is a type of marketing focused on creating, publishing, and distributing content for a target audience. Collectively, this content reflects a cohesive company brand that tells audiences an interesting story with the intent of motivating them to take action and ultimately become a customer. In an interview for this book, Robert Rose, Co-founder and Chief Strategy Officer of the Content Marketing Institute, stated that content marketing delivers value – education, inspiration, laughter, sadness – in order to build engaged and subscribed audiences with the goal of having an easier time reaching and influencing them.

Any company creating and selling new products has an uphill battle to convince consumers to believe in and ultimately purchase their product, and content marketing is a highly effective

DOI: 10.4324/9781003369103-1

means of achieving this outcome across product types. From promoting the latest smartphone to teenagers to introducing scientific-grade precision sensors to automotive test engineers, regardless of how seemingly dry or boring a product or service may be, marketers have the challenge and opportunity to create content that connects that product or service to the buyer's need and to elevate the story to a human level that makes the person consuming that content care.

We wrote this book so you can develop and execute a dynamic, integrated CM strategy. We chose to focus primarily on B2B content marketing strategies (i.e., purchases made for professional, business purposes) as marketers face distinct challenges from B2C markets (a consumer walking into a store to buy a pair of shoes). The differences between B2B and B2C buying decisions "are rooted in the nature and needs of [the] customers' buying criteria and purchasing processes, as well as in the impact of B2B marketing choices on business strategy" (Cespedes & Narayandas, 2019). However, many of the concepts explained, such as product positioning and developing buyer personas, apply across B2B and B2C markets; moreover, the process marketers follow to create a content marketing plan and the many types of content explained in the chapters of this book are similar across both markets. Any marketer working for any organization can use these concepts to create meaningful connections with current and potential customers.

We provide detailed plans and authentic examples to empower the reader to start their own content marketing plan.

- We first help you strategize your content – identifying your brand, researching your buyers, and positioning your message.
- We next help you create your content – drafting and editing persuasive content and creating the types of content across earned and owned marketing channels and those that B2B buyers value most, including product websites, white papers, videos, and customer testimonials.
- Finally, we help you gather and interpret the results of your CM strategy as well as learn about careers in content marketing.

We organized this book to help you complete content tasks that you might perform quarterly and annually in addition to providing a reference that you can use daily or anytime you are called on to create content. As a result, our book functions equally in both the workplace and the classroom.

CM is a relatively new term and still a nascent profession, and its role in and value to organizations is still not widely understood or cohesively implemented. Many of the tasks associated with effective CM are also tasks most everyone performs every day, including writing, speaking, and collaborating, so we may not associate them with requiring unique skill. After all, you write daily; what additional value would a content "specialist" bring to your organization? Therefore, before we relay the fundamentals of CM in the following chapters, we want to dispel six myths related to content marketing. Let's introduce and then bust the most common content marketing myths.

MYTH 1: TRADITIONAL MARKETING STRATEGIES WORK AS WELL TODAY AS YESTERDAY

The first myth assumes the traditional marketing strategies you used in the past are just as effective today. These strategies could include attending in-person trade shows or printing product catalogs.

The buyer journey has changed, and the strategies that were effective yesterday are less effective (and, in some cases, nearly obsolete) today. Technology has transformed whole industries, shifting the control of content delivery and consumption away from traditional publishers and empowering the individual user to choose what, when, and how to consume. In her first book, *Smart Marketing for Engineers: An Inbound Marketing Guide to Reaching Technical Audiences*, Rebecca explained the challenge modern business leaders and marketers face:

> "*Today, the buyer is in charge. For engineers [for example], who are voracious information seekers, it is nirvana. They can search and search and search online . . . without ever being interrupted or bothered. . . . With buyers in control, the marketer's challenge and opportunity is to get found where and when the buyer is.*"
>
> (Geier, 2016)

Over the last 20 years, companies have transformed how they market to consumers. Before internet search engines, as crazy as it sounds, buyers actually used their phones and called companies to ask questions as part of their product research. In turn, companies produced expensive educational content such as glossy print brochures and product catalogs they mailed to prospects that served as the cornerstone of their marketing efforts to drive awareness and consideration. Seemingly overnight, as early internet adoption grew, buyers started relying on company websites as their primary source of information. This marked the beginning of the digital transformation of marketing as a discipline with massive investments made in a company's website powered by new, original content published by marketing teams with support from subject matter experts including product information, videos, corporate news, and in-depth educational resources such as white papers.

While the sources that buyers value may have shifted from analog to digital, the reason they seek content remains the same. Consumers need high-quality information they can trust to help them make the best purchase decision to meet their needs. To meet them where they are, companies have had to pivot not only marketing spend but also marketing mindset. Where they used to control who received their catalog – the only way to get it was if you were on the company's mailing list or you called them to request a copy be mailed to you – today, customers don't wait for, or want, a 1,000-page annual product catalog to come in the mail. They go to their favorite search engine and trusted websites to search for the exact information they want, when they want it. They control, at their fingertips, what they read and research by scrolling and clicking through content they find relevant, interesting, and trustworthy.

In this post-COVID-19 era, even analog lead-generating marketing tactics that remain popular and valuable, such as trade shows and in-person meetings, are losing their value given that many have been canceled, and attendance has not returned to pre-COVID levels. The pandemic hammered the last nail in the coffin of companies who relied on outdated and expensive means of marketing. Sales and marketing teams who do not evolve with CM as a core focus will miss the opportunity to connect with their potential buyers where they are, struggle to compete, and risk failing all together. Digital CM strategies and their use of evolving technology have the potential to reach a larger audience for less money, delivering a greater return on investment (ROI) that's more efficient and provides a better experience for the consumer since they can find information when and where they want it.

MYTH 2: IF YOU CREATE IT, THEY WILL CLICK IT

The next myth assumes you recognize that your potential buyers' preferences and behaviors have evolved, and therefore, your content needs to pivot accordingly. You get that part and believe you just need to create persuasive content and the prospects will roll in. We wish.

Stop and consider the amount of content you are saturated with daily.

- How many emails did you receive today? Not only from colleagues or friends but also external audiences competing for your attention?
- Did you follow the news today? How did you receive this information?
- Did you visit a trusted website or listen to a podcast during your morning commute? Or check in on your go-to social media site?

How many results did you get from your last Google search? Despite the hundreds of thousands or millions of search results, did you advance past page two of those results? If you're like the majority of web users, the answer is no. Studies have shown that the vast majority of clicks on Google occur on the first page, and, in one that studied mobile usage, in all the results on the first page, 28.5% of clicks happen on the first result (Beus, 2020) (see Figure 1.1).

GOOGLE CTR PER RANKING

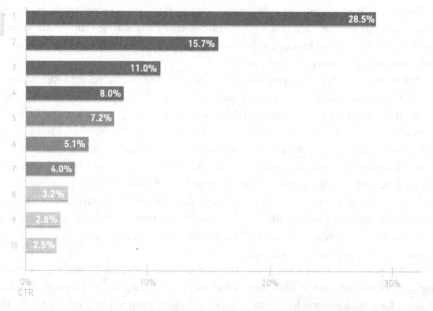

FIGURE 1.1 Despite the hundreds of thousands or millions of search results shown on a given search on a site like Google, most people don't advance past page two. Studies have shown that the vast majority of clicks on Google occur on the first page, including the chart shown here that shows the percentage of clicks by mobile users on ranked results on a search engine results page. The study found 28.5% of clicks happen on the first result, nearly double the clicks of the second ranked, which had 15.7% of total clicks.

Source: Beus, 2020.

Now, let's just think about the sphere of your company and target market. Consider the amount of content your company generates on its products and services and then add that to the amount of content your competitors generate on their products and services. How does your company's content rank on those search engine results? What's unique or more interesting about your content to encourage users to click on yours instead of your competitor's?

The internet doubles in size every two years, resulting in a 50-fold growth of content and data from 2011 to 2020 (Jones, 2019). Creating quality content is vital but no longer enough. The chances are small that you will grow awareness and trust at scale if your content does not rank high in your user's search; if your content is not trustworthy and uniquely valuable; or if your content is not immediately and sufficiently appealing enough to motivate the prospect to click in, open, and read more.

Your prospective buyers will always have unlimited and growing content choices, so your content strategy can never be static, and your content quality cannot just be good. CM is core to how companies build awareness and trust in our modern customer-controlled marketplace. You need an agile, fluid content strategy with high content-quality standards executed on a consistent basis, and that only begins with an ambitious and clear vision.

MYTH 3: CONTENT MARKETING ISN'T MY JOB

The third myth assumes you don't *do* content marketing. By this, we mean you assume CM is not part of your daily job duties. The reality is that, to some extent, everyone in a company is doing content marketing.

Let's take the role of an engineer for instance. In higher education, curricula for STEM degrees are packed with math and science courses (in part for accreditation reasons), which leaves little focus for strengthening interpersonal or writing skills. In fact, STEM majors identify little association between the quality of their verbal and written communication skills and overall career advancement and satisfaction (Pulko & Parikh, 2003).

However, if you are currently working in a STEM field, you probably write and communicate a lot. For example, engineers typically write for 30% of their workday, a percentage that increases for middle- and upper-level management positions (Leydens, 2008).

Even if writing and public speaking are not part of their direct role, effective content marketing can't happen without the input and direction of subject matter experts (SME). SMEs are often called upon by sales teams to provide pre-sales support with prospective customers or post-sales advice as a customer's project and application needs grow or change and by marketing to explain product-related topics to the media or investors or assist with creation of in-depth content such as white papers. The content that SMEs create or help develop – written, phone, presentation, or virtual – are all examples of content marketing and illustrate the critical role SMEs play in effective CM programs.

Most content marketing professionals have the skills to distill and communicate complex technical information but not the scientific knowledge to conceptualize and develop technical products and services. It takes both the STEM and the CM experts to successfully execute content marketing, especially in B2B technical markets. The same holds true in all other industries. A team-based environment that CM fosters benefits the marketers, the SMEs, and the work everyone does to create a valuable product or service.

MYTH 4: CONTENT MARKETING WON'T WORK ON TECHNICALLY MINDED, LOGICAL AUDIENCES

The fourth myth assumes marketing doesn't work for technically minded, logical decision makers, and content marketing by association won't either. There are two primary beliefs supporting this myth. First, there are many vivid stereotypes of slick marketing, such as the used car salesperson who suckers a vulnerable customer into buying a lemon. Or the countless infomercials that promise to make us fitter, healthier, and more attractive for only $19.99. This salesmanship and promising approach is especially suspect to the more analytical, technically minded audiences who make decisions with logic and evidence. Second, buyers who make decisions based on thorough analysis are concerned with reducing risk in their decisions, so special offers or the promise from brand alone are insufficient to convince the logical, analytical buyer.

It is for exactly these reasons that content marketing is, in fact, an especially valuable and effective means of marketing to a logical, technically minded audience. These buyers want information they can trust; they want to self-educate and find resources on their own from the sources they value and choose throughout their buyer journey. As a result, content marketing is actually one of the most effective marketing approaches you can use to build awareness and trust with these buyers since they want to be in control of what information they consume and how and when they it. This also underscores the critical importance of producing high-quality content prospective buyers find valuable and trustworthy. Said another way, content marketing must be as smart as the people it targets.

A story of one CM (content marketer) demonstrates this well. As he worked alongside recognized researchers in neurology, reproductive medicine, and musculoskeletal pathology to write federal funding grant proposals for the National Institutes of Health (NIH), he identified the features and benefits of the proposed study and then connected those to the broader impacts that NIH was seeking and emphasized how funding would advance public health and awareness. He was engaging these researchers in a content strategy to help them market their ideas more effectively. Researchers learned to connect their technical expertise with what the buyers (in this case, the NIH grant reviewers) wanted. The results were massively successful in achieving funding for important, future-oriented research.

MYTH 5: *CONTENT MARKETING* IS A BUZZWORD

The fifth myth is that *content marketing* is a buzzword that will fade.

In fact, *content marketing* was coined in 2008 by the Content Marketing Institute, and in its second decade in practice, it is continually gaining adoption in industry as a mainstream marketing methodology. Thousands of people attend the annual Content Marketing World conference, and you can access countless books, podcasts, articles, and blog posts on the topic. Careers for content marketing professionals have been trending up over the last ten years. As shown in data from Google Trends (No Author, 2013–2023) tracking "interest over time," the interest in "content marketing jobs" has trended up from a value below 50 in 2013 to frequently above 50 since then. As of the completion of this book in February 2023, global search interest had a value of 99, meaning it is near the peak score of 100 in popularity (Google Trends) (see Figure 1.2).

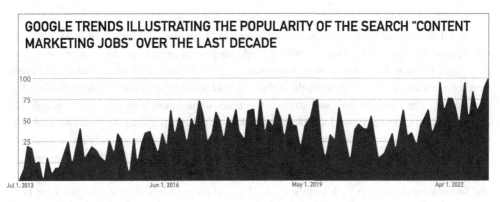

GOOGLE TRENDS ILLUSTRATING THE POPULARITY OF THE SEARCH "CONTENT MARKETING JOBS" OVER THE LAST DECADE

FIGURE 1.2 Careers for content marketing professionals have been trending up over the last ten years. As shown in data from Google Trends tracking "interest over time," the interest in "content marketing jobs" has trended up from a value below 50 in 2013 to frequently above 50 since then. As of the completion of this book in February 2023, global search interest had a value of 99, meaning it is near the peak score of 100 in popularity.

There is also significant growth in advertised content-related positions (and this might be a reason you picked up this book). For example, Contently.com reported a 33% increase in year-to-year positions for content manager, content director, and content marketing specialist (Skane, 2019). These results signal exciting news if you seek a future content marketing–oriented career. However, this also means you are a pioneer of sorts, working in unfamiliar territory, learning alternative methods of performing tasks, and working with colleagues who may be unfamiliar with the duties of a content marketer. The relative newness of the job title *content marketer* also means the associated skills and qualifications are expanding. Job titles like *content marketer* and *content strategist* are not attempts to rebrand something stale. Rather, these positions entail a series of skills that you must develop, apply, fail at, and then improve on over time.

MYTH 6: ANYONE CAN DO CONTENT MARKETING

The final myth is the assumption that anyone can do CM, and it doesn't take any special preparation.

This myth is actually partly true. Anyone *can* do it – but only after training and substantial planning. As we show throughout the book, CM is not simply publishing a blog, producing a white paper, or recording a webinar and then waiting as the prospects roll in. If it were merely about producing disparate pieces of content to the best of your ability, we wouldn't need to devote an entire book to explaining it. In fact, CM strategy should focus less on how many pieces of content you produce and more on the integrated approach and value you create with that content.

In an increasingly competitive market, companies are seeing the value of CM. Since 2000, over 50% of Fortune 500 companies have disappeared. We don't attribute this decline solely to poor CM; however, many of these companies disappeared because they could not weather the digital disruption that has forever changed how people communicate (No Author, 2018).

John Deere exemplifies the way a Fortune 500 company has adapted to and thrived through this digital disruption. They began publishing their own magazine, *The Furrow*, in 1895, when no other publication existed for farmers, with the sole purpose of providing education to farmers so they could be more successful in their work. Over 120 years later, 45% of its readers read every word of every issue, almost half go to the website to read about their products, and 90% of readers surveyed say *The Furrow* is their sole source of industry information (Jones, 2014). Through *The Furrow* and other content types, John Deere has used CM to drive traffic to their website, establishing the company as a trusted information source and establishing an engaged and captive audience.

While John Deere may have hypothetically seen satisfactory or even better near-term sales results by investing those same marketing dollars in advertisements in traditional agricultural and farming media outlets such as magazines, TV, and radio shows, they would not have built their own audience they could directly access and engage with; instead, they would be paying third parties to access those publications' readers, viewers, and listeners. By committing to creating and publishing *The Furrow* – a form of owned content marketing called branded magazines that we describe in Chapter 7 – John Deere has developed a trusting, dedicated audience they can communicate with directly.

WHY YOU NEED THIS BOOK

We began this chapter (and the book) by dispelling content myths because the perceptions of a topic are often the barriers to achieving success. You will encounter roadblocks and resistance to your content strategy. Any meaningful organization-wide content strategy involves change, and people are typically resistant to (at least initially) anything new. Understanding why these content myths exist – and why they are myths, not truths – will better inform how you begin your CM process, how you articulate this strategy to stakeholders, and how you can effectively collaborate with others in your organization to execute this strategy.

We wrote this book for anyone who has a story to tell about a product or service, such as:

- Engineers and scientists who need to promote their innovations and drive demand from potential buyers
- Small business leaders who want to showcase a different way to enjoy an experience
- Non-profits that seek to highlight how charitable donations transform the lives of young people

These professionals need insight on how to effectively invest limited resources to earn the greatest ROI. Content marketing is a newer solution to that age-old business need. This book is organized to explain content marketing in three successive sections:

- Section 1 of this book guides you through the foundational elements of content strategy including product positioning, buyer personas, and content planning aligned to integrated marketing and business goals.
- Section 2 shows you how to create persuasive content and provides in-depth instruction and real-world examples of the most common types of content. Chapter 6 covers earned

media content types such as news releases and thought leadership articles; Chapters 7 and 8 cover owned media types including the company website, blog, branded publications, and videos; Chapters 9 and 10 round out this section by describing product collateral and B2B content types, respectively.

- Section 3 focuses on the technology and tools driving content marketing and measuring its effectiveness. Additionally, we describe the transformation being driven by disruptive technologies such as artificial intelligence and virtual and augmented reality and the outlook on content marketing careers.

Everyone creates content. For the professional leading content marketing, this book serves as a guide to help you make your content memorable and appealing to your audience. Your role in the organization may be relatively new because the official job title of *content marketer* is still a nascent role. Even the most well-intentioned and supportive managers might not fully understand your skills and qualifications or what it takes to build and execute a CM program. Your list of expected job duties could be a simultaneous mix of the murky and unduly ambitious.

WHY WE WROTE THIS BOOK

With the growing adoption of content marketing in industry, the demand for skilled CM professionals is at its peak (see Figure 1.2). While there are many valuable and popular books available from professional practitioners, they differ from this book in various ways, such as:

- Lacking depth
- Solely targeting specific types of consumers such as entrepreneurs or business leaders
- Focusing on specific content types such as long-form books and courses or content for certain channels such as PR
- Lacking rigorous research

Unlike these more narrow, industry- or channel-specific books written for the current practitioner, this book is the first comprehensive, research-backed textbook written for academic instructors teaching college-level courses in the 3000 and 4000 level as well as introductory writing courses at the 2000 level. This book was written to become a trusted, useful resource for faculty who haven't built a content marketing arc or fully vetted a buyer's journey with professional examples that connect current trends with established theory, as well as learning objectives, test bank questions, and supportive instruction materials.

While the text is suitable for use by practitioners, *Strategic Content Marketing: Creating Effective Content in Practice* is primarily written for students who aren't familiar with the technical tools or the storytelling arc. The book includes specific strategies in jargon-free language that students can grasp and immediately employ and original interviews with prominent content marketers, including a foreword by Joe Pulizzi, founder of the Content Marketing Institute.

Another distinctive feature of this book is the authors. For over 30 years, Rebecca has worked with technical professionals to develop their brand and tell their company's stories to target audiences. She has worked in corporate marketing settings, founded and served as CEO of her own marketing agency serving B2B technical markets, and served as Chief Marketing Officer of two SaaS startups in the chemical industry and AI software. She has uniquely worked alongside engineers and scientists to develop specific, measurable content strategies and persuaded those who previously believed marketing doesn't work for skeptical, technical audiences. Named by *The Wall Street Journal* editors among America's Most Innovative Entrepreneurs, Rebecca has also dedicated time to researching the modern buying journey and published annual reports that are read by tens of thousands of engineering business leaders around the world. Based on her research and decades of practice, in 2016, she published her book *Smart Marketing for Engineers: An Inbound Marketing Guide to Reaching Technical Audiences*.

Dan Farkas is a Lecturer in Strategic Communication at Ohio State University, where he teaches courses on research, strategy, content creation, measurement, and analytics. The BBC and Mashable are some of the media outlets that featured Dan as a thought leader on the changing landscape of strategic communication and how we can make the most of it. He has helped clients receive media coverage from the *New York Times*, NPR, *Forbes*, ESPN, and the Associated Press. You can currently hear him on *The Strategic Communicator Podcast*, part of the Marketing Podcast Network.

Dan is also a business owner who practices the craft when not chasing late homework assignments. His latest venture is PassPR, a project that bridges the gap between higher education, employee needs, and student capacity.

In a former life, Dan earned more than 20 awards for his work in television news. His work appeared on CNN, MSNBC, and SI.com.

Collectively, our experiences represent the marketing and communication aspects that inform a winning CM strategy. Throughout this book, we share our experiences with CM and offer examples and heuristics we have created as part of our own work. We also include original interviews with industry-leading experts in CM to offer you the most current, substantive perspectives on content marketing and related topics.

Regardless of your CM needs, we wrote this book to support instructors, excite future CM practitioners, and serve as a foundation for current practitioners. The content in the upcoming chapters will challenge and inspire you to dive into the new and fast-growing world of content marketing – the industry needs bright, energetic practitioners excited and prepared to lead promising careers. If you're ready for these challenges, turn the page and let's begin.

CITATIONS

Beus, J. "Why (almost) everything you knew about Google CTR is no longer valid." July 14, 2020. Retrieved from: www.sistrix.com/blog/why-almost-everything-you-knew-about-google-ctr-is-no-longer-valid/#What-and-how-we-measured

Cespedes, F.V., & Narayandas, D. *Business-to-Business Marketing*. Harvard Business Publishing. December 2019.

Geier, R. *Smart Marketing for Engineers: An Inbound Guide to Reaching Technical Audiences*. Rockbench. January 2016.

Gourville, J.T., & Norton, M.I. *"Consumer behavior and the buying process."* *Harvard Business Publishing.* December 19, 2019.

Jones, C. "The content future: Content automation + personalization." *Content Science Review.* December 1, 2019.

Jones, C. *The Content Advantage (Clout 2.0): The Science of Succeeding at Digital Business through Effective Content.* New Riders. 2019.

Jones, D. "The original content marketers – John Deere and The Furrow." 2014. Retrieved from: www.contentmarketingworld.com/david-jones-original-content-marketers-john-deere-furrow-cmworld-recap/

Leydens, J.A. "Novice and insider perspectives on academic and workplace writing: Toward a continuum of rhetorical awareness." *IEEE Transactions on Professional Communication.* 2008.

No Author, DXC Technology. "Digital transformation is racing ahead and no industry is immune." *Harvard Business Review.* March 9, 2018. Retrieved from: https://hbr.org/sponsored/2017/07/digital-transformation-is-racing-ahead-and-no-industry-is-immune-2

No Author, Google Trends. "Interest over time." July 1, 2013–February 22, 2023. Retrieved from: https://trends.google.com/trends/explore?date=2013-07-01%202023-02-22&geo=US&q=content%20marketing%20jobs

Pulko, S.H., & Parikh, S. "Teaching 'soft' skills to engineers." *International Journal of Electrical Engineering Education.* 2003.

Skane, A. "Study: What 1,400 job posts teach us about content marketing hires." 2019. Retrieved from: https://contently.com/2019/04/11/content-marketing-hires-study/

SECTION 1

Content Strategy

CHAPTER 2

New Product Development and Positioning and Its Role in Content Marketing

---

LEARNING OBJECTIVES

1. Understand why companies develop new products, the strategies they use, and how this affects content marketing
2. Contrast a waterfall and an agile approach to product development and how a SWOT analysis is used
3. Examine the Four Ws of product positioning and why these are critical references for content marketing

---

INTRODUCTION

Products are the critical engine that drives revenue in companies. Without new products, companies must rely on existing products to support the business. That's a losing strategy in today's fast-moving technology-driven world because customers are apt to switch to competitors with new products that are better, faster, and cheaper. Thus, the ability to launch successful new products plays a major role in a company's competitiveness and value. New products may fulfill consumers' essential needs, or they may improve their lives along a dimension important to the consumer. New products are launched based on a company's competitive strategy and the landscape of competing products on the market (Miles et al., 1978; Dickson, 1992).

The challenge, however, is that creating new products is no easy feat. It requires intensive analysis, thorough development, and thoughtful consideration to position and differentiate products in the market.

To position a product, marketers must define the characteristics of a product that separate and distinguish it as different from and "better" than existing or competitive offerings. Scott Rust, Senior Vice President of **Global** Product R&D at National Instruments, said it best:

"Product positioning starts at the very beginning of the exploration and product definition phases of new product development. For National Instruments, that often starts with internal positioning within our

DOI: 10.4324/9781003369103-3

own portfolio. With tens of thousands of products that each accomplish key market objectives, often a new product fills a gap of features that, when combined with the right combination of other existing products, becomes valuable to promote to customers for specific applications."

(Scott Rust interview)

The CM's role is to showcase any product gap and help customers understand what makes a new product offering distinctive. How? Through effective positioning and messaging.

- CMs must first thoroughly understand the market, the positioning of competing products, and the customer needs and applications that ultimately led to each new and differentiated product.
- Next, a CM will transform the internal product positioning documentation into public-facing content that educates and motivates potential customers to purchase and use the new product.
- In particular, a CM must understand and communicate why the product was created and how it uniquely helps customers over other products on the market.

This chapter will provide CMs with an overview of new product development and examine how the process informs product positioning and content marketing.

COMPANY STRATEGIES FOR NEW PRODUCTS

There are four competitive strategies for developing new products: prospectors, analyzers, differentiated defenders, and low-cost defenders. Each strategy influences the speed at which companies commercialize new products, the extent to which products are customized, and how they are priced (Miles et al., 1978; Walker & Ruekert, 1987; Slater et al., 2007).

Prospectors take a "product leader" or "pioneer" strategy to rapidly develop and introduce innovative new products. Initial versions of technical products are often relatively limited in function and expensive when compared to future products. For example, Motorola commercialized the first cellular phone in 1983, which provided a maximum talk time of 35 minutes, had limited geographical reach, and cost nearly USD 4,000 (Gregersen, 2013; Edwards, 2018).

What a CM should know: Prospectors emphasize the new application enabled by new technology and appeal to early adopter consumers.

Analyzers are "fast followers" who quickly follow the prospector with their competing new product. Analyzers learn from the successes and mistakes of the prospectors, study customer use of new technology, and develop a product that offers either a technical improvement or a lower price (Shankar et al., 1998).

For example, a year after Sony introduced the PlayStation 2, Microsoft launched the Xbox, which provided consumers with faster processing speed, greater memory, and higher-quality graphics and audio.

What a CM should know: Analyzers also emphasize the same message as the prospectors – the new application that appeals to early adopters and the early majority – but further stress the improvement of the product and the corresponding limitation or weakness of the first product to market.

Differentiated defenders focus on small consumer niche markets and provide specialized tailoring of a product for a unique consumer group with premium customer service and higher prices (Walker & Ruekert, 1987). Differentiated defenders aim to maximize sales in the niche market through personalization of product design and high-quality customer relationships rather than competing on price or product technology improvements to win the larger market.

For example, Rackspace, an IT cloud services provider, provides customized solutions for Amazon, Google VMware, and other cloud partners' products to their customers and takes pride in being a leader due to their superior technical expertise and fanatical experience. This customer-centric, high-engagement approach led Rackspace to win the North America 2022 Partner Lifecycle Services Award by VMWare in partnership with IDC (No Author, April 2022).

What a CM should know: Differentiated defenders focus CM on specific segment needs and dedicate marketing and customer support resources to this group only.

Low-cost defenders appeal to consumers by providing the lowest-price alternative to competitors. They do this by optimizing production costs through supply chain, manufacturing, and distribution.

The prototypical low-cost defender is Dell, which introduced a direct seller model in the 1990s that eliminated the middle man retailer and offered built-to-order computers at a lower price than its competitors (Strickland, 1999). By 1999, Dell became the largest PC manufacturer and surpassed the sales of competitors such as IBM, Compaq, Gateway, and Packard Bell. The entry of low-cost defenders into a market marks the transition of a developing market into a mature market and the commodification of a technology that appeals to the mainstream market (Moore, 2014).

What a CM should know: Low-cost defenders emphasize marketing products more on price than on features.

THE NEW PRODUCT DEVELOPMENT PROCESS

Creating a new product takes shape over a series of phases inclusively referred to as the new product development (NPD) process. The NPD process includes a well-defined series of stages and gates at which teams explore innovative concepts, develop prototypes, evaluate products for performance, and analyze manufacturing feasibility (Griffin, 1997).

Companies use NPD to efficiently vet well-performing and profitable new product ideas. By adhering to a stringent process with thorough up-front analysis of new product ideas, companies save time and money by letting only the best ideas progress through each gate to the latter stages of development. This careful analysis also saves employees and departments significant work – including CMs.

From early feasibility and competitive research to market sizing and sales forecasting, the NPD process requires a cross-functional team. Members of different departments bring expertise in their discipline, work together through the process, share market knowledge and technical data, and own disparate pieces of a holistic schedule (Fredericks, 2005).

Most companies progress through NPD process in four stages: (1) identifying potential new products and conducting a business analysis, (2) product development, (3) performance evaluation and testing, and (4) product launch (Booz Allen Hamilton et al., 1982; Goulding, 1983; Griffin & Page, 1997; Grönlund et al., 2010).

Stage 1: Identify Potential New Products and Conduct a Business Analysis

In the first stage, companies identify new product ideas in alignment with their competitive strategy (Bhuiyan, 2011). Ideas for innovative new products may come from many sources, both internal and external (Goulding, 1983; Booz Allen Hamilton et al., 1982).

For instance, in technology companies, technical personnel in R&D departments have the primary responsibility for remaining on the cutting edge of technical innovations and identifying potential commercial products. Alternatively, employees in sales are closely aligned to customers, partners, and competitors to get ideas based on market interactions or observations (Kotler et al., 2006). Externally, a company may employ market researchers to provide new product ideas. The goal of this first NPD stage is to produce a breadth of ideas that the firm can select from to identify the most promising ones (Booz Allen Hamilton et al., 1982; Bhuiyan, 2011).

The expected return on investment (ROI), which is the difference between company expenses to produce the new product and profit realized from the new product after launch, influences whether new products proceed through the subsequent stages of the NPD process. Ultimately, organizations select competitive products they can profitably deliver to consumers (Kotler & Armstrong, 2010). The marketing and sales departments are responsible for positioning potential new products by identifying customer needs and desired product features and benefits and contributing a business analysis of competing products available on the market. This detailed business analysis helps verify the potential sales revenue forecast of a new product in target markets as well as expected development time and costs (Aulet, 2013; Hart, 2003).

What a CM should know: In particular, the business analysis data finalized in this stage offers valuable insights for CMs into target customer needs, key product features, and competitive products with points of differentiation.

Stage 2: Product Development

After a product concept receives a market evaluation, the development stage begins when a company specifies product features, builds a prototype, and evaluates the prototype's effectiveness. This phase shifts from research to development through combining product knowledge with market and customer needs (Fredericks, 2005).

As a product nears the end of development, the marketing department develops the marketing and CM plan. Without strong integration and communication between marketing and the product development team, the CM plan likely won't be ready for product launch, or the information will be incomplete or inaccurate.

For example, in the early days of Rebecca Geier's tenure as head of corporate communications at National Instruments, the company struggled with coordinating product launch
marketing with the product's actual readiness.

Based on the expected R&D schedule, the product marketing and communications teams
would organize the marketing content for the product launch for a certain month, week, and
often even specific day with activities such as web pages, white papers, product brochures,
videos, and scheduled press coverage all set for release at specific times. Unfortunately, as is the
case in many organizations, the development and manufacturing processes encountered issues
that resulted in the product being delayed.

Rescheduling a product launch creates an enormous amount of work for the marketing
team to reschedule and revise launch plans and secure activities such as postponing meetings with
the press, changing the timing of advertisements, and replacing planned new product messaging
and demonstrations at trade shows. Such changes would cost the company through additional
employee time, charges for changing or canceling activities, and risked diminished consumer confidence if news leaked to the public that the new product wasn't ready for its original release date.

After National Instruments adopted a more rigorous NPD process and improved communication between departments, product release delays decreased, and the organization became
more efficient in preparing for and executing new product launches.

What a CM should know: The features of a product often change during this phase. A CM
must be prepared for the preliminary product and content marketing plan to be continually
updated as the product definition changes. With the wide spectrum of new products, from a
new piece of software to a new medical device, this stage can take months or years to complete
and vary greatly in cost and complexity.

Stage 3: Performance Evaluation and Testing

Once the product is fully developed, it undergoes evaluation and testing so that the manufac-
tured product (rather than the R&D prototype) is fully validated and verified to ensure it functions according to specifications and performance claims (Hart et al., 2003).

At this stage, companies internally evaluate the product for quality control (QC) and may
evaluate externally with select consumers through beta testing. The nature of the product will
influence the length and logistics of this phase.

What a CM should know: This is when teams finalize marketing communications and content plans to prepare for the product launch. After testing is complete, the product is ready for
the final stage, the product launch.

Stage 4: Product Launch

The product launch is when a brand publicly announces the new product and makes it available
for sale. At this point, the primary responsibility of NPD shifts from the product development
team to the manufacturing, marketing, and sales departments.

During cross-functional meetings in this stage, the sales team uses CM materials created
specifically for sales sessions, referred to as sales enablement content. Feedback from sales helps

marketing improve product messaging because of salespeople's close customer relationships and their responsibility for ultimately selling the product in the market.

A product launch and market introduction process may last up to a full year or more, depending on how revolutionary the product is and how much effort it takes to educate the market.

Once a product launches, brands analyze the product's commercial success and make product improvements to further its position in the market. To remain competitive and avoid customers switching to a competitor's product, companies continually introduce newer versions of the product with improved features and different levels of products with various price points to appeal to different customer types.

What a CM should know: The marketing department's primary role is to promote the product and generate interest from potential buyers, known as demand generation. In parallel with marketing, the sales team works directly with potential customers, often meeting with them virtually or in person to demonstrate the product, understand their unique application and needs, and ultimately make a sale.

As products launch, evolve, and improve, so too will the marketing and content plan (explained in Chapter 4).

Managing the New Product Development Process

Two popular methods that teams use to manage the NPD process, as well as project management more broadly, are Waterfall and Agile. While both methods include the NPD stages listed in this chapter, the methods differ primarily in the speed of implementation and number of development cycles.

Waterfall is a more formal linear or sequential approach that follows the stage-gate model for new product development (see Figure 2.1). The Waterfall process is intended to be completed one stage or step at a time and requires approvals to move through the "gate" to the next stage.

Let's take the example of developing a new company website using the Waterfall method.

- In the first stage, developers define all requirements and plan all details of the website including site structure, hierarchy, design, and functionality, such as e-commerce, along with the development and hosting platform (such as Adobe, HubSpot, or WordPress). Next, all project stakeholders review these requirements. Upon approval, the project passes through the gate to the second stage.
- In the second stage, the website is designed with web page content, layout, and functionality features developed into a complete working model.
- After approval of all design features, the website moves into usability testing and performance evaluation.
- Only after testing is complete and all the errors, or "bugs," are corrected is the website approved for release and launch.

As shown in this website example, using the Waterfall method, the site is sequentially developed one stage at a time. A thorough and formal review and approval occurs at each gate to ensure the website project never has to go backwards.

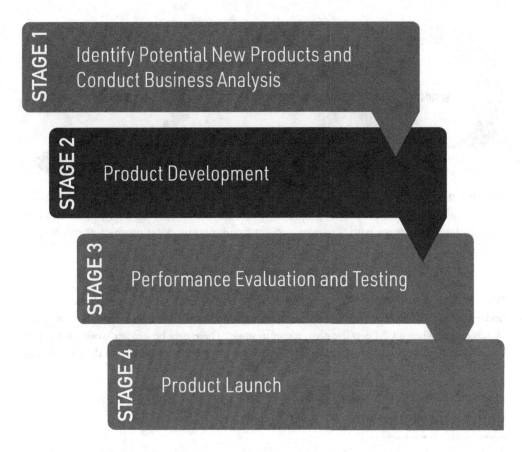

FIGURE 2.1 The Waterfall process is a formal, stage-gate model in which products are thoroughly defined in the initial stage and then progress through the NPD cycle once to release and launch.

In contrast, Agile is a more iterative approach that breaks the project up into small increments called sprints, in which the stages are repeated multiple times (see Figure 2.2). Software developers created Agile in the early 2000s to streamline development with an approach that offered an alternative to the significant up-front planning, documentation, intensive review, and approval at every stage required by Waterfall (Beck et al., 2001).

The Agile development process balances the need for rigidness and formality of the NPD with collaboration and continuous iteration. At the end of shorter time intervals, a working product is demonstrated that may be released to consumers.

For example, when developing a website using the Agile method, the first sprint may focus just on developing the home page. For that sprint, teams create a plan based on initial home page requirements; then it is designed, developed, tested, and deployed. The second sprint begins with the next website section, such as primary navigational pages. Using this method, the product is iteratively created and expanded and incrementally released after each iteration.

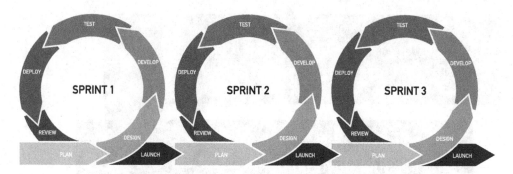

FIGURE 2.2 The Agile method follows similar processes to Waterfall's but divides a large project into several smaller projects, which are called sprints. In Agile, sprints are repeated multiple times with a narrow project focus and working product at the end of each cycle.

What a CM should know: Knowing the difference between Waterfall and Agile helps a CM understand their workflow responsibilities and deadlines. There's more hurry up and wait with Waterfall, but when a CM gets the plan, it's set in stone. There may be steadier work with Agile, but it's possible things may change, and a CM may have to start from scratch on their marketing story.

SWOT ANALYSIS

In the early stages of the NPD process, brands evaluate potential products against the company's existing product portfolio and competitive market position. To guide this evaluation, product development teams often conduct a SWOT analysis (strengths, weaknesses, opportunities, and threats), which organizes the advantages and disadvantages of a product relative to the competition in a four-quadrant profile. (See Figure 2.3 for a SWOT analysis for the wind turbine industry as an energy source. (Porter, 2008).)

The SWOT analysis framework allows teams to evaluate many different business objectives, from evaluating the viability of a specific product to improving department performance by understanding where it is most effective or has weaknesses.

What a CM should know: CMs may use a SWOT analysis to evaluate the performance of current content, such as identifying media sources that are driving the greatest consumer engagement (opportunity) or the existence of poor-quality content that is not effectively informing or resonating with potential consumers (weakness).

CMs should also understand a SWOT's value greatly depends on the quality and thoroughness of the information. It's easy to be overdependent on personal experience in a SWOT. It's also important to remember that a SWOT is only a snapshot of a particular time. SWOTs are quickly outdated, especially in a rapidly changing marketplace.

STRENGTHS

- Wind is a Source of Clean Energy: Wind is one of the most sustainable and renewable energy sources.
- Wind Power is a Sustainable Energy Source: One of the major concerns in using fossil fuels is its depletion.
- Wind Power is Cost-Effective: The running cost of wind energy generation is minimal once the wind farm is constructed; in several countries power generation from wind is the cheapest form compared to other renewable sources.
- Requires Less Space: Wind farm takes less space as opposed to solar farm and hydroelectric generation.

INTERNAL / ADVANTAGES

WEAKNESSES

- High Initial Investment: Although the running cost of wind power generation is minimal, the initial investment remains high.
- Noise Pollution: Noise pollution is one of the drawbacks of the wind technology. The noise of a single turbine can be heard from hundreds of meters away.
- Aesthetics: Some people argue the appearance and obstruction of wind turbines are undesirable.

INTERNAL / DISADVANTAGES

OPPORTUNITIES

- Focus on Renewable Energies by Governments: The environmental degradation and depletion of fossil fuels have pushed governmental and non-governmental organizations to focus on renewable energy sources such as wind and solar. The investment reported on renewable energy in 2011 was $257 billion which showed 17% increase from the previous year.
- Technology Advancement: The cost of renewable energy technologies has declined as a result of technology learning and economies of scale.

EXTERNAL / ADVANTAGES

THREATS

- Geographical Restrictions: A common weakness for wind energy generation is its limitation to geographical locations with adequate wind. As a result of low wind speed (less than 15 km/h), wind energy is not feasible in many locations.
- Fluctuation: The speed of wind is dependent on meteorological conditions. Thus, the power produced from wind energy is highly dependent on the wind speed.
- Established Fossil Fuel Technologies: Fossil fuels have been used as a primary source of energy for the last few centuries and changing energy sources will require a significant capital investment.
- Endanger Wildlife: Birds and bats die as a result of collisions with wind turbines (average of 5.25 per turbine per year); some other species are also adversely affected directly or indirectly in relation to the construction and operation of wind power facilities.

EXTERNAL / DISADVANTAGES

FIGURE 2.3 SWOT (strengths, weaknesses, opportunities, and threats) analysis for the wind turbine industry as an energy source. In a SWOT analysis, a complete list of factors contributing to (advantages) or undermining (disadvantages) the market success of a technical product is evaluated and organized by source as either within the control of a company (internal) or beyond the control of a company (external).

Source: Adapted from Guangul and Chala, 2019

PRODUCT POSITIONING

A defined discipline of marketing for decades, product positioning historically referred to its physical placement in a store – that is, its location along or at the end of an aisle or on a shelf (Karadeniz, 2009). For example, a bag of potato chips at the shopper's eye level in the middle of the shelf is "positioned" more advantageously than other products on the very top or bottom shelf (Sigurdsson et al., 2009).

This changed in the early 1970s when a series of articles by Al Ries and Jack Trout appeared in *Ad Age* that redefined positioning from a literal location in a store to how a product is subjectively positioned in the mind of the customer – specifically, how consumers define a product as a clear, distinct, and "better" product than all the other available products on the market (Dickson & Ginter, 1987; Kotler & Armstrong, 2010; Ries & Trout, 2001).

Anyone can see modern positioning daily in products from washing machines to automobiles. For instance, one car maker's brand position may emphasize power and engineering sophistication with high-performance vehicles while a competitor may focus on sustainable transportation, safety, and value through environmentally friendly and safety-conscious vehicles.

The essence of the product positioning is to be as specific and focused as possible – the more distinctive, even down to one word or memorable phrase, the more powerful the position in the consumer's mind (Ries & Trout, 1994). Examples of a memorable phrase conveying a clear product positioning message are the Bounty paper towel tagline "The quicker picker-upper" and Nike's "Just Do It."

Product positioning in the mind of the consumer is challenging because the same product can have different uses and benefits for different consumers. The same product can have different features that may be more important for different niche markets or consumer groups, and companies will launch new versions of their product for specific segments or groups of consumers.

For instance, Airbnb launched its higher-end hotel-like Airbnb Plus service for travelers who wanted a more consistent experience while Uber launched UberPool for price-sensitive riders who are willing to share a ride with other passengers to save money (Gupta, 2019). Therefore, product positioning requires a multi-step process of segmentation, targeting, and positioning (or STP) to identify potential customers and select which ones to pursue (Gupta, 2019).

- **Segmentation**: Group customers based on similar needs, such as price sensitivity or age group.
- **Targeting**: Assess attractiveness of each segment and select segments to target, including size of segment or competition.
- **Positioning**: The value proposition and benefits messaging for each customer segment. The value proposition and benefits messaging are lenses through which CMs tailor and apply the positioning of a product to a particular consumer segment, such as positioning a product's sustainably sourced ingredients for health-conscious consumers.

What a CM should know: STP is a critical process to define the business strategy, which, in turn, informs the tone, style, and content the CM develops. With a defined STP strategy, teams can estimate the size and potential revenue of a market to guide the level of marketing and content investment needed to meet product goals.

The Four Ws of Positioning Products

Positioning a product into a market of one or many target segments is a process that often involves people from multiple internal teams working over weeks or months. This process concludes with a deliverable called the positioning statement, a brief summary that defines the unique role of the product that becomes the foundational internal reference for external messaging to individual target segments and guides the selection of topics for broader content marketing and storytelling (Pulizzi, 2012).

Since the positioning statement is the core internal summary of a product that guides communication through all marketing channels, it must be as accurate and specific as possible and clearly convey the product's unique qualities in the marketplace.

Creating an effective product positioning statement involves in-depth analysis of the target audience and competition. Over hundreds of product positioning and launch projects while leading corporate communications at National Instruments, working with hundreds of B2B technical companies as CEO of TREW Marketing, and as Chief Marketing Officer of startups ChemVM Technologies and Monolith, Rebecca Geier developed the Four Ws for positioning products, a series of four questions, answered in sequence, to guide the development of product positioning statements that focus on the core target customer needs and product differentiation. Since being developed, the Four Ws for positioning products has helped position products in various B2B technical industries including cybersecurity, military, aerospace, semiconductor, manufacturing, chemicals, software, and communications. The four questions are:

- Who is the target customer? *Who* is the first of the Four Ws, which begins by identifying the individual(s) involved in the purchasing decision for the product or service. Your *who* may be one buyer who is the primary user of the product to be purchased and makes the ultimate decision to buy or a group of individuals in which one may be the primary user while another may have the budget authority to authorize the purchase. When multiple individuals are involved in the buying process, this is referred to as a buying committee; together, they make a collective decision to select a product for purchase. All individuals who influence the purchase decision should be identified in this first step. (For an in-depth explanation of developing the *who*, refer to "Buyer Personas" in Chapter 3.)
- *Where* is the second of the Four Ws: specifically, Where is the target customer working? *Where* builds on the *who* by identifying the environment, location, place, or situation in which the product or service would be primarily used. While *who* focuses on the relevant purchase characteristics and considerations of the buyer(s), *where* describes the specific geographies, company types, and departments, as well as size of the buyer's company.
- For the third W, *why*, we ask why the target customer/primary user needs this new product. *Why* describes the need(s) or want(s) of the target customer that lead them to seek the product. *Why* is the primary challenge the customer is facing or the opportunity they seek. *Why* is often referred to as the customer pain points or problem (the "pain") that each buyer is experiencing that leads them to seek a product to reduce or resolve the problem (Shewan, 2019).
- Lastly, the fourth W asks, "What does the product uniquely provide to the target customer/primary user that cannot be satisfied by current offerings?" In this last step, the goal is to define the unique or differentiating characteristics or qualities of a product, known as features, and the resulting benefits of those features or the unique value the features provide to the user.

What a CM should know: In content marketing, which serves to educate and influence buyers, it's important to thoroughly and accurately explain both features and benefits. For instance, the benefit statement "easy to use" is effective only if it is accompanied by a detailed description of the features that support the claim. The most effective marketing conveys both the benefits and the features. As explained by Adele Revella, founder and CEO of the Buyer Persona Institute:

> *"Buyers want answers to their questions about features and capabilities: How can you deliver that benefit? Why should I believe you're better qualified to deliver that than somebody else?*
> *We have got to stop teaching marketers that features are bad and benefits are good. We need to answer buyers' questions about how we deliver. We've got to stop blabbing our value propositions and*

our benefits . . . and thinking that that's going to impress anyone. What website were you on recently that didn't say that their product was 'the most flexible, scalable, easy-to-use solution'? Do people read on your website that your product is 'easy to use' and think 'Oh my gosh, where have you been all my life? I was looking for a solution that's 'easy to use'."

No! They want proof that it's easy. . . . You've got to get into that detail and explain: It's 'easy to use' because we've integrated these databases and provided this dashboard. And guess what, now we're talking features and capabilities."

(Adele Revella interview, 2019)

An Example of the Four Ws for Positioning Products

The W	Purpose	Description	Automotive Example
Who	Identify the target customer	Includes job title, gender, age, level of experience, and/or purchase influence/authority	Chief technology officers responsible for designing high-quality new vehicles on time and on budget
Where	The customer's location	Includes industries, regions, applications, size of company, etc.	Global automotive manufacturers and suppliers with revenue from $1B–$100B
Why	The customer's need	The challenge the customer is facing or the opportunity they seek	Engineering teams that are missing errors in engine design, risking quality and brand reputation
What	The product's goal	The product's differentiating feature(s) and benefit(s)	Software designed exclusively for engineering teams focused on improving quality and communication through the new product design process

To illustrate the purpose, description, and an example of each of the Four Ws of product positioning, let's look at how each would be used for a software product targeting the automotive market.

The Four Ws Applied

Let's apply the Four Ws for positioning framework to a real product, an external cloud storage for computer files used by different customer groups.

Each target group that seeks a file storage product has unique needs and pain points, and thus the same features translate into different benefits for different customer groups. For CMs, this translates into different content focus, types, uses, and messages for the exact same product.

The Who

Agreeing on the target segments of the product is the first critical decision in developing the product position. All the other elements of the positioning stem from this first piece. While it may seem easy, defining and prioritizing segments is a very difficult step explained further in Chapter 3. For this exercise, let's consider four different customer groups:

1. **Business owners** need reliable copies of important company information such as financial, customer, or employee records. Positioning the hard drive for the business owner would include a professional, serious tone that emphasizes reliability and value over price. It would also create ethically reasonable fear, uncertainty, and doubt (FUD) about using a competitor's product that may risk their business security and personal time.
2. **High school or college students** need to carry their work on portable devices that can quickly plug into computer systems in classroom labs. The approach to positioning for the student would focus on the device's light weight, low cost, and portability. It would also highlight an intuitive software interface that makes it easy to connect to any computer system, so when they are running late for class, they can quickly hook up the drive and get to work.
3. **Professional videographers or photographers** need extremely large, reliable storage for high-resolution files from client shoots. The positioning emphasis to these users is the device's massive storage capacity and the speed with which they can open and manipulate files. Similar to the needs of the business owner, the device's reliability is more important than price since redoing a photo shoot is costly and risks client satisfaction.
4. **Parents** want to have extra storage for music, photos, and personal files at a low cost. Since a parent cares most about getting the best device for the lowest price, the positioning would emphasize value and contrast various storage sizes at different prices.

This simple external hard drive example shows just how different customer segments can be in terms of their roles, responsibilities, and primary needs for the same product. By defining each potential customer segment, and then prioritizing or targeting them, you narrow down the first W – the *who* – of the product positioning.

Using the external hard drive product, our highest priority or number one target segment is the business owner, followed by the videographer/photographer segment. Both these groups care greatly about reliability and are willing to pay a premium to reduce the risk of losing critical business or client files. The student and parent buyer groups then become secondary target segments. By having the *who* segmented and targeted, the next steps in the positioning become clearer to define.

The Where

Identifying the second W – the *where* – helps further narrow down the buyer segment by describing their industry, company, region, or organization. Using the business owner segment, this customer can vary widely in the type or size of business, industry, or region.

For example, Richard Branson is an owner of many businesses, including Virgin Atlantic, a multi-billion dollar airline headquartered in the United Kingdom that does business on multiple continents. Contrast Mr. Branson to the owner of a restaurant with one location in Omaha, Nebraska. Even though they are both business owners, their businesses are radically different. This is why it's critical to further refine what we mean by this *who*. This is the purpose of *where*.

Let's continue with the external hard drive and define the *where* for the business owner target segment as the following:

- Company size: small business (fewer than 500 employees)
- Industries: professional services such as accounting, landscaping, legal, medical practices, small clinics, restaurants/bars
- Region: North America

We have defined the business owner as someone running a small business, which the Small Business Administration defines as having fewer than 500 employees. The geographic region for our business owner buyer is limited to North America.

The positioning is already becoming well defined. Of all the possible buyers of the external hard drive product, our focus is on the owner of a small business in any North American country with fewer than 500 employees in professional services, medical, and retail industries.

The Why

The next step in the positioning process, and one that top marketing teams invest in greatly to learn and understand, is to explore the buyer's use of the product in more depth and agree on *why* this buyer would need the product.

For the external hard drive, we want to know what challenges the buyer is facing that leads to needing this product. These are "customer pain points" – that is, what pain the customer is experiencing that prompts a purchase to reduce or remove their pain. For our North American small business owner customer, we define the *why* as follows:

- Duplicate copies of critical files
- Business risks if files are lost
- Reliable file storage that can be trusted to work every time
- Protection of data in case hard drive is lost or stolen

For the *why* in our positioning, we define the primary application or use of the external hard drive for this small business owner to be for storing important business documents, such as financial statements, employee documents, and legal filings. More specifically, this buyer needs to minimize the risk to their business of losing critical business files by choosing a product that provides a highly reliable storage solution. Finally, to protect their files in case the drive is ever lost or stolen, they need security features to control access. To address these needs, they are willing to pay a premium for a proven, secure solution.

The What

The three Ws to this point focus on the buyer: *who* they are, *where* they are, and *why* they need the product. It is critical that positioning teams focus first, and most, on the needs of the buyer and benefits they are seeking (Armstrong, et al., 2015).

Only after these first three Ws are defined can you move to the last step, the *what*, by combining these buyer needs with the unique differences in the product. With the *what*, we define how our product uniquely appeals to this particular segment's needs and is different from competitors' in terms of uniqueness, quality, cost effectiveness, and technical performance. For our external hard drive, we define the following features and benefits:

- Unique features

  - High-quality engineering
  - Security control
  - Value for the price (i.e., cost effective)

- Buyer benefits

  - Reliable storage
  - Protection of private business files
  - Affordable to a small business budget

For our North American small business owner, the *what* for the external hard drive focuses on the well-engineered product that provides high reliability and secure protection to store and retrieve critical business documents. In this case, the *what* doesn't position the hard drive as having the lowest cost or the largest storage capacity. Instead, the *what* focuses on what the buyer segment cares about the most – the product's reliability and secure access. To sustain their business, you must show the small business customer that their critical business documents will be accessible on the drive anytime they need them with security features that only allow them or others they authorize to access.

Positioning: The Foundation for Efficient and Consistent Content Development

The purpose of defining the Four Ws is to ensure alignment among internal teams and stakeholders on *who* the product is targeting, *where* they are, *why* they need it, and *what* the product effectively and uniquely offers to appeal to that customer's needs that competitors don't.

Once this work is thoughtfully done and a product is successfully positioned, it should rarely if ever be changed (Ries & Trout, 2001). Teams that take their time gathering customer data through internal and external research, analyzing the competition, and carefully working through the Four Ws will have a well-documented product position that makes it more efficient and effective to develop content and execute other aspects of marketing the product.

What a CM should know: For a product to become successful, customers must become aware of and interested enough in it to then decide to evaluate and ultimately buy it (Armstrong et al., 2015). To fulfill each of these steps a buyer takes to decide to purchase a product, a company must provide a great deal of content to educate them, build their trust in the product and company, and persuade them to buy the product.

CONCLUSION

To thrive and remain competitive, companies develop and introduce new products into the market. To determine which products to develop and how they will be created, teams follow a New Product Development (NPD) process that includes four distinct stages. With the plethora

---

Interview with the Experts: Q&A with Scott Rust, Senior Vice President of Global Product R&D, at National Instruments

Founded in 1976, National Instruments (www.ni.com) provides engineers and scientists with technical products to support their work. In this interview, we learn about their new product development process.

1. *How do you define the new product development (NPD) process at NI? Why is the NPD process important for the company?*
   The NPD process was introduced as a framework to enable teams to efficiently develop innovative products that grow revenue. The development of a new product requires the aligned actions of many groups across the company, with a particularly high need for aligned interactions between R&D, product management and planning, and manufacturing. NPD defines how the teams work together, and everyone knows how to move the product development forward.

2. *Which NPD approach, Waterfall or Agile, do you use and when? Why do you choose each method? From your perspective, what are the advantages and disadvantages of each method?*
   We use both a predictive (Waterfall) and iterative (Agile) model. NPD originally was designed around a predictive model as that lends itself well to brand new product development and initial product launches. This is especially true on hardware projects as many aspects of hardware development require long lead times and structured phases (e.g., working with suppliers to design and fabricate custom parts). We have teams that use an official iterative (Agile) variant

of NPD, such as our software teams, who tend to prefer an iterative model, especially on follow-up feature development to existing software products.

3. *What departments are involved in NPD at NI? What are the top three to five responsibilities of each?*

Product planning and R&D are the primary groups that use the NPD process. Manufacturing also plays a significant role within NPD for hardware products.

Product planning plays the largest role in the beginning phases (exploration and definition), owning the product/business strategy elements of defining and prioritizing projects to develop into products. They distill the needs of the business into product requirements and product development roadmaps for R&D to execute. Additionally, they work with R&D to translate and transition high-level product requirements into development requirements that R&D teams will design.

R&D plays the largest role from planning through launch (referred to at NI as "ship and ramp"), focusing on the execution elements of developing products/projects. They manage the resources it takes to transform product requirements from product planning into a complete product design that is production ready.

For hardware projects, manufacturing provides design for manufacturability guidance in the early stages of planning and early development. They produce and provide hardware prototypes for the R&D team throughout the development phase. At the end of the NPD process, they take a major role from the production verification phase through ship and ramp as we shift from the design stages into production stages of NPD.

4. *What percentage of new products initially proposed ultimately make it to and succeed in the market?*

One of the key objectives of NPD is that the early stages (exploration, definition, and planning) are meant to be a funnel – that is, you have many more ideas for projects during the exploration phase, and only the best ideas progress through each successive phase. The funnel and gates allow us to rule out the less successful ideas early in the process before we have spent a lot of time, development resources, and money. Because of this, it is rare that we have a project make it to the development phase that we don't take all the way to market. However, conditions do arise that can cause us to cancel a project while in development, such as a change in the market landscape that makes the project unattractive.

5. *What is the average length of time of an NPD process? How does the timeframe differ for software and hardware?*

Due to our wide breadth of products, there is a varied range of development times. Hardware projects typically range from 18 to 24 months, and software projects typically range from six to nine months. However, there are plenty of projects that may be shorter or longer than those typical ranges, depending on the scope of the product.

6. *At what point in NPD is the positioning of the product discussed? At what point in NPD does the formal process of positioning and messaging the product begin?*

That discussion often begins as early as the beginning phases of exploration and definition as we'll need to understand how this product idea will fit in the marketplace and how it enhances and/or expands our platform. This is one of the focuses of the exploration phase, and then, in definition, we shift our focus to how the positioning of the product should and will impact the features to be developed.

7. *Who leads the process for product positioning and messaging, and what are the primary steps?*

Product positioning is developed very early in the evaluation and justification phases of determining the feasibility and viability of any investments. This is led by the product managers. They determine the market opportunity, which includes segmented customer and market needs, disruptive trends, and competitive positioning. The team also develops buyer personas, which include critical customer pain points and key buying decision criteria. From there, buyer journeys are mapped, and key messaging, sales enablement, and outbound marketing materials are generated. Regional field marketing teams are also utilized to provide customer input and adapt material to regional market needs.

8. *What advice would you give CMs with respect to the NPD process?*

When developing marketing material to support a product launch, consider how the new product uniquely solves and supports the customer's needs in their workplace or application space. CMs should highlight and focus their understanding around how the new product is differentiated from existing and competing products in the marketplace. And finally, content marketers should highlight the benefits that both the product and the company's platform bring to the customer.

Note: *This description of the NI process was accurate at the time of creation in 2019. As with all good processes and strong innovative companies, we have continued to revise it to meet the evolving needs of our business. While this text remains generally aligned with our current process, we have continued to refine our processes to be more customer focused with more iterative and agile development practices to accelerate the delivery of value to our customers.*

of new products introduced annually and the thousands of promotional messages consumers receive each day, product positioning enables companies to reach their high-value customer target markets and influence consumer perceptions of new products.

Instead of leaving it to consumers to try and decipher a new product's features and benefits, CMs can reference the Four Ws positioning statement to develop consistent and effective content marketing for target segments. Answering the Four Ws provides a clear understanding of the target customers for a product (*who*), the context for use (*where*), the need(s) or want(s) of the target customer (*why*), and the unique or differentiating features and resulting benefits that are tailored to each customer market niche (*what*).

Well-researched and clearly articulated product positioning serves as the foundation for building and executing effective and successful content marketing.

CITATIONS

Armstrong, G., Adam, S., Denize, S., & Kotler, P. *Principles of Marketing*. Pearson Education. 2015.

Aulet, B. *Disciplined Entrepreneurship: 24 Steps to a Successful Startup*. John Wiley & Sons. 2013.

Beck, K., Beedle, M., Van Bennekum, A., Cockburn, A., Cunningham, W., Fowler, M., Grenning, J., Highsmith, J., Hunt, A., Jeffries, R., & Kern, J. "Manifesto for agile software development." 2001. Retrieved from: https://agilemanifesto.org

Bhuiyan, N. "A framework for successful new product development." *Journal of Industrial Engineering and Management*. 2011.

Booz Allen Hamilton. *New Product Management for the 1980s*. Booz, Allen and Hamilton. 1982.

Dickson, P.R. "Toward a general theory of competitive rationality." *Journal of Marketing*. 1992.

Dickson, P.R., & Ginter, J.L. "Market segmentation, product differentiation, and marketing strategy." *Journal of Marketing*. 1987.

Edwards, B. "The golden age of Motorola cell phones." *PC Magazine*. April 12, 2018. Retrieved from: www.pcmag.com/feature/360314/the-golden-age-of-motorola-cell-phones

Fredericks, E. "Cross-functional involvement in new product development: A resource dependency and human capital perspective." *Qualitative Market Research: An International Journal*. 2005.

Goulding, I. "New product development: A literature review." *European Journal of Marketing*. 1983.

Gregersen, E. "Martin Cooper: American engineer." *Encyclopedia Britannica*. 2013. Retrieved from: www.britannica.com/biography/Martin-Cooper#ref1180518

Griffin, A., & Page, A.L. "PDMA research on new product development practices: Updating trends and benchmarking best practices." *Journal of Product Innovation Management: An International Publication of the Product Development & Management Association*. 1997.

Grönlund, J., Sjödin, D.R., & Frishammar, J. "Open innovation and the stage-gate process: A revised model for new product development." *California Management Review*. 2010.

Guangul, F.M., & Chala, G.T. "SWOT analysis of wind energy as a promising conventional fuels substitute." *IEEE 4th MEC International Conference on Big Data and Smart City*. January 15, 2019.

Gupta, S. "Segmentation and targeting." *Harvard Business Publishing*. December 19, 2019.

Hart, S., Hultink, E.J., Tzokas, N., & Commandeur, H.R. "Industrial companies' evaluation criteria in new product development gates." *Journal of Product Innovation Management*. 2003.

Karadeniz, M. "Product positioning strategy in marketing management." *Journal of Naval Science and Engineering*. 2009.

Kotler, P., Armstrong, G. *Principles of Marketing*. London: Pearson Education. 2010.

Kotler, P., Rackham, N., & Krishnaswamy, S. "Ending the war between sales and marketing." *Harvard Business Review*. July 2006.

Miles, R.E., Snow, C.C., Meyer, A.D., & Coleman, H.J. Jr. "Organizational strategy, structure, and process." *Academy of Management Review*. 1978.

Moore, G.A. *Crossing the Chasm*. 3rd ed. New York: HarperCollins. 2014.

No Author. "Rackspace technology named winner of North America VMware 2022 Partner Lifecycle Services Award." April 19, 2022. Retrieved from: www.rackspace.com/newsroom/rackspace-technology-vmware-2022-partner-lifecycle-services-award

Porter, M.E. *Competitive Strategy: Techniques for Analyzing Industries and Competitors*. New York: Simon and Schuster. 2008.

Pulizzi, J. "The rise of storytelling as the new marketing." *Publishing Research Quarterly*. 2012.

Ries, A., & Trout, J. *The 22 Immutable Laws of Marketing*. London: HarperCollins. 1994.

Ries, A., & Trout, J. *Positioning: The Battle for Your Mind, 20th Anniversary Edition*. New York: McGraw-Hill. 2001.

Shankar, V., Carpenter, G.S., & Krishnamurthi, L. "Late mover advantage: How innovative late entrants outsell pioneers." *Journal of Marketing Research*. 1998.

Shewan, D. "Pain points: A guide to finding & solving your customers' problems." *Boston: WordStream*. August 26, 2019. Retrieved from: www.wordstream.com/blog/ws/2018/02/28/pain-points

Sigurdsson, V., Saevarsson, H., & Foxall, G. "Brand placement and consumer choice: An in-store experiment." *Journal of Applied Behavior Analysis*. 2009.

Slater, S.F., Hult, G.T., & Olson, E.M. "On the importance of matching strategic behavior and target market selection to business strategy in high-tech markets." *Journal of the Academy of Marketing Science*. 2007.

Strickland, T. *Strategic Management, Concepts and Cases*. New York: McGraw Hill College Division. 1999.

Walker, O.C. Jr., & Ruekert, R.W. "Marketing's role in the implementation of business strategies: A critical review and conceptual framework." *Journal of Marketing*. 1987.

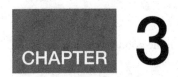

CHAPTER 3

Buyer Personas and Their Role in Content Marketing

LEARNING OBJECTIVES

1. Why buyer personas are important for content marketing
2. The two types of buyer personas – full-authority individuals and buying committees
3. How to create buyer personas using internal and external research
4. The elements of the buyer persona and a variety of persona templates

---

INTRODUCTION TO BUYER PERSONAS

In over 30 years of working with business leaders to develop and execute their marketing strategy, we've often seen substantial disagreement in answering these basic questions about the target audience:

Who are we talking to?
What do they want?
Where do they go for information?
How can we help?

When a business can't understand how to connect product value with customer wants, successful marketing is almost impossible; that's why healthy debating and defining of our potential customers is crucial before executing any marcom activity.

Too often, companies tend to remain insular focused instead of buyer-centric because it's easier and less expensive to rely on internal knowledge than investing time and money to conduct buyer and market research. The shortsighted risk of taking this insular, company-focused approach is that when the messages, content, and activities you create and execute do not resonate with your target customer, they don't buy your product.

DOI: 10.4324/9781003369103-4

Adele Revella, CEO of the Buyer Persona Institute, has seen the good and bad of this issue for decades. She said,

> *"The problem with our approach to marketing traditionally, and this comes out of our history, is that we, as marketers, think that we need to educate buyers and that we need to challenge their knowledge – and we need to somehow change them. But buyers aren't the least bit interested in that – buyers have a mission and a vision. In fact, the most effective way to do marketing is to forget all of that and really focus on what it is that the buyers are wanting."*
>
> (Adele Revella Interview)

Effective content marketing educates buyers about the benefits of the product using language and tone that specifically resonates with them and motivates them to take action and:

- Learn
- Consider
- Evaluate
- Ultimately make a purchase

To ensure content marketing appeals to the target buyer, you must first start with understanding who your buyer is and what their challenges/desires are.

How? It's called the buyer persona, a profile of your company's potential customer(s) that includes demographic, behavioral, and psychographic information. Buyer personas are important for CMs because they help you understand how your prospective customers make buying decisions. The buyer persona serves as a reference that empowers CMs to tailor content to address those specific needs, behaviors, and concerns. This is important since more personalized and customized messaging built on personas is shown to yield twice the average sales pipeline (Fullerton & Johnson, 2019).

By developing buyer personas, you ensure the greatest relevance and effectiveness in your messaging and content to drive your prospective buyer to trust and take action.

What a CM should know: Customer research is an investment in more effective content marketing, not an expense.

TWO TYPES OF BUYER PERSONAS

The individuals who influence and participate in the decision to make a purchase are known as the decision-making unit (DMU) (Gourville & Norton, 2019). The DMU can consist of one individual buyer or multiple individuals. In the book *The Challenger Customer*, researchers at the Corporate Executive Board (CEB) explained that "in a typical B2B purchase, [researchers] found an average of 5.4 different people formally involved in a typical purchase decision" (Adamson et al., 2015).

At face value, creating buyer personas for DMU participants may seem like a simple task of identifying educational levels, job titles, and product feature preferences. In reality, it can be incredibly complex when you consider the different types of customers and their varying degrees of influence and authority when making a purchasing decision.

High-performing marketing teams research and develop buyer persona profiles for each product or platform family, each of which may be an individual full-authority buyer or a buying committee with members serving various roles and levels of influence.

Full-Authority Individual Buyer Persona

This first type of DMU is an individual who has the full authority to select and purchase the product or service with little or no involvement of or approval from others. For the content marketer, this is the individual to educate or persuade. Information in the individual persona first identifies individual characteristics about the buyer, including (see Figure 3.1A):

- **Background**: identifies the primary responsibilities of the position, education, training, department, and reporting structure.
- **Demographics**: identifies prototypical personal characteristics, which inform the marketing style and media selection. Additionally, the demographics also identify the target industry and company size for which this persona is appropriate.
- **Identifiers**: further develop the personal characteristics that inform the marketing communication. Specifically, the demeanor is defined as typical behavior of this role, such as being an introvert or extrovert. Additionally, the communication preferences identify the sources that the buyer persona relies on to gather new information about the field.

Additionally, the persona includes the motivations or drivers the individual has for purchasing the specific product and how the product meets their needs, including (see Figure 3.1B):

- **Goals**: the relevant job responsibilities of individuals in this position (as relevant to the product being marketed).
- **Challenges**: derived from the goals by identifying the major obstacles and frustrations the prototypical customer experiences while trying to accomplish the goals listed previously.
- **Support and value**: lists specific methods of support and value to offer the buyer to guide the development of content marketing.

The final buyer persona step is naming the persona and selecting a representative photo or avatar. By giving it a name and often an avatar or even a picture of a real customer, the persona is humanized. Using alliteration in the name makes it easier for everyone to remember it for reference. An accurate persona photo brings meaningful insight to collective understanding and agreement on who the buyer is.

- Does the person wear a suit and tie and sit in a conference room during most of his workday?
- Does she wear a hard hat and work on the plant floor?
- Are they in their 40s and working in an office cubicle or in their 20s and working in the field?

**DEVELOPMENT
DIRECTOR DAN**

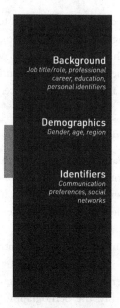

Background
Job title/role, professional career, education, personal identifiers

· Head of Software Development (titles: Director, Senior Manager)
· Computer science major, likely master's and maybe PhD
· Middle management, reports to VP of R&D
· 10+ years working, often at 1-3 companies

Demographics
Gender, age, region

· 75% of people in this role are male
· Age 35-50+
· SaaS industry

Identifiers
Communication preferences, social networks

· Uses LinkedIn for networking
· Attends relevant conferences, vendor events
· Sends staff to trade shows
· Has spam filters set up to block email solicitation

(A)

**DEVELOPMENT
DIRECTOR DAN**

Goals
Team, professional

· Reduce code bugs, product instability
· Work with Sales to get customer product feedback, new feature input
· Evaluate new processes, technologies to work smarter
· Ensure budget, timelines are met

Challenges
Departmental, professional

· Balancing solving customer issues with new product development
· Meeting growth goals on flat/reduced budgets
· Retaining top talent in tight job market

Support & Value
To overcome challenges, meet goals

· Industry benchmarks, relevant research studies
· Trusted 3rd party sources touting proven use, adoption, leadership
· Educational collateral detailing features, benefits
· User testimonials, customer references, case studies

(B)

FIGURE 3.1 In this full-authority buyer persona for Development Director Dan, information about the buyer characterizes the persona, including (A) the individual characteristics (*who*) and (B) the motivations for purchasing the specific product (*why*), and a representative photo or avatar of the persona in their professional environment.

Agreeing on the right photo can elicit other important features of the buyer such as age, work environment, gender, and even normal work dress. With the photo, a memorable name describes the role. This puts a human perspective on the aggregated data, such as the persona name in Figure 3.1A, Development Director Dan.

What a CM should know: When in doubt, look at the customer persona and think what he or she needs to succeed.

Personas on a Buying Committee

The second type of DMU is a committee made up of multiple participants who are responsible for collaborating on the selection, evaluation, and decision process. Buying committees are often used to make decisions on company-wide purchases when the price is a significant percentage of overall expenses. Defining these personas is complex since each committee member has a unique role and level of influence. That's why a more detailed buyer persona framework that specifies the role of each individual on the committee is often necessary to further identify their workplace role, concerns, and influence in the decision-making process.

Referring to the Sirius Decisions Persona Framework (Young, 2015) (Figure 3.2), there are four types of attributes to define for each buyer persona on the committee:

- **Functional attributes**: the relevant demographic data about the individual's job role and organization to understand the customer's responsibilities and the organization's history and decision-making culture.
- **Emotive attributes**: the goals, motivations, and concerns the individual has in the workplace. This provides the context to create relevant, compelling messaging and marketing content.
- **Behavioral attributes**: the activities and sources the individual prefers to consume work-related information and the media sources they use to develop their knowledge. This data informs the communication strategies of the marketing communication plan.

FUNCTIONAL ATTRIBUTES	EMOTIVE ATTRIBUTES	BEHAVIORAL ATTRIBUTES	DECISION-MAKING ATTRIBUTES
Job role, common titles, position on organizational chart, buyer center, firmographics	Initiatives, challenges, business drivers, buyer needs, vocabulary	Content asset preferences, interaction preferences, trusted sources	Buyer role, engagement level, provider selection drivers, category perceptions

FIGURE 3.2 Adapted from the SiriusDecisions Persona Framework, four types of attributes are used to identify each individual on a buying team and align the organization around a common understanding of the target buyer personas in the pursuit of creating personalized and relevant messaging and content.

- **Decision-making attributes**: the influence this buyer persona has in their role in an organization on the purchase decision and process.

CHARACTERIZING ATTRIBUTES

Characterizing Functional Attributes

The functional attributes include the individual's job responsibilities, which describe the position's purpose and job titles commonly used in companies and industries for that role. To infer the influence of each persona on the committee, identify the individual's position on the organizational chart and their role in the decision-making process.

As mentioned, a buying committee or buying center includes multiple individuals from different departments who have different goals, needs, and concerns. Identify all members who compose the buying center and prioritize each by most to least influential committee member.

Rounding out the functional attributes is firmographics, which are the relevant demographic features of the organization (i.e., the "firm") that influence the business needs and purchase procedure. The most conventional firmographics include the industry, number of employees, annual revenue, and geographical location. Unconventional insights include the organization's history and number of years in business (startup vs. well-established company), customers (B2C or B2B), and market segment. As with personal demographic information, the goal is to define the company's needs, abilities, and internal culture that influence purchase decisions.

What a CM should know: Use conventional and unconventional firmographics to better understand the industry, history, and culture of the buying committee's organization.

Characterizing Emotive Attributes

The second section outlines the emotive attributes that define the buyer persona's psychological characteristics in the position or role. These emotive attributes influence the personal motivation an individual has in the sales process. Referring to the Sirius Decisions template (Figure 3.2), there are four types of emotive attributes:

- **Initiatives**: the relevant career and workplace goals or objectives the individual has in the organizational role that influence the purchase decision.
- **Challenges**: the obstacles the individual encounters that hinder success. The challenges are similar to the needs, or pain points, described in the *why* of the Four Ws for positioning products discussed in Chapter 2 (specifically, why does the target customer/primary user need this new product?).
- **Business drivers:** the financial, operational, or strategic initiatives the persona is responsible for.
- **Buyer need**: referring to the challenges and drivers, a succinct description of the individual's ideal and prioritized outcomes and expected value.

- **Vocabulary**: the workplace language, common phrases, and communication style so CMs create messaging and content marketing that is relevant and resonates with the buyer.

What a CM should know: Collectively, the emotive attributes provide insight into someone's underlying motivation as they search for new products.

Characterizing Behavioral Attributes

The behavior attributes of the committee buyer persona identify the communication types, sources, and channels that CMs should use to reach each buyer. This attribute section includes three sub-types:

- **Content asset preferences**: the content formats and information sources valued most throughout the purchase decision process (e.g., blog articles, infographics, short videos).
- **Interaction preferences**: the media and communication channels the buyer values when interacting with potential vendors during the selection and purchase process.
- **Trusted sources**: the digital, print, and in-person information sources the buyer values and references during purchase decisions, such as specific industry or vendor websites, search engines, vendor meetings, third-party consultants, trade shows, online communities such as LinkedIn groups, and industry publications.

What a CM should know: Effective buyer personas ensure content development, presentation, and distribution channels are optimized, increasing the relevance and effectiveness of your efforts.

Characterizing Decision Process Attributes

The last type of attribute defines the influence and authority each buyer persona has on the committee and in the purchase process, including:

- **Buyer role**: the role, involvement, and considerations the buyer has on the buying committee (e.g., an economic decision maker who decides that change is needed and money will be spent).
- **Engagement level**: what stage of the buying process the persona participates in and their level of influence or authority at these stages.
- **Provider selection drivers**: factors important to the buyer when comparing potential vendors (e.g., price, references, brand reputation).
- **Category perceptions**: perceptions and biases about the segment or technology the vendor represents.

What a CM should know: By understanding each person's role and authority, as well as biases about the product, the CM can customize content to maximize relevance and value.

DEVELOPING BUYER PERSONAS

Having well-developed buyer personas sounds great, but where do you find all this information?

Much of this data is right inside or just outside your own organization. You can gather information using both internal and external methods. Depending on the size and complexity of the business, a company may have just one or two personas or as many as ten or more.

Internal Buyer Persona Research

Internally, robust buyer knowledge exists among company business leaders, especially in the sales and marketing departments. Interviewing these internal stakeholders, who often have years of experience working closely with customer buying teams (and may have even been a customer themselves at one point) can provide valuable insight into developing the buyer persona attributes. When developing committee buyer personas, you can similarly lean on internal colleagues who serve in roles such as finance or legal at your company to provide insight into these personas on your customer buying committee.

To supplement information gathered through internal interviews, CMs can gain valuable insights listening in on actual sales calls and meetings with potential customers. Hearing conversations, buyer questions and objections, pain points, and buying committee background helps CMs "hear it from the horse's mouth" to make content more relevant and customized to the persona.

What a CM should know: For many marketing teams, especially at smaller companies or those with only a few products or service offerings, internally gathered information may be sufficient to develop quality buyer personas.

External Buyer Persona Research

For companies with complex product offerings or enterprise-level sales or those that serve many industries across the globe, external sources will likely be necessary to supplement internal research to create accurate and thorough buyer personas. This may include informal research, such as online surveys or in-person interviews. In some instances, where in-depth research is needed, outside consultants may be hired to conduct qualitative or quantitative research, including global customer surveys or professionally facilitated customer interviews and focus groups.

When conducting interviews with external customers, the most effective interviewing style is journalistic in nature: the interviewer is inquisitive and curious and asks questions to truly understand how the buyer makes decisions, what information sources they use in the decision-making process, their role in the buying decision, and what questions they seek answers to along the way. Two ways to approach an interview are simply asking questions according to persona attributes or engaging in a guided conversational interview.

Attribute Interview Approach

A simple approach to prepare for the interview is to create a questionnaire that lists a set of questions covering all four attribute categories in the persona framework (Figure 3.2). The interviewer simply asks all the questions listed and uses the data from the interview to create a draft buyer persona.

The following are examples of questions you can ask for each category of attribute during a buyer persona interview.

Functional

- What is your job role?
- What degrees and/or certifications are required for this role?
- What are your primary job responsibilities?
- What are the most common job titles in the industry for this role?
- What is a typical day like?
- How are your performance and impact measured?
- Where does your role fit in the larger organizational structure?
- How are purchase decisions made in your organization, and what is your role in that process?

Emotive

- What are your goals in this role?
- What challenges do you face that could hinder success in your current projects or applications?
- How do you measure your personal success in your role?
- What are the primary risks you face (e.g., financial, job security, project deadlines)?

Behavioral

- What content types (e.g., white papers, webinars, case studies) do you most value during the purchase decision process and at which point?
- What are your communication preferences for interacting with potential vendors during the purchase process?
- What sources do you most value during the purchase process (e.g., vendor websites, vendor-produced content, internet search, in-person vendor meetings, third-party consultants, trade shows, online communities such as LinkedIn groups, trade magazines)?

Decision Making

- What job roles are represented when your organization makes a significant purchase decision?
- What are the key care-abouts of each role on the buying team?
- What is your role in the purchase decision? Would you describe your role as influencer or final decision maker?
- Briefly describe the decision-making process (e.g., phases, length of time)?
- How are purchase decision criteria developed, evaluated, and prioritized?
- How are potential vendors and/or solutions evaluated and selected?

INTERVIEW GUIDE

_____

1. Take me back to the day when you first decided you needed [category of solution]. *What happened to trigger that need?*
    - You probably needed [result mentioned just now] long before that day. What changed to make it a priority at that time?
        » Were there any other factors that made this the right decision?
        » [If the participant is struggling to be specific] Were you the person who decided this was a top priority, or who (role) did decide?
    - What were you hoping to achieve? What were your goals for this purchase?
        » You mentioned your goal for _, can you say more about that?
        » You also said you expected _ how would that help you?
        » With respect to _ was there a measurable objective for that?
        » Who in your organization had an interest in achieving these goals?

2. Once you decided to make this investment, *what did you do first* to determine which solutions you should evaluate?
    - What else did you do? (repeat up to three times)
    - What did you learn about the companies that seemed to be the most interesting?
        » You mentioned _, what was important about that?
        » Repeat prior question for other responses mentioned
    - What information was hardest to find?
    - How did the information you found impact your choice of providers?
    - Were you the only person doing this research, or were others involved?
    - How many companies were you evaluating at this point?

3. So you had (number from prior question] of companies/solutions in mind, *what did you do next?*
    - What did you learn from that?
    - What you said about was interesting. Tell me more about that
    - Who else from your organization was involved in this phase of your assessment?
    - Were there any external resources particularly helpful to you at this point?
    - How many solutions were you continuing to evaluate after [experience identified above]?
    - What distinguished those solutions from those you dropped from consideration?
    - Were there differences of opinion about which solutions you should continue to evaluate?
    - How many solutions were you evaluating at this point?

4. [In a very long or complex buyer's journey, where the evaluation included 4 or more solutions, repeat all questions from prior sequence]

5. What did you do to make the final decision about *which solution to purchase?*
    - Who was involved in the final choice of providers?
    - Did everyone in the evaluation agree that this was your best choice?
    - Who had to sign off on the purchase?
    - What information did you need to provide to get that approval?

FIGURE 3.3 Buyer Persona Institute interview guide: Using an interview guide is a more advanced approach in which the interviewer starts by asking one question and, based on the interviewee's answer, the interviewer then probes further with related questions. In this approach, the interview guide helps facilitate a conversation in which the interviewer is able to learn about the buyer persona and their buying decision process.

A Guided Interview Approach

A more advanced interviewing approach focuses less on specific persona attributes and instead guides the interview toward the buying decision specifically. This cascading interview guide, like the one shown in Figure 3.3 from the Buyer Persona Institute, starts with one question (1.0): "Take me back to the day when you first decided you needed [category of solution]. What happened to trigger that need?"

Based on the interviewee's answer, the interviewer then probes further with follow-on questions, such as "Were there any other factors that made this the right decision?" or, if the interviewee is struggling to be specific, "Were you the person who decided this was a top priority, or who did decide?"

Once that question has been sufficiently answered, the interviewer goes to another topic that starts with a question, such as: "What were you hoping to achieve? What were your goals for this purchase?" and includes related probing questions: "You mentioned your goal for [project/problem]; can you say more about that?" "You also said you expected [output/outcome]; how would that help you?" or "Who in your organization had an interest in achieving these goals?"

In this approach, the interviewer does not ask a list of attribute-specific questions, but rather uses the interview guide to facilitate a conversation to learn about the persona's role and buying decision process.

What a CM should know: Curiosity is a good attribute to have. Don't be afraid to ask questions.

FINDING YOUR INNER JOURNALIST

In addition to preparing an interview questionnaire or guide, a good interviewer builds rapport and sets expectations with the prospective interviewee/buyer. Pre-interview research, email communication, and phone calls to share interview objectives with the interviewee help everyone understand the types of questions that will be asked, the format, and the expected interview length.

To get to know the interviewee, spend a few minutes reviewing their LinkedIn profile to understand their professional background, such as where they went to college or how long they've been in their current role, as well as personal insights, such as what professional organizations they follow and their volunteer interests. This can serve as a helpful way to break the ice when the interview starts; you can comment on their alma mater if you know something interesting about it or mention an interest you both may share.

Once a CM sets the date, time, and length for the interview, send a formal email invitation to ensure the interviewer and interviewee are on the same page with meeting logistics, objectives, and expected outcomes.

Finally, the interviewer should record the interview if possible. This allows a CM to focus on the conversation rather than note taking. Being in the moment as an active participant allows for better follow-up questions and responses to interesting comments. Before any recording begins, you must gain permission to record from the interviewee for privacy purposes. This should happen in the email invitation. Then, when the interview begins, the interviewer should remind the customer that the interview is being recorded and have them verbally agree to the recording.

BUYER PERSONA TEMPLATES

There is no single or perfect template for buyer personas. They can vary greatly in depth, complexity, and layout/design from one slide to a multi-page report and include a variety of relevant data types and findings as well as verbatim quotes from interviews and research.

The key to an effective buyer persona template is to organize it to be robust, flexible, easily consumable, and visually appealing. For instance, the template in Figure 3.1 uses a basic design that focuses on a few key categories of information (e.g., background, demographics, goals, challenges) on the left and corresponding bullet points on the right with a name and picture of the persona at the top.

You can use this same template but add to it in both design and information, such as attributed quotes from customer interviews for buyer roles on a committee. For instance, in Figure 3.4, the

CHIEF INFORMATION SECURITY OFFICER OWEN

BACKGROUND
JOBS? CAREER PATH? FAMILY?
- Strategic, executive position in the company (VP, chief information security officer, chief security offer, director/ manager of information security, CIO who has no CISO but security responsibility)
- Policy and procedure comes from CISO, network IT implements it
- Reports CIO, COO or CTO, part of IT organization
- Technical degree, plus specific security certifications and accreditations. Often also advanced degree, sometimes military background

DEMOGRAPHICS
MALE OR FEMALE? AGE? INCOME? LOCATION?
- Male, 40+ years old
- Historically technically minded, but increasingly need to be business savvy
- Project management experience as well
- Needs budget approval from CIO, not a revenue generating source, budget is harder to come by
- Decision maker or influencer may need to get budget approved by the CIO
- They are not the end user

IDENTIFIERS
DEMEANOR? COMMUNICATION PREFERENCES?
- Always worried about the next threat so highly motivated to stay up to date with the latest technologies and threats. Spends a lot of time preparing for audits/ensuring they are complying with regulations.
- Gets Information from:
  - #1: Peers
  - #2: Conferences to learn about latest best practices (e.g., Gartner)
  - #3: Vendors, partners and professional service organizations (e.g., Meditology, HIMMS, CHIME)

CHIEF INFORMATION SECURITY OFFICER OWEN

GOALS
PRIMARY GOALS? SECONDARY GOALS?
- Prevent attacks and protect critical assets
- Understand system vulnerabilities and have a plan of action to fix it
- Protect equipment, ensure it functions with integrity, ensuring that it hasn't been compromised due to cyber activity (have to measure risk to do this)
- Bring awareness of risk throughout the organization

CHALLENGES
PRIMARY CHALLENGE? SECONDARY CHALLENGE?
- Adversaries are always changing, always has to stay in an arms race with what everyone else is doing and the latest threats, bad guy only has to find the weakest link - just needs one way in
- Many blind spots because new devices are added all the time, issues compounded by rapid growth, traditional IT tools are not designed for this level/volume complexity
- Understanding ever-changing regulations and compliance
- Security tooling fatigue - complex market with so many tools that only solve part of the challenge, these guys are the inroad for the next +1
- Limited budgets, resources, and skillsets (talent shortage) - have to invest a lot of time to get buy-in and support for security initiatives, especially when going above compliance

WHAT CAN WE DO?
...TO HELP OUR PERSONAS ACHIEVE THEIR GOALS?
...TO HELP OUR PERSONA OVERCOME THEIR CHALLENGES?
- Give them the ability to remediate and/or investigate security breaches
- Segmentation to protect equipment in a systemic way - protection vs. reaction
- Visibility: ease of getting insight, understanding what you are protecting, what the risk is, whether it is vulnerable, if there are active threats, whether it's been compromised
- Prioritize their efforts: informing them what systems they should care about and speed up the process so you can understand the problem and fix it (integrated tools in a very clean way)
- Help them save time, labor and number of tools required to inventory, assess vulnerabilities, and implement plan of protection

FIGURE 3.4 (Continued)

CHIEF INFORMATION SECURITY OFFICER OWEN

CISO JOB ROLES

WHAT JOB ROLES ARE REPRESENTED AT THE TABLE AND HOW DOES EACH INFLUENCE THE BUYING DECISION?

CISO

> I'm responsible for risk management and technology security. I report to the CIO.
> -Paul

> At my company, I would have been the buyer... [I'd] assign a team to go evaluate. [I'd] be looking to spend $1M on this product to roll out. I'd then invite members of the business in to also consider how to add security into our managed services or Honeywell connected products...could become a marketing message to differentiate the product in the market.
> -Rich

> Security team is setting the policy, recommendations to the organization and IT team is more operational to implement.
> -Peter

IT DIRECTOR

> 90% of the time, it's the IT or security groups that make the purchase decision.
> -Andrew

CIO

> [I] told [my] security team manager - You guys gotta check this out - I think it will help solve our biomed problem. At my company, we don't have a CISO:
> • Hard to come by. Super expensive.
> • I have an IT security and risk manager that has a team of analysts responsible for security deterrents and access for the organization do all the rick assessment.
> -Tom

> I report to the COO and she gives me full power to determine the solution and decide on the vendor. I would make the decision. I would include the IT director and possibly one other person from operations. I would include it in my budget and present to the BOD.
> -Brock

FIGURE 3.4 This buyer persona template uses the basic template in Figure 3.1 but has a more visually appealing layout and design. It is extended to add a third page for quotes from interviews with three different personas on the buying committee: Chief Information Security Officer (CISO), IT Director, and Chief Information Officer (CIO).

PROCUREMENT MANAGER PATTY

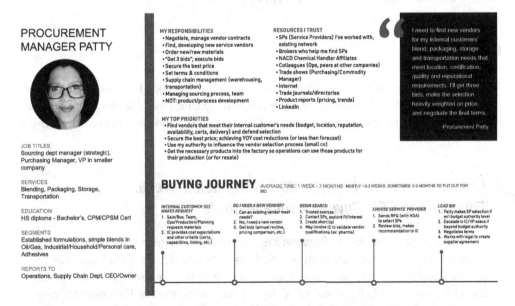

MY RESPONSIBILITIES
• Negotiate, manage vendor contracts
• Find, developing new service vendors
• Order new/raw materials
• "Get 3 bids"; execute bids
• Secure the best price
• Set terms & conditions
• Supply chain management (warehousing, transportation)
• Managing sourcing process, team
• NOT: product/process development

MY TOP PRIORITIES
• Find vendors that meet their internal customer's needs (budget, location, reputation, availability, certs, delivery) and defend selection
• Secure the best price; achieving YOY cost reductions (or less than forecast)
• Use my authority to influence the vendor selection process (small co)
• Get the necessary products into the factory so operations can use those products for their production (or for resale)

RESOURCES I TRUST
• SPs (Service Providers) I've worked with, existing network
• Brokers who help me find SPs
• NACD Chemical Handler Affiliates
• Colleagues (Ops, peers at other companies)
• Trade shows (Purchasing/Commodity Manager)
• Internet
• Trade journals/directories
• Product reports (pricing, trends)
• LinkedIn

> I need to find new vendors for my internal customers' blend, packaging, storage and transportation needs that meet location, certification, quality and reputational requirements. I'll get three bids, make the selection heavily weighted on price, and negotiate the final terms.
> -Procurement Patty

BUYING JOURNEY AVERAGE TIME: 1 WEEK - 3 MONTHS MOSTLY: ~2-3 WEEKS, SOMETIMES: 2-3 MONTHS TO PUT OUT FOR BID

JOB TITLES
Sourcing dept manager (strategic), Purchasing Manager, VP in smaller company

SERVICES
Blending, Packaging, Storage, Transportation

EDUCATION
HS diploma - Bachelor's, CPM/CPSM Cert

SEGMENTS
Established formulations, simple blends in Oil/Gas, Industrial/Household/Personal care, Adhesives

REPORTS TO
Operations, Supply Chain Dept, CEO/Owner

INTERNAL CUSTOMER (IC) MAKES REQUEST
1. Sale/Bus. Team, Ops/Production/Planning requests materials
2. IC provides cost expectations and other criteria (certs, capabilities, timing, etc.)

DO I NEED A NEW VENDOR?
1. Can an existing vendor meet needs?
2. No, I need a new vendor
3. Get bids (annual routine, pricing comparison, etc.)

BEGIN SEARCH
1. Trusted sources
2. Contact SPs, explore fit/interest
3. Create short list
4. May involve IC to validate vendor qualifications (ex: pharma)

CHOOSE SERVICE PROVIDER
1. Sends RFQ (with NDA) to select SPs
2. Review bids, makes recommendation to IC

LEAD BID
1. Patty makes SP selection if w/ budget authority level
2. Escalate to IC/VP execs if beyond budget authority
3. Negotiates terms
4. Works with legal to create supplier agreement

FIGURE 3.5 This in-depth buyer persona template, Procurement Manager Patty, is one illustration of a one-page, in-depth buyer persona that provides a comprehensive report of individual buyer attributes as well as the buying decision process. Adding to the information shown in Figures 3.1 and 3.4, this template includes information such as organizational reporting, job responsibilities, priorities, and trusted resources, as well as a story written in the first person to capture the persona's care-abouts and buying process for selecting a vendor. An infographic visually illustrates the persona's steps in the buying journey.

first two pages include the same categories as the template in Figure 3.1, but the layout and design are more visually appealing. Additional information is included on a third page with quotes from three different personas on a buyer committee: Chief Information Security Officer (CISO), IT Director, and Chief Information Officer (CIO).

Going even deeper, Figure 3.5 illustrates a different way to design a one-page in-depth buyer persona that provides much greater detail on the individual buyer attributes as well as the buying decision process. The template titled Procurement Manager Patty is a persona for a manager in procurement in the chemical services industry served by the company ChemVM. You find similar information such as photo and persona name, job titles, typical education, certifications, and whom she reports to and sections with further information on her responsibilities and priorities and resources she trusts.

Also included is a story written in first person to capture the types of chemical services Patty sources and what she cares most about (location, quality, reputation) as well as her process for selecting a vendor (get three bids, compare prices, and negotiate terms).

Further in-depth information includes her decision criteria when making a purchase. An infographic visually illustrates the steps in the buying journey, which starts with an internal customer making a request for a new chemical service to deciding if an existing or new vendor is needed. Then she begins her search, leads the bid process, and chooses a chemical service provider.

This buyer persona template may also include verbatim quotes like those in Figure 3.4 taken from customer interviews regarding their role on the buying team, success factors, perceived barriers, decision criteria, and the buying journey process.

CONCLUSION

Whether using a simple approach and interviewing internal stakeholders in sales and management or taking a more in-depth, research-based approach to developing more complex buyer personas, they help sales and marketing teams become much more aligned and efficient in reaching target

Interview with the Experts: Q&A with Adele Revella, Founder and CEO, Buyer Persona Institute

Founded in 2010, the Buyer Persona Institute (www.buyerpersona.com) provides organizations with research, best practice resources, and consultative services to create buyer personas and deliver buying insights. We interviewed Adele Revella, founder and CEO of BPI and author of *Buyer Personas*, named by *Fortune* magazine as a "Top 5 Business Book," to learn her firsthand thoughts and guidance for the next generation of content marketers regarding buyer personas.

1. *What is your working definition of a buyer persona?*

   First of all, it's not fictional. A buyer persona in an ideal case that tells you what they want by explaining to you everything buyers do and think about as they make decisions to buy from you or buy from someone else.

2. *What is the most important thing to emphasize when creating buyer personas?*

   The most important part of [the buyer persona] is to understand how [customers] make decisions – because most people, when they build buyer personas, are focused on *who* the buyer is but never *how* they make decisions.

   Ultimately, as a marketer, I'm trying to influence a decision or a series of decisions because, in fact, in a complex buying decision, buyers are making a series of decisions. They're making a decision first that the status quo is unacceptable, and they need to change and find the money or the resources to change. Then there's decisions about how they are going to do research to figure out what they should buy, so that's a decision. Are they going to do that online; are they going to ask their peers? How are they going to get the information they need to make the decision? Then there's decisions about the companies they are going to consider initially, followed, at a later point, by deciding how to pare the universal list of potential providers down to the ultimate decision of whom to buy from.

3. *What are marketers missing about buyer personas?*

   Basically, the problem with our approach to marketing traditionally is that we, as marketers, think that we need to educate buyers, challenge their knowledge, and somehow change them. But buyers aren't the least bit interested in that. Buyers have a mission and a vision and problems and challenges. In creating buyer personas, we should seek to understand from the buyer's perspective. What do they believe is wrong in their companies? What do they think needs to change? What do they think will get better? What do they think is important about a solution? What marketers are missing is that it's about what the buyer wants. What can they teach us?

   By listening to the buyers and what they want, we see the buying decision through the buyer persona's eyes. Only then can we know which target markets we should approach and how to do that effectively.

4. *What are the most important questions to ask in a buyer persona interview?*

   First, you want to make sure you are interviewing a person who is involved in the end-to-end evaluation of the solutions and had to evaluate multiple providers so you can glean information about how to influence that decision process. Most buyers think that there's three or four providers that can all address their needs perfectly well. At the end of the journey, when they decided what companies to consider, I want to learn how they ultimately decided which one.

What I really want to know is why. However, I never just ask the question "Why did you do that? Why did you choose that company?" because people get resistant when you ask them directly. Instead, I ask, "How did you come to the decision that [Company X] was the best company?"

Interviewers need to think more like journalists and ask questions like "That's interesting what you said; tell me more about that" or "Can you elaborate on what you mean and explain why you took that approach?" It's about being in a state of inquiry and being curious and just asking the person to share more.

5. *Does it require a particular person or department to create a buyer persona?*

No, it just should *not* be somebody in sales or a person who's going to go in and try to overcome objections and actually turn it into a sale. It goes back to constantly being in a state of inquiry and seeking to learn from the buyer. What's more important is the person's level of curiosity and ability to listen and inquire more than their title or role.

If the buyer is in a highly technical role, such as a design engineer at a semi-conductor company, it's important the interviewer is at least able to understand what the buyer is saying. If they don't, they will miss opportunities to inquire with those follow-on "Tell me more about that" questions. If the interviewer doesn't understand what the buyer is talking about, it will be hard for them to follow and really engage in the interview for maximum learning.

While it's important to be able to understand generally what they're talking about, it's most advantageous if the interviewer is not a subject matter expert as they're less likely to have the buyer elaborate and share their point of view or feelings about a particular aspect of the solution or decision criteria. By not being that expert, the person is more likely to inquire further by asking questions like "I'm not an expert on that; can you explain why that was important?"

6. *Is there an optimal number of buyer personas for a company?*

The number one question I get in every interview about buyer personas is "How many do I need?" The only answer I can tell you for sure is it's way less than what you think. The way to find the answer is to understand differences in how people make decisions.

Let's say I'm targeting four industries, and there's three critical people in the buying committee. Doing the math, I need 12 personas. Now, let's say we go to market in North America, Asia Pacific, and Western Europe. That's three regions times 12 personas, so now we're up to 36 personas. When I speak to audiences about this topic, I'll ask if anybody in the room has 36 personas or more, and I always get four or five hands. I ask, "Okay, how's that working out for you?"

What we really want to understand is the differences in how people make decisions across those regions, across those industries, and across those job titles and roles. When we do that, we often find that instead of 36 personas, we have two or three. Of the demographics such as geography, industry, company size, and job title, the one that is least likely to have an influence on the buyer persona is geography. Industry is next. . . . [I]ndustry and job title are kind of a close match. And age is absolutely not going to make a difference – we don't even ask about age in our work.

7. *Can you explain why categorizing buyer personas as influencer vs. decision maker is, in your words, "old-school thinking"?*

My point of view is that there are two decision makers. There's one decision maker who decides to change and invest because they're not happy with the status quo. This is the economic buyer. Then there's another, more important decision maker, which is the buying committee that works together to evaluate companies to consider and ultimately selects the winning solution.

From a content marketing standpoint, the most important decision makers are the people doing the evaluation, serving on the buying committee. Sales people will say that the "decision maker" is the economic buyer who has to sign off on the deal, but that's at the end of a whole long period of evaluation.

8. *What advice do you have for the next generation of content marketers and writers regarding buyer personas?*

First, be helpful to your buyers. The buying experience is going to win. The chances in a B2B market that you're going to differentiate because you're the only ones that can deliver some unique value is really thin. If you've got that, by all means, go for it. Chances are you're going to end up at a company where, from the buyer's perspective, the product will do the job as well as two or three other providers. How you're going to win that business is going to be based on how you and your sales and marketing teams work together to make that experience of buying the best.

B2B buyers buy on value and perceived value as a function of their belief and trust that you're going to be the best at delivering the solution to them and their company at this time. That's going to be a function of how authentically and honestly and openly you answered their questions about what could go right and what could go wrong. And that comes down, in part, to great content.

Second, my most important advice is if you're going to be a marketer, work at a company where you love the core business. When I was 25, my boss gave me the best career advice I ever got in my whole life. He told me that I would never get ahead in my life unless I loved the company's core business. I was working for a big bank at the time, and I just hated banking, so I got out. You've got to love the core business and then you've got to go learn about that business. The salespeople are a really good place to learn about that. So invite a salesperson to lunch . . . and be curious.

Third, I teach people never to start a sentence with "I think." To get ahead in your career, you want to start your sentences with "The buyers want . . ." People will listen when you are speaking for your customers, and your sources are credible.

buyers. A telltale sign that a buyer persona is successfully adopted inside an organization is when the buyer becomes personified and "alive" in the conversation, such as "Sam would not respond to this white paper because it focuses on hardware, and his primary focus is software."

What a CM should know: Without understanding the buyer, the content will not be as effective in resonating with the prospective buyer. With buyer personas understood and defined, you can create highly relevant content, such as web pages or white papers with messaging that aligns to the customer's job function, goals, challenges, and decision-making role.

CITATIONS

Adamson, B., Dixon, M., Spenner, P., & Toman, N. *The Challenger Customer: Selling to the Hidden Influencer Who Can Multiply Your Results*. Portfolio. September 2015.

Fullerton, E., & Johnson, J. "The new requirements for building a modern B2B marketing experience." *Slides 11, 19*. August 28, 2019. Retrieved from: www.slideshare.net/AcquiaInc/open-marketing-what-every-modern-marketer-needs-to-know

Gourville, J., & Norton, M. "Consumer behavior and the buying process." *Harvard Business Publishing*. December 19, 2019.

Young, R. "The B2B buyer persona framework." *Slide 8*. November 22, 2015. Retrieved from: www.slideshare.net/SanDiegoAMA/ibm-sirius-decisions-transforming-marketing-through-buyer-profiles-and-personas-55380279

CHAPTER 4

Content Marketing Planning and Integrated Marketing Communications

LEARNING OBJECTIVES

1. An introduction to common marketing frameworks, including the 4Ps, the 4Cs, and the AIDA model and how these frameworks are used to understand the buyer journey and where content marketing fits in.
2. What an integrated marketing plan is and why it's important to ensure consistency of message as the number of promotional channels continues to grow
3. The steps in creating an integrated marketing communications plan and marcom campaigns and how they serve as a foundation for content marketing.
4. The content marketing planning process from strategic purpose to tactically mapping out what content to write, what elements to include in a content calendar, and the importance of repurposing.

INTRODUCTION TO INTEGRATED MARKETING COMMUNICATIONS

In its simplest form, marketing involves the comprehensive set of business activities used together to bring products (or services) to target customers. The essence of marketing has been around since the beginning of time and continued to expand with new inventions from the printing press in the 1400s to industrial manufacturing and the mass production of goods in the 1800s to the internet and thousands of cable channels in the 2000s. With these changes, it's not surprising that how teams develop their strategic marketing plan has continuously changed as well. For instance, in the 1960s, a framework called the 4Ps was introduced to help internal teams develop a marketing strategy to bring products to market (McCarthy, 1960):

- **Product**: physical product (or service) being offered to the customer
- **Price**: amount the customer pays for a product
- **Place**: where the customer can access and purchase the product
- **Promotion**: marketing communications (marcom) plan to educate, influence, and drive consideration and purchase of the product to prospects and customers

DOI: 10.4324/9781003369103-5

This format was criticized as being too company focused, and in 1990, a new framework known as the 4Cs promised a more customer-oriented version (Lauterborn, 1990):

- **Customer:** What does the customer want and/or need?
- **Cost**: What are they willing to pay for it?
- **Convenience:** How easy is it for them to find and purchase the product?
- **Communication**: Every touchpoint that is used to deliver information to the customer.

No matter the framework, one thing remains the same – the number of touchpoints consumers can use to learn about products and make buying decisions continues to expand, creating a growing challenge for marketers to deliver a consistent message across so many channels. As we see in Figure 4.1, the number of channels the marketer had to contend with before 1990 pales in comparison to those after 2014.

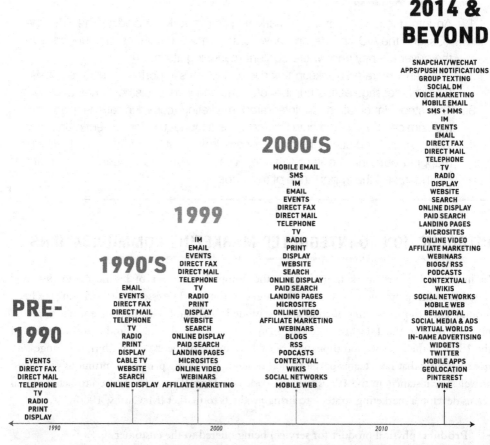

FIGURE 4.1 The number of channels the marketer had to contend with before 1990 pales in comparison to today. As a result, the number of touchpoints consumers use to learn about products and make buying decisions continues to expand while the challenge for marketers to deliver a consistent message becomes more and more difficult.

Source: Adapted from a presentation by Jeffrey Rohrs, October 2014

In 2014, the channel expansion of the previous 20+ years seemed like a revolution. Little did we know what the next ten years would bring. The explosion of social media and other channels since 2014 is best illustrated by the Conversation Prism, a visual representation of the social media landscape created by Brian Solis and interactive agency JESS3 (Figure 4.2).

This is why, with so many choices, in order to be effective and drive the greatest return on the investment of finite marketing resources, it's critically important to first define the message (explained in Chapter 2) and the target customer (explained in Chapter 3). With these in place, in order to achieve consistency of message, marketers then develop an integrated marketing communication (marcom) plan. By taking an integrated approach, rather than treating each channel, such as public relations or advertising, in a silo, the developed

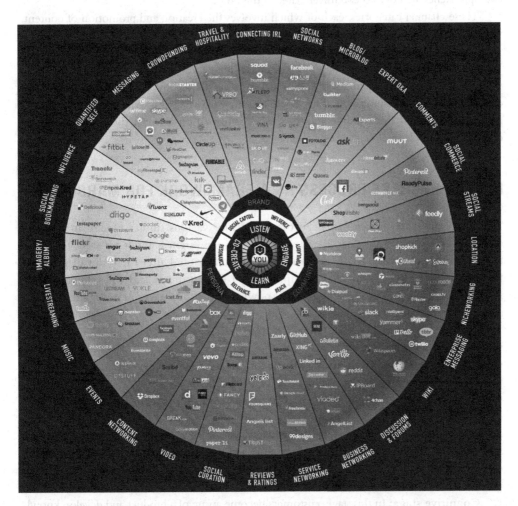

FIGURE 4.2 In 2014, the channel expansion of the previous 20+ years seemed like a revolution. Little did we know what the next ten years would bring. The explosion of social media and other channels since 2014 is best illustrated by this graphic, known as the Conversation Prism: a visual representation of the social media landscape created by Brian Solis and interactive agency JESS3.

plan is cohesive and considers how the customer will consume a "flow of information from indistinguishable sources" (Schultz et al., 1993). Starting with the target customer (explained in Chapter 3) in mind, the marketer can then work backwards to determine where to best communicate the message.

A core component of today's integrated marcom plan is creating original content and promoting or marketing that content across channels. Thus, the form of marketing that today is called content marketing. Content that CMs create can apply across any number of channels. A modern way of organizing the growing number of channels is to group them into four categories, referred to as the PESO model, which stands for "paid" (e.g., advertisements), "earned" (e.g., publicity), "shared" (e.g., posts on LinkedIn), and "owned" (e.g., your website or blog) (Deitrich, 2014).

Both earned and owned media require extensive involvement from a CM, and thus these two approaches are covered extensively later in the book.

These channel categories, each of which involves the creation and promotion of content, work together to educate and persuade buyers along their purchase journey.

What a CM should know: The more channels where a CM's content can work, the more value a CM has to an organization. It's crucial to think about how a core story can work in diverse forms of communication. That doesn't mean a CM has to rewrite everything; it does mean a CM should think about how to rework information to meet the needs of diverse communication channels and diverse audiences.

BUYER PURCHASE PROCESS AS A FRAMEWORK FOR MARCOM

The buyer purchase process has been organized into various similar models in which a customer transitions somewhat linearly from a lack of awareness about a product through to the point of purchase. Many contemporary models extend after the point of purchase for a continued, long-term relationship between the customer and the company. The AIDA model (Figure 4.3) is the most well known and has four stages of buyer thought and action (Barry & Howard, 1990):

- **Attention**: Gain initial awareness of a new product.
- **Interest**: Develop interest in and increase knowledge about the product.
- **Desire**: Create a feeling of wanting to own or use the product.
- **Action**: Instigate the actions necessary to purchase the product.

AIDA and similar models consist of three broad stages of buyer thinking: cognitive, affective, and behavioral. By understanding the information needs of the buyer at each stage, the CM can create the most effective content that resonates with the buyer:

1. **Cognitive stage**: In this stage, customers become aware of a product and develop knowledge about the product attributes (features) and useful applications (benefits). In this rational stage, the purpose of content marketing is to raise the awareness of the buyer about the product, demonstrate the company's understanding of the buyer's needs or pain points, and even provide entertainment to promote a positive brand image.

THE AIDA MODEL

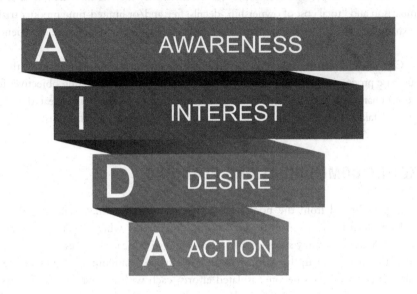

FIGURE 4.3 The buyer purchase process has been organized into various similar models in which a customer transitions somewhat linearly from a lack of awareness (A) about a product to interest in the product (I) to a desire for the product (D) through to the point of taking action to purchase (A). Many contemporary models extend after the point of purchase for a continued, long-term relationship between the customer and the company.

2. **Affective stage**: At this stage, customers develop attitudes and feelings towards the product (and perhaps the company that provides the product) and increase their affinity for it. Through engagement with marcom activities, customers:

   - First gain an interest (to learn more about a product).
   - Then begin liking the category of products (recognizing that the type of product is beneficial or desirable).
   - Next, build preference (preferring a specific product over the alternatives).
   - And finally, develop conviction (an intention to purchase).

   At this stage, content marketing should change and develop attitudes and feelings, including building trust in the product and the company. This typically includes informative product comparisons that distinguish one product from others in the class, lengthier content such as white papers (explained in Chapter 9), webinars (explained in Chapter 10), as well as case studies (also explained in Chapter 9). The goal of this content is to provide in-depth details about the challenges the customer faces, explain how the product solves them, and demonstrate the company's expertise and adoption by similar buyers to build trust and lower objections or feelings of fear from risk.

3. **Behavioral stage**: This is when customers reach a point of action to purchase a product. The primary intention of content marketing at this stage is to enable the buyer's purchase process and the salesperson's selling process. Content may include information such as cost comparison and "total cost of ownership" details, free and/or limited-time product trials, and an explanation of the purchase process and expectations of the post-purchase experience.

What a CM should know: The AIDA model, although an oversimplification of the actual buyer purchase process, provides a useful framework to develop the marketing objectives for different PESO channels and helps CMs consider the role of the content being created.

Now let's take a look at the marcom plan and where content marketing fits.

MARKETING COMMUNICATIONS PLANNING

The saying paraphrased from the book *Alice's Adventures in Wonderland* and popularized by George Harrison in his song "Any Road," "If you don't know where you're going, any road will take you there," accurately sums up why planning is so critical to success.

Without a marcom plan, the road, or goals and expected outcomes, are not defined, and as a result, marcom activities become isolated efforts, each with its own cost and measure of success. In contrast to this, by defining the road your marcom efforts will take, you have a plan or blueprint for achieving agreed-upon goals. In this organized planning approach, teams coordinate marcom activities to reach potential buyers efficiently and to effectively drive awareness, preference, and conviction of potential buyers to take action. The marcom plan is the framework used in marketing to define and document the integrated approach and expected outcomes along the marketing and sales funnel.

Developing the Marcom Plan

Marcom planning is a step-by-step process used to outline the promotional strategy for a product and is a deliberate effort by company and marketing leaders to ensure the company meets the needs of the prospective buyer and achieves the organization's goals for the product (Lamb et al., 2011). With so many channels from which to choose, the role of an integrated marcom plan is to ensure consistency across channels and efficiency within each channel to achieve the best results.

There are varied models of marcom planning. Most include these key elements:

- **Target customer profile** – as described in Chapter 3, the target prospective buyers' attributes and information about how buying decisions are made.
- **Plan goals** – the expected outcomes of the overall marcom effort, written in SMART goal format to be specific, measurable, attainable, realistic, and time bound.
- **Campaigns** – subsections of the plan used to organize activities and measured objectives for a common theme or initiative, such as the launch of a new product, focus on a particular application area, or expansion into a new market or geography.
- **Prioritized media channels** – with an understanding of the buyer personas, scrutinizing the strengths and weaknesses of each PESO channel category to concentrate on the most effective ones to achieve the plan and campaign objectives.

- **Content plan** – the topics your content will focus on, as well as the types and quantity of content needed to appeal to the target customer along the marketing and sales funnel, written with a consistent tone that allows for easy adaptation and repurposing for different genres (explained in detail later in this chapter).
- **Timeline** – a visual overview of the key projects, activities, and milestones of the marcom plan, usually shown in the form of a Gantt chart.
- **Metrics dashboard** – the quantitative measurements, or key performance indicators (KPIs), tracked and analyzed monthly, quarterly, and/or annually to monitor whether activities are achieving the plan objectives.

Marcom planning usually occurs on an annual basis to align with business plans to ensure the investment made in marketing delivers results in areas where the company is investing. For instance, if a company-level goal is to increase revenue in a particular product line or expand in a new geographic region or application area, this informs where marketing should invest.

With business goals defined, the first step in planning is to define the marcom goals. These are often quantitative in nature, such as increasing the number of leads for a particular product line or expanding awareness in a specific sector through earned media. Using these two examples, when written using a SMART format, marcom goals are written similarly to the following two examples:

- Generate 550 new leads in a segment X in the next 12 months.
- Double the number of earned mentions in our top five automotive publications this year.

Usually a marcom plan will include between four and seven goals like these examples. It's not recommended to have more goals than this as it can dilute the effort toward any one goal and diminish the marcom team's ability to impact the business in a given time period. A more in-depth discussion of marcom goals and measurement occurs in Chapter 11.

What a CM should know: If a marcom plan doesn't have clearly defined goals and objectives, it is next to impossible for a CM to succeed in their work. Make sure everyone on the team understands and agrees to the same clearly defined goals and objectives before starting the content creation process.

The marcom goals encompass the top four to six priority outcomes the team needs to achieve in a year. Then the question is "How do we accomplish these goals?" In reality, the goals are accomplished through a myriad of activities, from a global product launch to a website redesign, executed across channels within a defined budget. To bring focus and organization to these major initiatives, a campaign framework defines the set of activities and primary PESO channels needed to best achieve each campaign's objectives.

Referring to the first marcom goal of expanding into a new segment, the example in Figure 4.4 shows how a medical device manufacturing company, ATL Technology, defined a campaign focused on generating leads and establishing thought leadership in the minimally invasive segment, targeting surgeons who use these specific types of medical devices to limit the size and number of incisions in patients' operations.

The first element of the minimally invasive campaign is the marcom objective or purpose statement. In ATL's case, the objective of the campaign was to "Establish ATL as the thought

---

CAMPAIGN: *MINIMALLY INVASIVE*

OBJECTIVE

Establish ATL as the thought leading manufacture of Minimally Invasive device connectors that results in generating leads and qualified opportunities for the sales team.

CHANNELS & ACTIVITIES

EARNED
- Build relationships, share news and expertise with key trade editors

SHARED
- Promote content at least twice weekly on LinkedIn, YouTube and Twitter
- Ensure ATL executives post on LinkedIn at least weekly
- Auto-publish blog to social platforms

OWNED:
- Content marketing: publish 6 blog posts, 1 white paper, 1 webinar
- SEO: optimize content, web pages for search
- Website
  - Create Minimally Invasive application page
  - Update website navigation to bring prominence to Minimally Invasive application

QUARTERLY KPIs

- Achieve 100% of content publishing plan
- Generate 24 new leads with interest in ATL Minimally Invasive manufacturing
- Achieve a 20% conversion rate to generate 5 Minimally Invasive sales qualified leads
- Achieve at least 3 mentions in articles published in top trade magazines

FIGURE 4.4 To bring focus and organization to major marcom initiatives across channels during a given time period, campaigns like this one from ATL Technology are used. The first element of the campaign is the objective, which states the purpose. The next elements are the PESO channels and specific activities within each channel that will be used to achieve the campaign objective. The third element of the campaign is the KPIs, which are the quantifiable outcomes of the activities, in this case measured on a quarterly basis.

leading manufacturer of minimally invasive device connectors that result in generating leads and qualified opportunities for the sales team."

With this objective in mind, the ATL marcom team then scrutinized all the channels and selected those that would help them position ATL as a thought leader and generate leads in this specific application area. For this campaign, the three PESO channels chosen were earned, shared, and owned, with the specific activities planned quarterly listed under each channel type. By executing these activities, the team defined four expected outcomes, or KPIs, of the campaign, measured quarterly:

1. Achieve 100% of content publishing plan.
2. Generate 24 new leads with interest in ATL minimally invasive manufacturing.
3. Achieve a 20% conversion rate to generate five minimally invasive sales qualified leads.
4. Achieve at least three mentions in articles published in target trade magazines.

With so many elements to a marcom plan, it is helpful to have a bird's-eye view of the timeline showing the schedule for key projects, activities, and milestones in each campaign by PESO channel throughout the year. An effective project management tool to use for this is a Gantt chart, illustrated in Figure 4.5. A horizontal bar across the top lists the months when activities are scheduled to occur, in this case from January to July. The vertical column on the left side of the chart is grouped by campaign, with specific channels prioritized under each campaign.

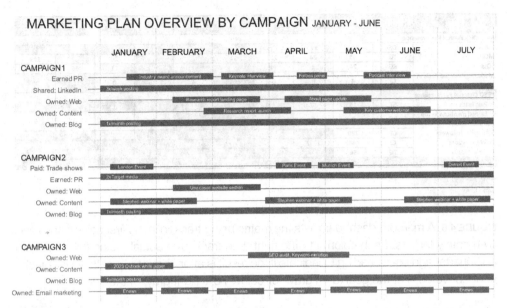

FIGURE 4.5 It's helpful to have a bird's-eye view of the marcom plan schedule for each campaign by channel type. Using a Gantt chart, a horizontal bar across the top lists the months from January to July when activities will occur while a vertical column on the left side lists the planned campaigns with channel categories prioritized for each. To the right of each channel category are the specific activities that will occur for that channel, placed under the month when they will occur.

To the right of each channel are the specific activities that will occur for that channel, placed under the month when it is scheduled. For example, below Campaign #1 for the earned PR channel, there are four specific activities that are planned: industry award announcements in January and February, a keynote interview in March, a *Forbes* panel in May, and a podcast interview in July.

The last piece of the marcom plan is the metrics dashboard. Much like the dashboard of a car, which includes a gauge to alert you when you are low on gas and indicator lights such as those that measure the pressure in your tires, a marcom dashboard tracks the performance of your activities.

Chapter 11 goes over measurement ideas in more detail. For the sake of a marcom metrics dashboard, a CM should provide the information needed to compare results to your intended goals in a simple format. This way, it's clear what's working and where corrective actions are necessary to get the plan back on track. The metrics in a marcom dashboard depend on each campaign's objectives and channels. Additionally, the layout and design of the marcom dashboard can vary widely. The dashboard shown in Figure 4.6 lists two approaches – one by funnel and the other by campaign:

- Marketing funnel performance (similar to the AIDA model)

  - **Leads** – new contacts.
  - **Marketing qualified leads** (MQLs) – contacts that meet a basic set of qualification criteria.
  - **Sales qualified leads** (SQLs) – contacts that meet a higher level of qualification criteria.

Metric	Owner	Monthly Targets	Jan	Feb	Mar	Q1 Total	April	May	June	Q2
Marketing Funnel Performance										
Leads	DF	100	88	144	192	424	180	144	216	964
MQLs	TG	40	24	20	32	76	15	20	32	143
SQLs	RG	24	8	21	26	55	10	21	16	102
Marketing-sourced deals in pipeline	CJ	4	0	0	4	4	2	0	24	30
PESO Channel Performance										
P: Paid leads	ST	16	12	44	60	116	100	44	76	336
E: Earned mentions in top tier publications	RG	2	1	2	2	5	0	0	0	5
S: LinkedIn followers	DF	220	57	50	154	261	154	50	185	650
O: Web sessions	CJ	3,452	2892	4180	4512	11584	1121	1047	1398	15150
O: Online leads	TG	56	72	88	132	292	18	22	27	359

>=90%
75% - 89%
<75%

FIGURE 4.6 A marcom dashboard lists the metric being tracked in the first column followed by monthly targets. Each column to the right then tracks the actual metric for the month and quarter and uses shading to indicate if the result is at or above 90% of the goal (black), at or above 80% of the goal (dark gray), or below 70% (light gray) of the goal.

- **Marketing-sourced deals in the pipeline** – new revenue opportunities that are created directly from marketing efforts.

- PESO channel performance – these metrics can vary by marketing team and include the critical KPIs that must be met to achieve channel and thus campaign performance:

  - **Paid** – metrics such as impressions or leads from paid media activities.
  - **Earned** – metrics may include mentions in articles, feature coverage in third-party news and trade media, or share of voice of your brand versus competitors in defined outlets.
  - **Shared** – metrics to track reach, such as social media followers, site traffic, and leads to measure content performance.
  - **Owned** – metrics along the funnel, including site traffic, inbound leads, and time on site.

The metrics tracked on the left include the owner responsible for the metric, the monthly target, each month's results, and a quarterly summary. Using a simple color-coding approach, the result for each metric in each month is shaded to indicate if the result is at or at or above 90% of the target (black), between 75%–89% of the target (dark gray), or below 75% (light gray) of the target. The quarterly results are similarly color coded. By quickly viewing this dashboard, the marcom team can understand what metrics are on track (black) or nearly on track (dark gray) and what areas of the marcom plan are not achieving results (light gray) and require immediate actions to improve performance and achieve the desired results.

What a CM should know: Many people outside marketing use the metrics dashboard as the sole evaluation of marketing work. That's not perfect or ideal, but it happens. A CM should feel comfortable with the metrics measurement process and what success looks like. A CM should also expect that it's impossible to reach every benchmark. Be comfortable knowing why winning and losing occur, and learn from both.

CONTENT MARKETING PLANNING

With the marcom goals and campaigns developed, the CM has a foundational framework to develop the content marketing plan. This plan's purpose is twofold, one strategic and one tactical:

1. Strategically, create a connected story that your target customer values and wants more of.
2. Tactically, identify the specific content assets along the customer's buying journey, noting when each will be published, which campaign it supports, and how it will be measured. Chapter 11 goes into further detail on measurement.

While content marketing teams must demonstrate ROI toward achieving marcom and business goals to receive continued investment, content marketing plays a much broader role than driving leads or generating new sales. In its purest form, content marketing's ultimate purpose is to build a growing audience that values and trusts what your company has to say. Over time, as your audience grows, this becomes a competitive advantage that is harder and harder for your competitors to compete against. This is the true ROI measure of a successful content marketing program.

This is why we are writing this book – to not only explain tactically how content marketing is done also but to illustrate the impact CMs can have at the highest levels of a business or organization.

What a CM should know: While the CM role often sits in the marketing organization and needs to be well versed in the business and marcom goals, growing an audience that trusts and values your brand is the holy grail for a CM leader.

Developing the Content Marketing Plan

The first step in creating the content plan is defining the strategic story by deciding what your content should focus on – e.g., Why is a particular topic important to your audience? How will it help them? How will it, in turn, help your company build awareness and interest and, ultimately, grow their trust to drive desire and action (i.e., AIDA)?

Joe Pulizzi, founder of Content Marketing Institute and a global expert, speaker, and author of many books on the topic of content marketing, gave the following description of content purpose in an interview on his podcast, *Content Inc.* (Pulizzi, 2021):

> "*Do you know the "why" behind your content? Or are you jumping from article to podcast to video without truly understanding the purpose for creating it? You have to remind yourself of this all the time. I know I do. Maybe in your situation you are asked to create content to drive immediate sales . . . but you know in your heart and soul it's not serving the customer or audience. While these activities might help short term, they will kill you long term. We have to learn to say no.*"
>
> "*Here's what I ask of you: Right now, stop creating all the "whats" and really put some thought into your "why." Find a "why" that has purpose for you as well as a deep purpose and meaning for your audience. Once you find that, all the "whats" will easily present themselves.*"

For the CM, the *why* behind the content should be derived in part from the marcom goals and campaigns but also from higher levels of the business to flesh out that "story." There are many ways to begin the process of defining the purpose and focus of your content; one simple way is to define content themes. To get ideas for content themes that will build a growing audience aligned to business and marcom goals, here are a few ways to start:

- Create a list of relevant topics identified during the process of creating your positioning statement, messaging, and buyer personas (described in Chapters 2 and 3).
- Analyze topics your competitors have written about.
- Interview salespeople and internal subject matter experts to learn what questions potential buyers most often ask or would value learning from your team.
- Conduct a Google search to browse the content that comes up in the search results for related words and phrases.

From this research, you will have a list of disparate topics to group and rank according to your company's unique expertise; target segments and customers; product offerings; and competency to write compelling, high-quality content on each topic. In reviewing your list, group together related ideas to form a cluster of topics that emerge as a content theme.

Keeping with the earlier marcom campaign from ATL focused on the minimally invasive segment, a theme by the same name is at the center, and related content topics are identified,

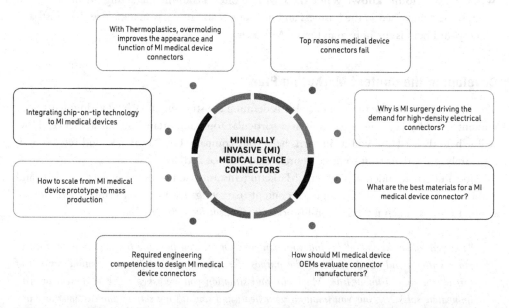

FIGURE 4.7 Through the process of interviewing and researching potential content themes, topics are grouped and ranked together to form a content theme. By creating a content theme that groups related topics, a story emerges that demonstrates ATL's expertise and interest in educating prospective buyers throughout their buying process as they investigate and select solutions in the minimally invasive segment.

such as "Top reasons medical device connectors fail," "How should minimally invasive medical device makers evaluate connector manufacturers," and "Required engineering competencies to design minimally invasive medical device connectors" (Figure 4.7).

By creating content themes that group related topics, a story emerges that demonstrates ATL's expertise and interest in educating prospective buyers throughout their buying process as they investigate and select solutions in this segment. Additionally, when the content is published on the company's website and linked to a web page devoted to the theme, called a pillar page or cluster page, the content in the cluster performs better in search engines such as Google. Linking content within a cluster to the pillar page and vice versa programmatically alerts Google that there is a semantic or interrelated relationship between the linked content and thus improves the chance that each piece of content in the cluster will be ranked higher in search engine results and discovered by potential buyers searching for information related to that theme.

CONTENT TYPES ALONG THE FUNNEL

FIGURE 4.8 Similar to the AIDA model described earlier (Figure 4.3), another common way to visualize the buyer journey is through a simple marketing and sales funnel that describes four stages: attract, convert, close, and retain. At the top of the funnel, the goal of content is to attract prospective buyers who are strangers and turn them into visitors to your company's brand online or in person. In the middle of the funnel, the goal of content is to convert visitors who are aware of your brand into leads who are considering your company and want to evaluate your expertise and offerings more seriously. At the bottom of the funnel, content is used to help further qualify and close sales opportunities by converting leads who were considering your company into customers who purchase your product.

What a CM should know: Clusters often have overlap, which some CMs see as a sign of inefficiency. In fact, it's the opposite. It's a sign a CM is on to a powerful insight that can help create measured results. Welcome clusters!

With the strategic part of the content plan defined, it's now time to move to the tactical aspects of content marketing planning: specifically, identifying the content assets along the customer's buying journey, when each will be published, which campaign it supports, and how it will be measured. Like the AIDA model described earlier (Figure 4.3), another common way to visualize the buyer journey is through a simple inbound marketing funnel that includes four stages: attract, convert, close, and retain (Figure 4.8). In this framework, anonymous prospective buyers are attracted to your content, which they find during their online search, decide to visit your website, and engage from there along the next three stages (Geier, 2016).

At the top of the funnel (ToF), the goal of content is to attract prospective buyers who are strangers and have not heard of your company and turn them into visitors to your company's brand, either online or in person. Providing content that is freely available to the public educates prospective buyers and exposes them to your company's products, solutions, and expertise. The primary purpose of content at the top of the funnel is to demonstrate your company's knowledge and expertise by educating readers on topics such as industry or technology trends, providing advice and guidance, and sharing useful resources. Types of content most often used at the top of the funnel are top-level web pages, blog posts, introductory videos, and infographics.

In the middle of the funnel (MoF), the goal of content is to convert visitors who are now aware of your brand into leads who are considering your company and want to evaluate your expertise and offerings more seriously. This content is often referred to as gated or lead-generating content. This means the user must provide information such as name, email, job title, and employer to receive the content (i.e., "open the gate"). When the visitor completes the form, they become a known person whom the marcom team can further engage. Common examples of gated content used in the middle of the funnel that requires form completion to access include webinars and white papers, described in detail in Chapters 8 and 10, respectively.

In the third stage of the funnel, referred to as the bottom of the funnel (BoF), content helps further qualify and close sales opportunities by converting prospective buyers who were considering your company into customers who purchase your product. At this stage in the funnel, the purpose of content is to strengthen the buyer's trust in your company's ability to solve their application, differentiate your company's products from competitors, and enable sales with content to persuade and inspire action to purchase. Examples of bottom-of-the-funnel content used to convert qualified leads to buyers are customer case studies, product demonstrations, sales presentations, and product comparison guides.

In the last stage of the funnel, content is used to retain existing customers and build loyalty with them so they're inspired to become promoters and advocates of your product, company, and brand. Examples of content at this stage include customer newsletters and areas of the website with specific content that supports a positive customer experience that only customers can log in to and access. When customers have a positive experience with your product and company, they become promoters who are enthusiastic to share their positive experiences with others. These promoters are ideal candidates for CMs to work with to publish testimonial quotes and case studies (explained in Chapter 10).

What a CM should know: While in no way an exhaustive list of content types for each stage of the funnel, this provides a way of thinking about where a certain content asset will most likely be consumed in the buyer's journey. At the same time, the reality is that prospective buyers may consume any type of content at any point in their journey. What's important for the CM is ensuring each and every piece of content supports and strengthens the story they want to tell in the content theme in a way that the prospective buyer will value and find helpful. In his book *Stop Selling. Start Helping.*, Matt White (2016) explains,

> *"One of the major benefits of helping instead of selling is being a resource in such a way that, over time, you're in the right place at the right time with the right product or services. As you educate, inform, and entertain your customers and prospects, you're priming the pump, so to say, for that time six months, 18 months, or two years from now when your prospect is ready to make a purchase."*

CONTENT MAPPING

With your content themes defined and having considered how content may be consumed throughout the buyer journey, you are ready to create your tactical plan: what specific content pieces you will create in what format and when they will be published.

Focus x Format

	People	Basics	Details	History	Process	Curation	Data	Product	Example	Opinion
Writing	●	●	●	●	●	●	●	●	●	●
Infographic	●	●	●	●	●	●	●	●	●	●
Audio	●	●	●	●	●	●	●	●	●	●
Video	●	●	●	●	●	●	●	●	●	●
Live Video	●	●	●	●	●	●	●	●	●	●
Image Gallery	●	●	●	●	●	●	●	●	●	●
Timeline	●	●	●	●	●	●	●	●	●	●
Quiz	●	●	●	●	●	●	●	●	●	●
Tool	●	●	●	●	●	●	●	●	●	●
Map	●	●	●	●	●	●	●	●	●	●

From your friends at StoryFuel. Learn more at StoryFuel.co

FIGURE 4.9 The Content Fuel Framework provides a simple matrix system to map out content focuses and content formats, which, when filled in, provides 100 different content ideas. Going through this exercise unlocks ideation and demonstrates just how many ways you can tell your story from different angles, called the 10 Focuses listed across the top row, and types of content, called the 10 Formats listed along the left-hand side.

It's important to understand what types of content your buyer prefers. For instance, in B2B technical markets, in which purchase decisions are high involvement and can last months, the most valued types may be longer-form technical white papers and in-depth datasheets that provide detailed product specifications. Contrast this with consumer markets, in which purchase decisions are more emotional and even spontaneous, and the preferred content type is a 20-second video on Instagram or a colorful, easy-to-read infographic. It's the responsibility of the CM to understand the prospective customer's preferences and put a plan together that aligns to what they value most.

In her book *The Content Fuel Framework*, Melanie Deziel provides a simple matrix system to map out content focuses and formats, which, when filled in, provides 100 different content ideas (Figure 4.9). Going through this exercise fuels content ideation and demonstrates just how many ways you can tell your story from different angles (called the 10 Focuses) listed across the top row and types of content (called the 10 Formats) listed along the left-hand side (Deziel, 2020):

In the framework in Figure 4.9, the content types are listed by how the CM creates them, such as writing, audio, video, or design in an infographic or map. Just as with the explosion of media channels shown in Figures 4.1 and 4.2, the list of content formats or types continues to grow and change as well. (TikTok didn't exist at the start of writing this text and now is among the most popular platforms to be educated and entertained.)

A sample of the more common types of content CMs are responsible for creating are listed below according to the chapters in which they are explained in this book:

1. **Chapter 6 – Earned Media**

   a.   Presentations and speeches
   b.   Thought leadership articles
   c.   News releases

2. **Chapter 7 – Owned Media (Part 1)**

   a.   Websites
   b.   Blog posts
   c.   Branded publications

3. **Chapter 8 – Owned Media (Part 2)**

   a.   Webinars
   b.   Videos
   c.   Podcasts

4. **Chapter 9 – Product Collateral**

   a.   Product web pages
   b.   Brochures
   c.   Fliers

5. **Chapter 10 – B2B Content**

   a.   White papers
   b.   Case studies

With specific content pieces defined, a content calendar helps organize and schedule content publishing throughout the year. Housed in a simple spreadsheet, the content calendar includes a variety of information such as:

- Content title
- What theme the content supports
- Content writer
- The buyer persona the content is written for
- The content type to be created, such as blog post, webinar, or white paper
- Estimated date the content will be published
- Who will be credited as the public author of the content, where applicable
- What stage of the funnel the content is intended to serve
- The call to action where the reader will be pointed to learn more
- Keywords the content supports in search engine optimization
- What channels will be used to distribute and market the content
- How the content will be repurposed

Regarding this last point on repurposing content, best-in-class content plans list not only the original content to be created but also the additional ways the content will be used in other formats and further distributed and promoted. As explained in Chapter 10, a high-quality white paper takes significant time and effort to produce and involves multiple internal reviews to ensure quality and accuracy standards are met. Once the white paper is published, as shown in Figure 4.10, the approved content can be efficiently repurposed into a blog post series and used as a transcript for a

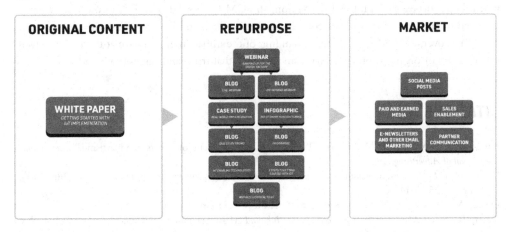

FIGURE 4.10 A high-quality white paper takes significant time and effort to produce and involves multiple internal reviews to ensure quality and accuracy standards are met. Once the white paper is published, the approved content can be efficiently repurposed into a blog post series and used as a transcript for a video or a script and slides for a webinar. The blog posts, video, and webinar can then be individually marketed across additional shared, paid, and earned channels and shared with sales and partners, multiplying the return on the investment of the original white paper.

video or a script and slides for a webinar. The blog posts, video, and webinar can then be individually marketed across additional shared, paid, and earned channels and shared with sales and partners, multiplying the return on the investment of the original white paper.

What a CM should know: Repurposing content is vital for a CM. There are too many different ways to communicate for a single person to oversee. Reworking what teams already have approved is much easier than starting from scratch. It also allows a CM to empower others to help create, repurpose, and share content ideas.

CONCLUSION

This chapter introduces the strategic and tactical steps involved in content marketing planning and how it fits into the larger context of integrated marketing communications. The marcom planning process and its key elements are introduced, including SMART goals, marcom campaigns, PESO channels, measurable objectives, and using a marcom metrics dashboard to track performance to plan. The chapter then details the key strategic and tactical elements of the content marketing planning process. This begins with defining the purpose of content and the strategic role content marketing plays in building an audience and creating competitive advantage over time. The process of creating content themes is described to organize and focus your content on key topics relevant to target buyer personas. Content marketing planning tactics are then explained, including identifying content types along the marketing and sales funnel and developing a content calendar to track specific information about each content piece, such as when it will be published and how it will be repurposed. With this information, the CM has a solid overview of the role, what is involved in creating a best-in-class content marketing plan, and how it aligns with the marcom plan. Moreover, the CM gains an understanding of the impact they can have at the highest levels of a business or organization by growing an audience that trusts and values the brand.

CITATIONS

Barry, T., & Howard, D.J. "A review and critique of the hierarchy of effects in advertising." *International Journal of Advertising.* 1990.

Deitrich, G. *Spin Sucks: Communication and Reputation Management in the Digital Age.* Que Publishing. February 25, 2014.

Deziel, M. *The Content Fuel Framework.* StoryFuel Press. February 23, 2020.

Geier, R. *Smart Marketing for Engineering: An Inbound Marketing Guide to Reaching Technical Audiences.* Rockbench. January 2016.

Lamb, C.W., Hair, J.F., & McDaniel, C. *Essentials of Marketing.* Cengage Learning. 2011.

Lauterborn, B. "New marketing Litany: Four Ps passé: C-Words take over." *Advertising Age.* 1990.

McCarthy, E.J. *Basic Marketing: A Managerial Approach.* McGraw-Hill. 1960.

Pulizzi, J. "Q&A with comedian Michael Jr." *Content Inc. Podcast.* July 15, 2021.

Rohrs, J. "Audience – The flip side of content marketing." *Slide 118.* October 2014. Retrieved from: www.slideshare.net/KC_BMA/audience-the-flipside-of-content-marketing-by-jeffrey-k-rohrs/2-JEFFREY_K_ROHRS_VP_MARKETING

Schultz, D.E., Tannenbaum, S.I., & Lauterborn, R.F. *Integrated Marketing Communications.* NTC Business Books. 1993.

White, M. *Stop Selling. Start Helping.* CreateSpace. April 14, 2016.

Creating Persuasive Content

INTRODUCTION

It's so simple.

"Create good content."

Countless experts go through incredibly intricate models to develop impactful marketing solutions for content marketers (CM) and clients. The only thing you need to keep the flywheel turning: good content.

This is the equivalent of telling someone they can lose 50 pounds by just not eating unhealthy foods, then taking them to a buffet with pizza, wings, and enough fried carbs to feed a football team.

Creating good content is easy to say and hard to do. This chapter will offer a brief synopsis of why we need to focus on the persuasive story in content marketing, how basic message theory can help, what diverse methods a CM can use to build an audience in which language can help or hurt, and how to create an easy-to-use storytelling structure for any audience.

Full disclosure: creating good content won't be simple at the end of this chapter. It will be easier to navigate and more likely to achieve goals in a manageable way for a CM and their team.

DOI: 10.4324/9781003369103-6

WHY PERSUASIVE STORIES ARE VITAL FOR CONTENT MARKETING

See. Think. Do. Feel.

There are many ways to describe a customer's buyer journey. Some will describe it as a sales funnel or sales cycle. Others believe it's a sales circle. Regardless of how many steps are in your favorite definition, the process for the customer remains consistent.

- They notice something exists.
- They consider if it will help them.
- They decide to do something: i.e., buy the product.
- They feel something about the product experience and communicate those feelings to an audience.

When Lisa Gerber of Big Leap Creative talks with her clients about the power of business storytelling, she finds a way to mix personal and professional.

> *I love helping people shed the "so what?" content – the meaningless drivel – and show up as themselves. Stories reveal your essence, give people something to latch onto, and help you develop a community.*

As discussed in previous chapters detailing buyer personas and content marketing planning, the core of CM revolves around delivering the right message to a potential customer when they are in the moment and being able to offer them helpful information to build trust and inspire them to engage and take further action.

That's why diverse storytelling is vital to reach an intended audience when they are in the moment. Diverse storytelling can appeal to a mix of logic, reason, and emotion. Diverse storytelling also means adapting your story as needed based on the target audience and delivering it through their preferred channels.

That combination serves as the gravity to move your audience down the funnel.

MESSAGE THEORY'S ROLE IN EFFECTIVE CONTENT MARKETING

Dr. Eddith A. Dashiell joined the E.W. Scripps School of Journalism at Ohio University in 1992 and serves as the School of Journalism's director. "Dr. D." is a national leader in helping students understand and apply communication law, ethics, and diversity. She applies all these skills in Journalism 1010, The Future of Media, a course every first-year journalism student takes in their first semester on the Athens, Ohio, campus.

"Storytelling should drive technology and not the other way around," Dr. D. tells students on the first day of class.

Tools evolve. Video has been around for less than a century. Streaming audio is under 30. YouTube launched in 2005.

Tools decay. Myspace was once popular. Tout and Vine once existed. Twitter was once a place where thoughtful conversation occurred.

When content creators chase tactics, the inefficient effort comes at the expense of the story. Aristotle may not have had a great Myspace page, but his principles of ethos, pathos, and logos still apply to anyone with a story. That means it applies to anyone who works in CM.

Ethos (Credibility) and Content Marketing

Merriam-Webster (No Author, 2023, *Ethos*) defines *ethos* as "The distinguishing character, sentiment, moral nature, or guiding beliefs of a person, group, or institution."

For a CM, this is argument currency. Web links to other sources are valuable ways to create currency that help validate a claim.

According to Moz's *Guide to Link Building* (Morgan, 2023), "Within SEO, link building plays an important role in driving organic traffic via search engines, especially in competitive industries."

There are two kinds of web links. **Internal web links** take you from one page of your website to another page on your site. If a content marketer writes a post and links to another post on the same website, that's an internal link. Internal links show depth of knowledge, which search engines value when trying to rank content for key aspects such as relevancy and trustworthiness.

While an internal link, as the name implies, lives within one website, **external links**, in contrast, take you from a page on your website to a page on another website or vice versa. While it may seem counterintuitive to move a user off your site to somewhere else, Google values diversity in thought. External links showcase that diversity. A content marketer may write a post and link to a news article from *The New York Times* that addresses the importance of the issue being discussed in the blog post. This provides value to the reader and, in turn, builds the credibility of your content.

When looking for good external links, consider the Moz Domain Rating and Page Authority scores from www.moz.com. The higher they are, the better the link. When those high-ranking pages link back to your work, that helps with search engine rankings.

A CM should have a link for every 75 to 100 words of copy (No Author, 2023, *Moz*). Too few and Google crawlers can't see the thought leadership; too many and Google thinks your site is spam. Both are bad.

When writing link copy, be specific. "Click here" is a link you likely see all the time, but not because it's effective. It's one of the worst links imaginable because Google crawlers don't know what "Click here" means. The link loses all value. "See course offerings" allows readers and crawlers a sense of what they will get when they click on the link. "Contact Dan Farkas" lets readers and crawlers know there is a way to reach the co-author.

What a CM should know: Links are the best way to create digital ethos – or credibility – for Google.

Pathos (Emotion) and Content Marketing

Merriam-Webster (No Author, 2023, *Pathos*) defines *pathos* as "An element in experience or in artistic representation evoking pity or compassion."

For a CM, this is a reason to believe (RTB). This happens in two ways we can all likely understand:

The heart: When I asked my mom for money in college, I appealed to the emotional reasons of how I would use that money to make the most of the one time I had in college, the greatest experience of my life, a chance to make moments that last a lifetime.

The head: When I asked my dad for money in college, I mentioned how I would specifically use it to advance my educational experience and become a better candidate for jobs and internships.

I knew what worked with my parents. As a CM, you may not have that full transparency, so it makes sense to appeal to both heart and head with messaging. There are two ways a CM can achieve these diverse needs – knowing the *"Why"* and getting past *"Says Who?"*

What's the *Why*?

When a brand or non-profit is able to connect its efforts to how it impacts or solves a societal problem, it creates a deeper, more emotional connection with potential buyers that goes beyond a financial transaction. One example of this is communicating your company's corporate social responsibility (CSR), such as the commitment to reducing its carbon footprint and energy consumption or building a diverse and equitable workforce. It is one of the growing areas of business management and marketing because it brings a degree of humanity to brands of all sizes (Amaydin, M., et al, 2020). As a CM, creating content with a narrative that goes beyond simply the benefits and features of a product and ties in the larger meaning of why a product or service makes the world a better place aims to establish a deeper connection between the company and its target audience.

Pass the *Says Who?* Test

Many of us have heard the saying "You can't put all your eggs in one basket." To strengthen your content and appeal to the head, you have to go beyond your own SME's personal opinion or what one customer may have experienced. Secondary research sources validate arguments and build trust, especially with complex levels of communication, such as those involved in healthcare (Seegert, 2019). When you speak with different stakeholders who have different perspectives (e.g., doctors, nurses, patients, pharmacists) as part of your research and content development process, you're able to incorporate different story elements that resonate with different readers, making your final piece more believable and helpful to a broader audience.

Author Liz Seegert explains it this way: "If you're only talking to one group of experts, you're missing out on vital sources which can add rich, diverse perspectives to your stories."

Content sourcing must also be diverse (Gynn, 2020). Author Ann Gynn wrote, "Truly diverse and inclusive content – the kind that resonates consciously and subconsciously with your audience . . . requires thinking more deeply, from your audience research to your team structure, from your style guide to your user experience." Consider using available demographic and psychographic data, attend industry events, conduct focus groups, do competitive research to see how peers in your industry communicate important concepts, and ensure an inclusive point of view in your final piece.

What a CM should know: Secondary sourcing and humanization both offer an opportunity to create impactful external links to help humans and Google better understand a company's value to consumers.

Logos (Logic) and Content Marketing

Merriam-Webster (No Author, 2023, *Logos*) defines *logos* as "the divine wisdom manifest in the creation, government, and redemption of the world and often identified with the second person of the Trinity."

For a CM, this is how well a writer conveys the argument. In this book, we explain how to create specific types of content. This space is for the actual process of writing.

The goal is to convey everything a reader needs in as little time as possible. There are many 2,000-word posts that could be 1,000 words. However, there are many 300-word posts that miss key points.

A CM needs to be as direct as possible. You've likely heard that a human's attention span has declined from 15 seconds to under eight seconds; a goldfish's attention span is nine seconds (Hayes, 2023).

Direct writing is an entirely different book. For a CM, subject, verb, object (SVO) is the most important thing to consider as the content creation process evolves.

SVO writing helps eliminate passive voice and increase clarity. In every sentence, something does the work. The sun rises. Rebecca gets a coffee. The table leg breaks. When the item doing the work is the subject, the sentence becomes clearer to the reader. This is vital when understanding the evolution of modern content.

- A 2022 Exploding Topics study found 62% of web use is on a mobile device (Howarth, 2023).
- A 2022 HubSpot study found nearly half of all emails are read on a mobile device (Kirsch, 2022).
- The growth of 5G access will likely only increase those numbers.

The people reading CM content are overwhelmingly doing so on a phone or tablet. However, reading on a mobile device isn't as effective as reading on a printed page. The Educational Research Review studied 171,000 readers and found they retained more information reading on paper than on a screen (Ackerman et. al., 2018). Why?

- It's easier for the device to create a distraction that prompts people to leave.
- It's harder for people to mind-map content with screens than with a page.
- Our eyes blink less looking at a screen, creating more stress and exhausting eye stamina.

A CM's audience is likely on the move and easily distracted. While passive language with jargon is not ideal, it's something people can slow down and tolerate in print. Online, the reader can leave in a second and never come back.

What a CM should know: The best writing happens in revision. As a CM, it's easy to write a first draft in passive voice. An effective CM budgets time and resources to rework copy to ensure it is active and easy to understand.

BUILDING DIGITALLY SOUND, ETHICALLY RESPONSIBLE, AND INCLUSIVE LANGUAGE

How do we minimize the distance between the ask and the answer? The answer: concise writing with ethically appropriate language.

It looks easy on paper. In practice, it's a mountainous climb. Our journey begins with Mount Google and will continue into the clouds of humanity.

Key terms: This is how Google compartmentalizes the entire internet. A CM can do this in three ways:

- Branded key terms are something the client owns. I can only get a Big Mac at McDonald's.
- Non-branded key terms are something the client has but others do too. There are plenty of places to get a cheeseburger.
- Competitive key terms are specific alternatives. The Whopper at Burger King is a competitor of McDonald's.

Any of these key terms can also be short-tail or long-tail. When someone searches for a midsize sedan, that non-branded key term will come up with dozens of different options. That's a short-tail key term. When someone searches for a midsize sedan with a V6, heated leather seats, keyless entry, and a premium sound system, that's a long-tail key term.

A good CM piece has between three and five key terms. At least one is branded. At least one is non-branded. At least one is short tail. At least one is long tail. The rest is the CM's choice. Key terms should then be appropriately placed throughout the copy in conversational ways written for humans and not machines.

What a CM should know: Many writers are too broad with key terms. *Training* can mean 1,000,000 different things. *"Best ways to stretch your hamstrings before a marathon,"* is much easier to understand.

Positive Emphasis

Tony Dungy and Lovie Smith were the first two Black coaches to lead their teams to the Super Bowl. Dungy's Indianapolis Colts defeated Smith's Chicago Bears, but both earned business recognition for their treatment of players. Dungy and Smith replaced the screaming yeller mentality made famous by Bill Parcells and Mike Ditka. As Carol Hymowitz (2007) of the *Wall Street Journal* wrote, this quieter style emphasized accountability and calm.

> *Both believe they can get their teams to compete more fiercely and score more touchdowns by giving directives calmly and treating players with respect.*
>
> *This doesn't mean they aren't demanding or don't push hard. Mr. Dungy has a grading system that counts players' "loafs." If someone isn't running at full speed, or eases up or fails to hit an opponent when he could have, those are loafs, and it's hard to get through a game without getting at least one.*

When Mr. Smith . . . gets mad, he stares straight ahead in silence. His players call it "the Lovie Look" and say it's more frightening – and more of a warning to play better – than a torrent of angry words.

This notion of positive emphasis isn't limited to sports. Martin Seligman created the PERMA model for well-being. Communicators using these themes create better environments for people to thrive (Park et al., 2004; Seligman, 2012; Seligman, 2018):

- Positive emotions
- Engagement
- Relationships
- Meaning
- Accomplishments

Language with these elements inspires individuals to want to do something, not feel like they have to do something. The proactive approach of positive emphasis empowers consumers and builds brand loyalty because the consumer views the source as an ally in their life's journey.

Empathy Index

Dungy's mentor was Pittsburgh Steelers head coach Chuck Noll. Dungy tweeted that Noll's best advice was to think beyond the game:

"Don't make football your life."

It's impossible for a CM to understand everything a person is dealing with at a particular moment. It's likely that things at home, school, and the world impact a person. Noll wanted his coaches to be home for dinner and bedtime because he believed balanced people played and coached better on Sunday.

A successful CM can look for ways to identify this balance. In 2020, Brian Carroll found a way to index empathy the same way Lisa Gerber does with sales.

See. Think. Do. Feel.

The approach allows a CM to understand challenges and use common language to create understanding and connection, two human qualities customers crave in a digital world.

Inclusive Language

Every year on the first day of school, Dan's wife tries to get a photo of their kids, Leah and William, before they start the new year. At the beginning, it was easy. As middle school became a reality, it got a bit tougher. So Dan used four words that are a part of any parent's lexicon when asked why these photos had to be taken.

"Because I said so."

Parents can occasionally play this card. A CM can't. And as communication strategist, futurist, and owner of Volume PR, Elizabeth Edwards believes they shouldn't. Edwards studied a combination of human motivation and behavioral science in the decision-making process. What she found was that common leadership, marketing, and communication often fail to use inclusive language, unintentionally turning potential customers away in the process. Her advice:

"Thicken language."

In many cases, we use common language in an honest attempt to help, find common ground, or explain the unexplainable. Who hasn't heard these statements?

- You win some. You lose some.
- It is what it is.
- Everything happens for a reason.

Edwards describes these statements as "thin language" that subtly tells people someone isn't open to listening or hopes to end an uncomfortable conversation.

Thick language removes words that can trigger a response and replaces them with clearer language that better explains a situation. For example, the word *crazy* has connotations that involve mental health. The word *unexpected* may more accurately explain a decision you weren't expecting. Calling the decision *crazy* or *weird* would be thin language. Calling the decision *surprising* or *unexpected* would be thick language.

Putting It All Together with the Message Triangle

In an ideal world, any brand should have three main points it conveys in a message. For a CM, ethos, pathos, and logos are the colors within the triangle. Mixing and matching the three increases the chance that a customer will remember what you want them to remember. It also makes it easier to determine what kind of content to write and what kind of research to conduct.

THREE-ACT STRUCTURE FOR CONTENT MARKETERS

Syd Field (1979) likely never saw a content funnel, but his 1979 book *Screenplay: The Foundations of Screenwriting* does a masterful job of explaining how a CM should think through the CM writing process. At the core is a three-act play:

- Act 1: The Setup
- Act 2: The Confrontation
- Act 3: The Resolution

A CM can use this tried-and-true formula to develop a compelling story that moves people into and through the sales funnel.

Act 1: The Setup

This is where writers introduce the plot and characters. A CM can look at this and think of a problem, situation, or opportunity at hand.

- It's hard to eat healthy during the holidays.
- The supply chain is really tough to manage right now.
- Student debt relief can help millions of Americans.

Jason Hellerman (2018) offers a five-step checklist for anyone thinking about a great first act. Here are those questions with some modifications for a CM:

- Where are we in the world? What is the state of the industry?
- What year is it? Where are we in the buyer's journey?
- Who do we meet? Who or what causes problems or offers solutions?
- What are the stakes? Why does this matter to a customer?
- What can we expect to happen over the course of the movie? How does your CM offer a map to help the reader?

Act 2: The Confrontation

Tension mounts as stakes get higher. The protagonist uncovers allies and enemies while enduring ordeals and reaping rewards. Hellerman's checklist for Act 2 offers additional ideas, modified here for a CM building their story:

- Do your characters have a clear goal? What is the solution?
- What are the hurdles they will have to face to clear their goal? Insert solution for goal.
- Can you introduce a time lock? Deadlines spur action.

Act 3: The Resolution

The conflict reaches its apex when a victorious hero overcomes obstacles and deescalates the conflict through resolved ideas that tie up all loose ends. In this case, Hellerman's checklist offers two questions, modified here for a CM:

- How are they fully realizing their goal? Choose your product.
- What do they do to get it all back? Use your product.
- How do we tell the audience our story is complete? Share client delight.

Ideally, every step of the customer journey should have this three-act structure. A CM can do this in one single post or in three separate posts connected through internal links.

In the Communication 2321 class Dan teaches at Ohio State University, his final assignment is a content marketing piece. Students set up a problem impacting their lives. They then create tension surrounding that problem and how it can impact their college experience or life.

The resolution allows the reader to solve the problem and highlights a specific brand that empowers the reader to overcome the obstacle at hand. Dan leaves the subject matter completely up to the student, and that blank canvas can be intimidating.

One student came up to Dan after class and asked what he should write about for his final. Here's Dan's account:

> I told him to write about what you care about or something on your to-do list. He wasn't exactly sure; so, I came back and asked what stressed him out. He told me he really wanted to go to Japan after graduation, but he didn't want his parents to be mad. I told him to write about how you can convince your parents to travel overseas after graduation. So here's what he did.

- He explained the situation with a first-person account and secondary sourcing.
- He found solutions. It was a mix of affordable ways to justify the experience, secondary studies on the value of international travel, and job/internship opportunities in Southeast Asia.
- He found an organization that allows English-speaking postgraduates to work in Japan for a semester or a year. That turned out to be his client.

MERGING OLD THEORY WITH MODERN PRACTICE

VIVO Growth Partners is a human resources firm that helps growth-minded companies scale talent. Its founder, Molly Eyerman, made it a priority to be extremely agile when it comes to working with different software providers and vendors; this way, VIVO can offer custom solutions to any client and adapt those solutions as its clients continue to grow.

VIVO's core messaging triangle revolves around three main themes that drive most of the company's internal and external communication:

- Attract talent in competitive landscapes, like strategic communication, through a 90-day onboarding process.
- Develop talent through better career planning and performance reviews.
- Retain talent through better employee engagement, cultural development, inclusion, and equity.

With that messaging in place, the next step was to envision ethos, pathos, and logos in a digitally friendly way.

Ethos is about credibility. In 2021 and 2022, finding mid- and senior-level talent in the public relations space was increasingly difficult. Twelve external links in a 1,000-word piece of content showcase diverse thoughts on emerging issues for hiring managers and how to strategically reconsider alternative benefits to find and keep talent.

Pathos reflects emotion. Language like *headaches* and *24/7/365* in the lede tries to draw emotional attention to the exhaustion that comes when a hire goes awry. The section "Attract Talent With Time" discusses the emotional benefits to employees' having more time to balance work and life. A section about personal growth highlights the social and emotional success that comes with finding joy in the workplace.

Logos tries to convey the argument in a way that balances concise and thorough. In this case, the 1,100-word post is broken into eight different sections. The longest paragraph is five lines to make it easier for people to read the material on a phone or mobile device. The core messaging of "attract, develop, retain" is in the beginning, middle, and end of the post to reinforce core themes and increase the probability people will remember VIVO's main message triangle.

The post also applies the concept of the three-act play. The first act establishes characters and conflict. Here, the competition for talent and the stress of not having the right people are the challenges that threaten the protagonist (any PR firm trying to grow their teams).

The second act involves working through the situation, identifying unforeseen pitfalls, and finding potential allies. VIVO's content expands on common barriers to finding quality candidates. The body content includes having money to pay for alternative benefits, making sure staff members get appropriate feedback, and ensuring there's an opportunity for work-life balance.

VIVO serves as an ally on two fronts. The content provides external links that offer diverse sources on how hiring managers can affordably attract talent. At the end, VIVO explains how its "*Professional Development Map*" builds an infrastructure that clients can use to take these concepts and turn them into viable strategies in their own workplaces.

The third act is the resolution (Figure 5.1). VIVO uses the conclusion to reinforce its core messaging of "attract, develop, and retain." It also empowers the reader to use this diverse pool of knowledge to address staffing issues, with a subtle call to action that VIVO can help readers bring these ideas to life. The breakout also offers a checklist that helps readers address issues with current staffing.

What a CM should know: It's possible to use decade- and century-old communication and storytelling theory in today's digital communication landscape. Thinking about content in the context of a message triangle and a three-act play will give content marketers new and creative ways to tell brand stories.

Three Words to Help Find and Attract Talent in 2021 and Beyond

Finding and keeping talent is a 24/7/365 job. With the war for talent and the Great Resignation stealing headlines and causing headaches, it's hard to find a starting point.

Our recommendation . . . the flowerhorn cichlid.

According to Fishkeeping World, it's one of the most colorful fish you can put in an aquarium. In a world full of fish, sticking out is crucial. To be the flowerhorn cichlid in the public relations industry, we want everyone to think through three key words:

- *Attract*
- *Develop*
- *Retain*

Any hiring effort that doesn't attract, develop, or retain should be a nonstarter for the employer and employee. Ideally, any hiring effort should intertwine attracting, developing, and retaining talent. Let's walk through from the beginning.

Attract Talent Affordably

In 2021, alternative benefits are a way to stand out in a world full of people seeking talent. It's unlikely a small business can bring sleep chambers into the office. Affordable alternative benefits do exist, and there are plenty of hacks to make the most of your investment in talent.

When VIVO Growth Partners has done this with clients and industry leaders, these benefits seem to spark the most interest:

- Student loan repayment assistance. Student debt tops $1.7 trillion. Fewer than 4% of businesses offer repayment support. Small and midsize businesses can control student loan repayment assistance and help alleviate a massive mental strain on their talent. That investment will help attract and retain talent over time.
- Pay for an employee's vacation. A peer nomination process to help team members earn a trip can incentivize effort and build loyalty. Other businesses are offering timeshares that team members can reserve at a reduced price. Both ideas offer fixed costs that are easily budgeted.
- Parental leave. It's easy to expand this for moms; dads; adoptive parents; postnatal support; and employees with fertility issues and even aging parents.

Survey your team. They'll let you know what matters to them. In turn, that helps develop and retain the people you want to keep.

Attract Talent With Time

Who doesn't want more time? Transparent PTO, work from home, and family leave options are as important for some hires as salary. Many businesses are also looking at when an employee works, with child obligations, home schooling, and other realities making nine-to-five work unfeasible for many parents and care providers. Flexible work schedules are among the things that team members want most.

For businesses that want or need people onsite, entice efficiency. Onsite fitness equipment, massages, dry cleaning pickup, and coffee delivery can help team members find better balance when at the office.

Develop a Compensation Sheet

Financial literacy skills are a work in progress for many. Present a total compensation package sheet that highlights salary, standard benefits, and alternative benefits so that candidates can see the total investment the company will make. The apples-to-apples comparison will help prospective hires understand the competitive advantage your business has with its offer and can help steer potential hires your way.

Develop New Timelines

The old rules around how long people stay at entry-, mid-, and senior-level jobs are antiquated. The average person will have 12 different jobs in their lifetime, and one recent study found that 80% of people in their 20s have thought about switching careers.

As employer/employee relationships change, it's reasonable to see employment timelines change as well.

- Under a managerial level: Do not to expect to see someone with more than two years at a job on their resume.
- Managers and above: Do expect to see two to four years.

As you attract talent, ask why a person is thinking about leaving. This is a subtle way to learn about a candidate's personality and how they might fit into your company culture. It also helps you look for ways to retain that hire over time. Remember, in many cases, the fit is as important as the skill set.

Hiring managers should also understand that employment gaps aren't a scarlet letter. Ask people what they did during their employment gap to boost skills. Volunteering and online courses show initiative; being honest about providing for family shows empathy. You want those skills in your next hire.

Retain Talent With Personal Growth

Employees want to feel nurtured and want to find intrinsic value in their work. It's the biggest trend we see among our clients and partners.

Covering professional development fees and association dues is a start. States like Ohio offer workplace training vouchers to help businesses and employees offset costs.

Personal growth can also apply in social, emotional, and physical settings. Footing the bill for a recreational sports team and offering an employee discount to a fellow small business owner are alternative benefits to make team members feel different, special, and connected.

Retain Talent With Professional Development Maps

Yearly reviews aren't enough. It's an alternative benefit to offer a clear professional development map that shows how team members can grow and develop within your small or midsize business. Developing that employee handbook, updating job descriptions as needed, offering consistent feedback, and using company swag to visualize key points also help with attracting and developing the right candidates.

Any of these alternative benefits are easy to customize. While VIVO Growth Partners recommends health insurance/other insurance on the date of hire, a three-to-six-month waiting period is also common for alternative benefits. To maximize your investment, we recommend requiring that employees must stay employed for a six-to-twelve-month period after they've received the benefit.

This is a small sample of alternative benefits. There are hundreds of other options out there. As you determine what works best for your business, we encourage you to siphon everything into three words.

- *Attract*
- *Develop*
- *Retain*

Any alternative benefit should do one of these three things. Ideally, an alternative benefit will do all three. An ocean's worth of opportunity awaits. Make the most of it.

SIMPLIFIED STORYTELLING THEMES AND WHERE TO FIND THEM

Storytelling for CM starts with newswriting.

Whether writing for an internal audience, external audience, business to business, or business to consumer, there has to be some degree of news value. Why will someone who has had an incredibly busy day stop what they're doing and pay attention to your message?

What is newsworthy content?

There are dozens of different written definitions that don't encapsulate the biggest challenge a CM will face: there is no one single definition of news.

In Dan's Writing for Strategic Communication courses, he takes students through this experience.

Imagine a space alien comes down from the sky and sees you. The first thing he asks is, "What is news?" Here's the catch, you only get three words. They can be any three words, and they don't have to make up a sentence.

Each participant will list one word. Dan gets three because he teaches the class. In reverse order, each student takes one word off that list until there are three words remaining. Over 11 years, here's the percentage of students who had all three words, two words, etc. make the final cut (Figure 5.1).

THREE WORDS	TWO WORDS	ONE WORD	ZERO WORDS
2%	5%	58%	35%

FIGURE 5.1 Students in the same large Midwestern university, nearly all of whom were communication majors, had very different senses of what news meant to them.

In a class of like-minded students of similar ages and backgrounds, there's minimal consensus on what news is. That means a CM must first determine what news is to them and then connect those values to the values of others. That doesn't mean a CM should compromise their values; rather, you need to find common ground with different people who have different perspectives.

Absent any viable definition of news, these themes tend to resonate in many forms of news content. While it is impossible to have every theme in every piece of content, there's a higher chance your content will resonate the more themes it reasonably has.

Timeliness: Ideal CM content will be timely at the moment of consumption. That's different from "new." When a celebrity passes away, older feature stories about those individuals become timely.

Prominence: How many of you reading this ever received a speeding ticket? Our hands are raised too. Hopefully, the situation was safely resolved with a fine and reminder to slow down. Likely, your name didn't end up in a news article. However, when a celebrity or famous race car driver gets a speeding ticket, their experience is more likely to capture attention.

Proximity: News is local in terms of geography and area of interest. A car accident near your house is more important than one 100 miles away because the one near your house might impact the morning commute or someone you know personally.

In the CM space, consumers want relevant content, and often the location or source of that content isn't a factor. If someone can help you solve a problem and that person lives in Portland, Oregon, it's local to you regardless of where you call home.

Significance: Is a Kardashian or a Jenner news? That's highly subjective and part of the reason customer research is so vital in CM.

- Universally significant themes (curing cancer, feeding the hungry) have impactful value.
- A sale on USB drives is likely not significant to most people.
- A new menu item may not be significant unless there is a special connection (gluten-free Mexican food) that makes it significant to a specific audience.

Unusual: In the movie *Anchorman: The Legend of Ron Burgundy*, a "Channel 4 news exclusive" involved Nutty, the water-skiing squirrel. Indeed, that squirrel can water-ski.

When we see things that don't happen very often (dare I say viral?), it's an example of something unusual. There's value in making someone look twice.

Human interest: Mail carriers work every day. But if there's a mail carrier who is 80 years old and retiring after 60 years on the job, it personifies the United States Postal Service's notion that "Neither snow nor rain nor heat nor gloom of night stays these couriers from the swift completion of their appointed rounds."

Think of it this way. If someone destroyed your phone and deleted all your contacts, how many people could you call from memory alone? Your favorite pizza place doesn't count.

There's value in finding humanity. Many of us struggle to remember numbers. We are really good at remembering people and seeing something distinctive about their experience. This also makes complex ideas easier for people to understand.

Conflict: Watch TV news for four minutes and you'll find it. For the sake of CM, view your client's service offering as a connected protagonist, a tool that helps the consumer become the hero of their story. For example, when there are concerns about personal information being hacked and disagreement over who is to blame, a software service provider can offer guidance to help people remedy any potential liabilities.

Newness: Many established brands need ways to reinvent themselves and look for new ways to view an established product. Every month, McDonald's has a new promotion, contest, or menu item.

Newness doesn't have to involve a calendar. Where have you seen people eat ranch dressing? There might be ten different things mentioned before someone mentions a salad. There are new ways we can use existing services to create value that might be of interest to a potential customer.

What a CM should know: Great content ideas have at least two news values, and possibly more depending on the circumstance.

HOW DO WE FIND NEWS?

There are ways to find news and create news. The key in either situation is to go back to news themes and make sure there is a clear correlation. Here are easy ways to review existing business material and identify ideas you could use to create helpful content for your target audience:

Internal sources: Any company likely has a mix of white papers, annual reports, and website pages that have never seen the light of day and internal communication to empower associates and team members. It's highly likely that a new set of eyes, including those of a CM, can find information of interest to a potential audience.

Seasoned staff: Every company has certain individuals who know the place inside and out. They don't have to be C-suite or even B-suite, for that matter. Information is power, and seasoned staff have it in bulk. Ask them questions. The worst-case scenario is you meet with the person and get free lunch or coffee out of it.

What a CM should know: It's okay to ask questions. You aren't supposed to know everything.

External news sources: Following current events is a must for a CM. What happens in the world impacts your client, your organization, and your world. It's also a way to interject expertise into the conversation.

Primary research: Brands conduct surveys, focus groups, in-depth interviews, and countless other forms of research to learn more about customer preferences, market trends, etc. Some of this information may be proprietary, but not all of it is. Mixing qualitative and quantitative information in a consumer-friendly way helps potential customers better understand the situation at hand and how your brand can help.

Trade publications: There are thousands of trade publications that cover only one genre. For example, *Space News* covers outer space. That's it. Many journalists will take niche story ideas from a trade publication, advance certain concepts, and broaden the scope to a larger audience. A CM can do that too.

Pseudo-events: Those traditional ribbon cuttings, check presentations, and product releases have worked for decades because people like seeing new things come to life in a visual way. A CM can find value and efficiency in working with the larger marketing department to review events and cover them as part of their CM funnel.

PUTTING THIS ALL TOGETHER

Robert Rose, one of the world's most recognized experts in content strategy and marketing, said, "Storytelling is not a unique skill set, it's a muscle that we build when we give ourselves the patience, time and space to actually develop it. Most of the time, especially in today's world, we don't give ourselves the flexibility, the freedom and quite frankly the courage to go there."

There's structure to storytelling. When content marketers and their colleagues can agree on the structure, the storytelling becomes more efficient because everyone is working from the same framework.

Ann Handley (2020), author of *Everybody Writes* and a partner at MarketingProfs, condensed much of what's covered in this chapter into a single framework (Figure 5.2). While it isn't 100% comprehensive, it guides a CM through a process that can humanize a product, clarify need, and connect what consumers want with what your product offers. For those working in engineering or development, the framework serves as a way to translate technical

---

A Brand Storytelling Framework

Ann Handley's framework, adapted here as a Mad Libs-inspired exercise, helps you understand the actual problem you and your business solve for your customer—not the ones you *think* you solve.

Once upon a time, there was _____ . It has the capacity to
                                                          (your product)

_____ . Some people doubt it because _____
(your product's superpower)   *(what the doubters might claim)*

But one day, _____ . Which means
                              (something happens)

_____ . To help _____ .
(how your would-be customer now needs your product)   *(the people your customer serves)*

And that matters because _____ . That
                                        (how your customer becomes the hero)

brings together a community of _____ .
                                              (the larger market of those whom your product serves and brings together)

FIGURE 5.2 Adapted from Ann Handley's storytelling framework, this guides a CM through a process that can humanize a product, clarify need, and connect what consumers want with what your product offers. For those working in engineering or development, the framework serves as a way to translate technical jargon into something potential buyers can more easily comprehend. For the CM, it serves as a checklist to ensure the brand story is compelling and comprehensive.

jargon into something potential buyers can more easily comprehend. For the CM, it serves as a checklist to ensure the brand story is compelling and comprehensive.

Rose has a simple summary of the importance of bringing these diverse elements together: "Every single business on the planet is dealing with humans in some form. At the heart of every great story is a human."

CONCLUSION

Create good content. It's so simple . . . or not. A good CM has to develop a persuasive story, merge centuries-old theories with emerging technology, and identify ethically responsible language for people and for Google. It's Aristotle, Toni Morrison, and Bill Gates wrapped in one job description.

How does a CM wear all these hats? Structure. Solid messaging empowers a CM to use their storytelling skills to create impactful content. Structure guides a CM when fatigue or confusion sets in. Structure quiets outside noise that makes the journey harder to navigate. A CM who can build that structure finds freedom and can (dare we say) create good content.

Interview with the Experts: Storytelling Q&A with Robert Rose, Content Marketing Author and Chief Strategy Advisor at Content Marketing Institute

1. *How would you define and explain storytelling? How do you differentiate between storytelling and content marketing?*

   I would say that storytelling is a piece of a larger strategy called content marketing.

   When we're trying to provide a singular framework for someone who's creating media/content, we want to pull trust forward and deliver value first, and typically, that value is to change or persuade you to make you want to do something differently because that's the whole reason for this. I'm not doing this from a purely artistic or altruistic standpoint; rather, mostly I'm doing this because I want you to buy some stuff. The whole point of this is that I ultimately want you to believe something different than you did when you went into this piece of content. The easiest framework to illustrate that arc of believing something different on the back end than you did on the front end is classic storytelling frameworks – introducing you to some tension or conflict, and because of the experience of that tension or conflict, you come out believing something different, or you are changed on the other end of that experience. That's classic storytelling 101 structure.

   What that means is when we're creating content, we can use that idea and the pillars of classic story structure in order to build the "product" that is our content experience, whether that's a blog post, an email, a presentation, a white paper, or even an entire resource center, magazine, theme park, television show. Whatever the experience is, at any hierarchical level, it should be able to conform – not necessarily comply – but conform to some of the classic pillars of story structure which will then make the content stronger as a result.

   When you think about the hero's journey . . . not every great story conforms with every single step of Campbell's hero's journey, but every great story complies with more of them. In other words, the greater the story, the more it complies.

   You can use the great tenets of storytelling to architect a piece of content, and if it complies mostly or completely with lives within the physical world of great storytelling, it's got a much greater chance of being fulfilling, satisfying, valuable, of differentiating and ultimately changing the behavior of that customer we're trying to change.

2. *How do you tell a "story" about a seemingly boring B2B product, such as a newly improved digital signal processor or a conservative and/or sensitive market such as military and aerospace or chemicals?*

   Every single business on the planet is dealing with humans in some form. At the heart of every great story is a human. This is another argument for audience personas – not necessarily buyer personas because that limits your thinking in many ways. If you are to say, "We make this boring product, so how are we going to make something people are going to care about that focuses on that product or service?" (29:07). If you think about them from the buyer's perspective, you may be right that it's actually a boring industry.

For example, ADP sells the point-of-purchase terminals at car dealerships: those old computer terminals with black screens and green type along with the routers and connectivity systems that mechanics use to type your work orders in when you bring your car in for service. How do you make that sexy and build thought leadership around that? Well, there is someone who cares deeply about that system. That boring computer terminal and point-of-purchase system may be the most expensive asset that a small family car dealership business owner spends money on that year, so it's an emotional purchase for that person. You've got to elevate what you do to not just solve the efficiency of the auto mechanic getting their work order submitted; you've got to elevate that experience to something that the car dealership owner cares about writing a check for a couple thousand dollars. . . . That's content. That's delivering value through content, whatever format that content ultimately becomes.

Coming back to classic storytelling, no matter how seemingly boring your product or service, it's about elevating the story to something that's at a human, emotional level that makes the person consuming that content care.

3. ***Does it take a special person to become a great storyteller? What skills are required?***

It's not a skill set. What I learned from John Klease, when I sat down and talked to him about this, he said creativity is not a talent; it's a process.

Storytelling is not a unique skill set; it's a muscle that we build when we give ourselves the patience, time, and space to actually develop it. Most of the time, especially in today's world, we don't give ourselves the flexibility, the freedom, and, quite frankly, the courage to go there. Someone comes into your business and starts talking about the higher emotional levels of a computer chip; you're like "I don't have time for this. . . . I just need the sales guy to make more calls." Having the courage and the "intestinal fortitude" to actually go there is the key, and it can be uncomfortable for many classic businesses and marketers, especially on the B2B side, who have never had to do this before.

It's always been the approach to lean back on facts and figures and the classic tenets of marketing and advertising from the 60s and 70s because someone somewhere at some point is going to need our stuff. And when someone needs our stuff, we'll compete on the merits and differentiators of our product, and we'll win some of those, and we'll lose some of those, and the skill we build in marketing is to sharpen our persuasive message on the merits of our product. But you can't do that anymore. One, you can't rise above the noise. Two, as I like to remind everyone, it's not just about the technology around content, the internet, and the web that has evolved so much; it's everything we do in business has evolved so much. Your widget that you've spent years developing the differentiation for because you can mill it and manufacture it better than anyone else . . . no, the guy down the street can do that with a 3D printer now and can do that as well. Your designs are not as differentiated anymore, and quite frankly, some of the major four Ps are not going to be, as the investment community calls it, motes anymore – competitive advantages – because it's too easy to develop technological solutions that can duplicate what you do.

Don Schultz, whom many call the father of marketing communications, once said at Content Marketing World that everyone can do what you do from a product and market standpoint. The only differentiator today is communicating how you do it.

4. ***Should we think of "stories" in terms of a quantity, like we need 15 "stories" this year? Or is a story more of a message that is told in various ways, and woven through all content types?***

My typical answer to the question of how much content we need to produce is as little as possible to create the change you're trying to create. Others may argue you need to produce as much as possible on every possible channel. For me, content marketing is so much better as an integrated piece of the overall marketing strategy. We still need to invest in the other channels – we still need to do paid media and other things we've classically done, maybe in different ways. Content, and storytelling as a subset of content, is only going to be to one part of our portfolio.

CITATIONS

Ackerman, R., Delgado, P., Rakefet, C., & Vargas, S.L. "Don't throw away your printed books: A meta-analysis on the effects of reading media on reading comprehension." *Educational Research Review.* 2018.

Apaydin, M., Jiang, G.F., Demirbag, M., & Jamali, D. "The importance of corporate social responsibility strategic fit and times of economic hardship." *Wiley Online Library.* April 19, 2020. Retrieved from: https://onlinelibrary.wiley.com/doi/full/10.1111/1467-8551.12402

Emde , K., Klimm, C., & Schluetz, D. "Does storytelling help adolescents to process the news?" *Journalism Studies.* 2016.

Field, S. *Screenplay: The Foundations of Screenwriting.* Bantam Dell. 1979.

Gynn, A. "Diversity and content marketing: How brands can be more inclusive." June 5, 2020. Retrieved from: https://contentmarketinginstitute.com/articles/diverse-inclusive-content-marketing/

Handley, A. "Storytelling framework." 2020. Retrieved from: https://annhandley.com/ah/wp-content/uploads/2020/12/Ann-Handley-Storytelling-Framework.pdf

Hayes, A. "The human attention span." February 2023. Retrieved from: www.wyzowl.com/human-attention-span/

Hellerman, J. "Three act structure: Breaking down acts one, two, & three in movies." November 6, 2018. Retrieved from: https://nofilmschool.com/Three-act-structure

Howarth, H. "Internet traffic from mobile devices." February 2023. Retrieved from: https://exploding topics.com/blog/mobile-internet-traffic#mobile-internet-top-stats

Hymowitz, C. "Two football coaches have a lot to teach screaming managers." *The Wall Street Journal.* July 29, 2007.

Kirsch, K. "The ultimate list of email marketing stats for 2022." November 30, 2022. Retrieved from: https://blog.hubspot.com/marketing/email-marketing-stats?__hstc=150320169.4745567e558fb352b 00a8fb8af3f5bc3.1668873941616.1668873941616.1668873941616.1&__hssc=150320169.1.1668873 941616&__hsfp=231856096

Morgan, P. "The beginner's guide to link building." Cited February 21, 2023. Retrieved from: https:// moz.com/beginners-guide-to-link-building

No Author. "Ethos." *Merriam-Webster Dictionary.* 2023. Retrieved from: www.merriam-webster.com/ dictionary/ethos

No Author. "Logos." *Merriam-Webster Dictionary.* 2023. Retrieved from: www.merriam-webster.com/ dictionary/Logos

No Author. "Pathos." *Merriam-Webster Dictionary.* 2023. Retrieved from: www.merriam-webster.com/ dictionary/pathos

No Author. "What are internal links?" Cited February 23, 2023. Retrieved from: https://moz.com/ learn/seo/internal-link

Seegert, L. "Diversifying your sources can improve your reporting." *Association of Health Care Journalists.* May 5, 2019. Retrieved from: https://healthjournalism.org/blog/2019/05/diversifying-your-sources-can-improve-your-reporting/

SECTION 2

Content Delivery

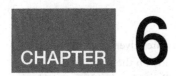

CHAPTER 6

Earned Media and Its Role in Content Marketing

LEARNING OBJECTIVES

1. Overview of the earned media channel and how it compares to other channels in the PESO model
2. Learning the best practices of creating a news release, the cornerstone content type for earned media, and how it can be utilized across other channels and for search engine optimization
3. Understanding the essential information a journalist needs to know and how to use the five Ws of journalism
4. The role and structure of contributed and thought leadership articles written for third-party media
5. Effectively developing content for awards and speaker applications

INTRODUCTION: EARNED MEDIA

In the early 1900s, the richest man in the world, John D. Rockefeller, hired Ivy Lee to change his public image from vilified oil baron to well-loved philanthropist. Rockefeller knew changing public opinion would make his work and life easier. He also knew he couldn't pay his way into changing public opinion, nor could he do it in one persuasive speech. He knew he had to earn it, which takes time.

Earned media is the practice of producing statements of truth that can be fact-checked and validated by third parties (in the case of PR, these third parties are journalists, bloggers, social media influencers, and others who are perceived as trusted experts by their readers and followers), who then write about the person, company, or product through their authenticated filter (e.g., magazine, blog, LinkedIn page, etc.). Earned media, of which public relations (PR) is the most well-known form, is generally understood to include the practice of both informing and influencing the attitudes and behaviors of the public – that is, external stakeholders, such as customers, investors, donors, prospective and retired employees, etc. (Treadwell & Treadwell, 2005).

DOI: 10.4324/9781003369103-08

Think about your favorite online or print magazine. There are advertisements mixed in with editorial articles. While both forms of content live side by side on the pages of the magazine, the decision of if, where, and how they are placed – as well as who decides – could not be more different. Marketing teams purchase the advertisement in outlets and on websites and social media platforms and are in control of when, where, and how the advertisement is executed – what it says, what page it appears on, how often it runs. They pay to play.

Placing an editorial article is a completely different journey. In this case, it is the editors and journalists who are fully in control of the article, including what, if any, brands, people, or products are mentioned; what prominence and length the article is given; and what the article says about a given topic (i.e., what angle it takes). Unlike in advertising, the marketer has no control over if, when or how the coverage appears or if it shines a positive, neutral, or negative light on the company or product.

That is why the key word of this media channel is *earned*. Content created for earned channels faces a momentous challenge: to earn the awareness and trust of the third-party target audience and influence and persuade their opinions and decisions.

What the CM needs to know: While many companies will have dedicated PR teams led by trained and seasoned PR practitioners, CMs are often critical partners of their PR colleagues. A good PR writer works hand in hand with the technical content developer, often through internal interviews with business and product leaders, to understand the competitive landscape, unique product positioning, and newsworthiness of specific media outlets. In this way, the CM is not only a valuable sounding board but also helps explain and ensure consistent messaging between pure PR and other content types.

Additionally, PR content, such as news releases, can serve as a valuable resource for CMs to repurpose into other content types, such as white papers or podcast episodes (Abdow, 2020). Finally, on smaller marketing teams without dedicated PR, CMs will have direct responsibility for developing PR content. Given the strategic nature and potential impact (positive or negative) of content for earned media, the best CMs have a deep understanding and appreciation for developing content for this channel.

Traditionally, earned media was synonymous with PR, and the desired outcome was publicity for the company in its target publications through activities including:

- **Media relations** – building relationships and maintaining consistent dialogue with journalists and editors covering their space
- **News releases** – official documents written by PR writers and distributed to media announcing company news, such a new product or business expansion
- **Press interviews** – in-person or phone meetings with members of the media to discuss a specific topic, such as company news or a current event or industry trend
- **Press tours** – a dedicated set of meetings with target media over a series of days or weeks to share time-sensitive news (most often used for major product launches) and secure significant coverage

> • **Press kits** – a set of content bound together in a "kit" or folder, written and distributed specifically for the media audience, including news releases and additional background material such as datasheets, white papers, and partner and customer testimonials
> • **Press conferences** – live events held at specific times and locations in which company spokespeople share news and invited media have the opportunity to ask questions

THE CONTENT CORNERSTONE OF EARNED MEDIA: THE NEWS RELEASE

The cornerstone of earned media is public relations (PR), which embodies the collective efforts of using third-party channels to build awareness and trust. Today, the news release remains a very strategic, widely used, and proven form of earned media content in building awareness for a company and its offerings. (See "Q&A with a Journalist" at the end of this chapter for tips on what makes a compelling news release.)

When a CM writes a news release, there's a simple first question to ask:

"Is this news?"

When companies publish even a few news releases that lack news and are more style than substance in the eyes of a journalist or editor, both begin to subconsciously or consciously distrust the brand as self-serving and promotional. That means future news releases receive less attention and may not even get read.

What a CM should know: A CM has the opportunity to serve as the front-line filter to ensure a news release has actual news value, protecting the company from losing trust with the journalists who cover their industry.

The main elements of a news release are as follows:

- **Headline** – first words of the release that introduce the leading message of the announcement
- **Sub-headline** – an optional second headline that communicates a secondary message of the news
- **Dateline** – the date the news is announced
- **Opening sentence** (a.k.a. lede) – the first sentence of the release, which elaborates on the headline and explains the news
- **Body paragraphs** – structured sections of the release dedicated to explaining key messages of the news, such as underlying technology, industry or application context, data, features, and benefits

- **Quotes** – an optional section devoted to opinions, testimony, and commentary from important stakeholders, including company leaders, industry analysts, and customers. Only use when the quotes have adjectives or emotion
- **Calls to action** – links to further reading the journalist can include in their article to direct readers to learn more about the news, such as a dedicated product or event web page, related video, or in-depth white paper
- **Boilerplate** – a paragraph at the end of the release describing the company, its position, and product and service offerings
- **Contact information** – the company's website, telephone, and social media contact information

When writing a press release, it's helpful to reference the inverted pyramid format, shown in Figure 6.1, in which the most important facts are at the beginning of the release while supporting information and useful but less essential information appears later. This method helps journalists quickly craft articles from the release and empowers them to add or delete information when deadlines are tight (Bejerman, 2011).

Although the headline and sub-headline are the shortest in length compared to the other sections of the news release, they are arguably the hardest and most important to write. Journalists read the headline and sub-headline first. If they don't capture the reporter's attention, the

INVERTED PYRAMID NEWS WRITING

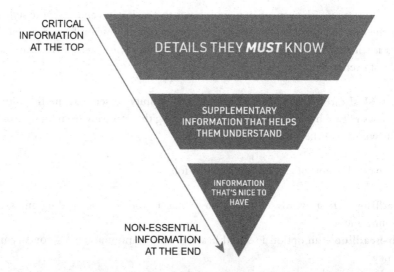

FIGURE 6.1 The inverted-pyramid approach to news release writing places information the reader must know at the beginning of the release, followed by additional information that is less essential or interesting. This ensures the most critical information comes at the beginning, and the remaining information cascades in order of significance throughout the release to increase the chance the journalist will continue reading the news announcement and consider writing about it, creating publicity for the company.

rest of the release may not see the light of day, and your company's publicity chances go out the window. To provide essential information to the journalist, the headline, sub-headline, and opening paragraph, including the lede, should include the five Ws of journalism:

1. Who is the news about?
2. What is the news?
3. When did the news occur?
4. Where did the news occur?
5. Why is the news important?

Looking at the example in Figure 6.2 from the Texas Academy of Medicine, Engineering, Science, and Technology (TAMEST) announcing a new report on K–12 science, technology, engineering, and math (STEM) education, we see the five Ws are explained:

Who: Texas's top scientific, academic, and corporate experts
What: A call for world-class K–12 math and science education
When: December 9, 2008
Where: Texas
Why: To announce a new report that outlines the critical steps to solving the math and science crisis facing the state of Texas

The *who* are the members of the organization: leading scientists, engineers, and university and industry leaders in Texas. In further explaining who TAMEST members are, the CM aims to establish the organization as a highly credible voice to comment on and recommend to the state of Texas how STEM education needs to change. In this paragraph, we also learn more about the *what*: that TAMEST has issued a report titled *The Next Frontier: World Class Math and Science Education for Texas* that includes four key findings and recommendations the leaders call on Texas lawmakers to heed in the next legislative session. We also learn the *why* of the news, which is to offer "critical steps to solving the math and science education crisis facing our state" and to "set a world-class bar for science, technology, engineering, and math education."

TAMEST *Texas Academy of Medicine, Engineering, Science & Technology*

**Texas' Top Scientific, Academic and Corporate Experts Issue
United Call for World-Class Math and Science Education**

*Vision for the Next Frontier Starts With Training, Supporting and Paying
High-Quality Teachers – Now*

AUSTIN, Texas – December 9, 2008 – Texas National Academies Members, Nobel Laureates, university and industry leaders – joined together as the Texas Academy of Medicine, Engineering, Science and Technology

(TAMEST) – have issued a report offering critical steps to solving the math and science education crisis facing our state. *The Next Frontier: World-Class Math and Science Education for Texas* calls for the state to set a world-class bar for science, technology, engineering and math – or STEM – education, and outlines four key findings and recommendations that TAMEST members hope will move Texas lawmakers to even bolder action during next year's legislative session.

"We're not here to criticize; we're here to energize," said Dr. Kenneth Shine, Interim Chancellor of The University of Texas System, past president of the Institute of Medicine and TAMEST member. "We're applauding the efforts of Texas' policymakers and education leaders up to now. And today, we're letting them know we stand united – ready to respond to the opportunity of this next frontier, ready to raise the bar high in Texas, and ready to help them accomplish even more."

The report, created by the TAMEST Education Steering Committee, draws upon President John F. Kennedy's inspirational 1960 vision of a New Frontier for America, and illustrates Texas standing at the edge of the next frontier – science and technology – at risk of future failure for our children, our economy and our state as a whole. The Committee's call for action follows the release of unfavorable statistics on the status of science and math preparedness, not only in Texas, but also across the country.

"The United States is being left behind," said Committee Co-chair Dr. William Brinkley, Senior Vice President for Graduate Sciences and Dean of the Graduate School of Biomedical Science at Baylor College of Medicine – Houston. "In China today, over 40 percent of college undergraduates earn engineering and science degrees, while in the U.S., only 5 percent of students do. And Texas is in the bottom half among the states – our students consistently score lower than the national average on math and science proficiency tests. This is simply unacceptable."

"If we, as Texans, don't roll up our sleeves and work together to begin providing our children with the science and math knowledge they need *today* – starting with training, supporting and paying great teachers – then our kids and our state will not succeed tomorrow," added Dr. Mary Ann Rankin, Dean of the College of Natural Sciences at The University of Texas at Austin and Committee Co-Chair.

The *Next Frontier* report's findings and recommendations center around four key areas of STEM education:

- **Teachers**: Recruiting, rewarding and retaining high-quality teachers;
- **Curriculum**: Developing curriculum that piques and holds student interest;
- **Accountability**: Modifying the accountability system to reward improvement, and better preparing students for college and careers; and

- **Guidance**: Establishing a statewide advisory council to oversee and coordinate Texas' STEM education efforts.

Leaving Behind a Weakened Economy

Experts agree the number-one priority for STEM education is to stop the hemorrhage of good teachers from Texas' public schools. The ripple effect is shocking:

- *An educated workforce requires passionate teachers who are fully certified in their subjects and willing to spend their careers teaching.*
  Last year, about 4,000 math and science teachers left Texas classrooms for other professions or retirement – costing the state an estimated $27 million to replace them.
- *A shortage of good teachers negatively affects student performance.*
  Nationwide last year, Texas ranked 37th on students' SAT math scores; on the ACT, Texas scores ranked 39th in science and 36th in math.
- *Poor academic performance is one of the reasons students drop out.*
  Texas' overall graduation rate is among the lowest nationwide – in fact, every hour of every school day, an astounding 90+ students drop out of Texas schools.
- *In an increasingly knowledge-based economy, college-readiness means workforce readiness.*
  Almost 40% of students at two-year Texas colleges and about 25% of students at four-year Texas universities are enrolled in at least one remedial course – at an annual cost of $300 million to our state.

Making the Most of Past Progress

The *Next Frontier* report highlights several programs already successfully improving STEM education in Texas, including:

Math and Science Scholars (MASS) at Texas A&M University, which works to enlist the brightest students to become secondary math and science teachers, employing a mentored, field-based, hands-on approach to certification;

UTeach at The University of Texas at Austin, which provides new teachers with up to five years of induction support and additional training. Nationally, only 50% of new teachers are still teaching after three years, while 80% of UTeach graduates are still teaching after five years. UTeach was recommended in the National Academies' *Rising Above the Gathering Storm* report, and the National Math and Science Initiative is supporting the replication of UTeach across the country, including three Texas universities in the first phase, with the goal of making UTeach the national standard for math and science teacher preparation; and

Advanced Placement Strategies (AP Strategies), which features an incentive program that promotes strong teaching and testing of college concepts by providing monetary stipends for successful high-school teachers and students. Within a decade, the number of Texas students passing the AP exam with a score of 3 or higher rose from 361 to 1,300.

"Great teachers are the foundation upon which we will build world-class science and math education here in Texas," said Committee member Kurt Swogger, Executive Vice President Investments, Planned Innovation® Institute. "Thanks to attention, ideas and funding from our state leaders, Texas already has many programs proven to recruit, reward and retain great teachers. But we must go further to take Texas from our ranking at the bottom of the U.S. to the top of our class, to create a workforce ready to compete globally, and to take on the next frontier."

About TAMEST

The Academy of Medicine, Engineering and Science of Texas (TAMEST) was founded in 2004 by U.S. Senator Kay Bailey Hutchison and Nobel Laureates Dr. Michael S. Brown and the late Dr. Richard E. Smalley. It is comprised of Texas' 10 Nobel Laureates and 200+ Texas members of the National Academies – the National Academy of Sciences, the National Academy of Engineering and the Institute of Medicine – working together to strengthen our state's position as national research leader and hub of achievement within these fields, and to help cultivate the next generation of Texas scientists.

For further information, please visit www.tamest.org.

FIGURE 6.2 This news release from the Texas Academy of Medicine, Engineering, Science and Technology (TAMEST) details five 5 Ws of effective news release writing, including *who*: top Texas scientific, academic, and corporate experts; *what*: a call for world-class K–12 math and science education; *when*: December 9, 2008; *where*: Texas; and *why*: to announce a new report that outlines critical steps to solving the math and science crisis facing the state of Texas.

Following the lede, the body of a release consists of additional information that further elaborates on the five Ws, including quotes from important stakeholders such as company leaders, industry analysts, and customers. In the TAMEST news release, the first body paragraph following the lede is a quote from Dr. Kenneth Shine, who the release states is the chancellor of the University of Texas system and past president of TAMEST. For a journalist who covers K–12 education in the state of Texas or even nationally, this is likely news they would decide to cover, given the prominent and credible voices speaking out and being quoted endorsing and supporting this news, as well as the fact that this group of scientific and engineering leaders has issued an official report with findings and recommendations for legislators.

The TAMEST release is a lengthy example, with eight total body paragraphs providing supporting information, findings and recommendations of the report, and additional stakeholder quotes.

The last paragraph of the release with the heading "About TAMEST" is the boilerplate paragraph. In a few sentences, the reader can learn about the organization, its purpose, and its position. Following this boilerplate is information on how journalists can contact the organization and the call-to-action website address they can visit to get details about the report.

The Expanded Role of News Releases: Optimizing for Search and Social Sharing

The TAMEST release is from 2008 and showcases core steps that still work to this day. While the CM should write press releases primarily for the media, news releases are a valuable content tool read by a wide variety of audiences including customers, prospects, partners, industry analysts, investors, and employees.

A 2022 example from the Greater Columbus Sports Commission (GCSC) offers a very different example of how news release principles can help with content marketing, media relations, and search. GCSC earned the right to host the 2027 NCAA Women's Final Four basketball tournament. Figure 6.3 shows underlined key terms that also feature a mix of internal links to the GCSC website and external links to outside sources like the NCAA website. The article also tries to incorporate storytelling elements that explain why the event is so important for the city. Adding these components enables journalists to craft more compelling content that is appealing to readers (Kulkarni et al., 2022).

In the two days following the announcement in November 2022, *Sports Illustrated*, the Associated Press, and *USA Today* were among the more than 600 media outlets that picked up the story. Media outlets with strong domain and page ratings help a CM with search, especially when links and key terms are aligned and repurposed within the release.

GREATER COLUMBUS SPORTS ★ COMMISSION

Columbus to Host 2027 NCAA Women's Final Four

Columbus earned global recognition for its hosting of the 2018 Women's Final Four.

COLUMBUS (Nov. 21, 2022) – The NCAA Women's Final Four is returning to Columbus in 2027

Columbus has been a key ally in showcasing NCAA student-athletes and competitions, having hosted more than 100 events over the last 20 years. One of those events was the 2018 NCAA Women's Final Four, which received SportsTravel magazine's Sports Event of the Year, beating out the Super Bowl and Olympics.

"We are grateful to be a hub for women's sports through our partnership with the NCAA," said Linda Logan, CEO and President of the Greater Columbus Sports Commission. "We raised the bar globally with our work on the 2018 Women's Final Four and embrace the challenge to elevate the event even higher in 2027."

Starting from a pool of 15 cities, Columbus was selected as one of seven finalists to host the event earlier this year. Following that announcement, the Greater Columbus Sports Commission, The Ohio State University and Nationwide Arena submitted a final bid and hosted a site visit from the NCAA in August.

"Incredible things happen when we come together in the name of sports," said Gene Smith, Senior Vice President and Wolfe Foundation Endowed Athletic Director, Ohio State University. "These championship events will have a profound impact on our university and community."

The 2018 event brought in $21.7 million in direct visitor spending to the region. More than 80% of visitors were from outside of Ohio, with 60% making their first trip to Columbus.

"The 2018 Women's Final Four was a thrill culminating in two OT semi-finals and a buzzer beater. We cannot wait for the opportunity to host a future tournament and welcome players, coaches, programs, families and fans from all over the country to Nationwide Arena," said Michael Gatto, COO of Columbus Arena Management and Senior Vice President, Nationwide Arena.

Read the NCAA's full Women's Final Four selection release here.

About the Greater Columbus Sports Commission

The Greater Columbus Sports Commission's mission is to rally Columbus to compete and win sporting events, providing a singular athlete and fan experience and positively impacting image, economy and lifestyle. Since 2002, the Greater Columbus Sports Commission has brought nearly new sporting events to Columbus, generating an estimated $625 million in direct visitor spending.

FIGURE 6.3 This news release from the Greater Columbus Sports Commission highlights how links, key terms, and other digital currency can easily be incorporated into a news release. For a CM, this is an easy way to efficiently create trackable content for consumers and search engines.

What a CM should know: News releases almost always end up online, so a well-written news release can drive improved search engine optimization performance of your company's website with proper links, language, and social sharing.

To optimize the release for search performance, a CM should include relevant keywords early in the headline as sites like Google will only include the first 160 characters in the listed search result, known as the meta description (No author, 2023, *Moz*). These first 160 characters (about 25 to 40 words) are your opportunity to explain and inspire the searcher to click to read more.

For instance, in the TAMEST education report news release, the keywords *Texas, math and science*, and *education* all appear in these first 114 characters. Incorporating these keyword elements in critical sections of the release, such as the headline area, strengthens the optimization of the news content, resulting in your content ranking higher in search results for relevant topics.

For further SEO effectiveness and to create a helpful reader experience, include the relevant keywords throughout the release and add internal links taking readers back to relevant web pages or related content to learn more.

By interviewing stakeholders as a journalist would and ensuring the announcement is truly newsworthy, following the inverted pyramid format, answering the five Ws, and keeping in mind the wider audience of today's news release by incorporating keywords to improve optimization and shareable content to promote social sharing, technical content writers can create highly valuable news releases that build awareness, trust, and demand for their company and products.

OTHER COMMON EARNED-MEDIA TYPES

There are several other common types of content development a CM may support or spearhead. Each has its own purpose, structure, and writing approach:

- Contributed or thought leadership articles
- Speaking/awards submissions
- Presentations/speeches
- Customer case studies (explained in detail in Chapter 10)

Contributed Articles

To create more thought diversity, some publications allow outside authors to write a contributed article about a topic on which they are an expert. With shrinking editorial staffs at news outlets, there is a heavier reliance on relevant, contributed content that suppliers can provide via contributed articles (Walker, 2021). Moreover, the expert is close to the customer and hears about their challenges, which makes their experiences valuable to publication and its reader.

A contributed article is a trusted, valuable form of earned media that a reputable third-party publication chooses to publish. Contributed articles can be hundreds or thousands of words and focus on a specific topic. Where editor-written articles will include quotes and perspectives from competing companies, and CMs will cite industry experts, you will not want to include quotes or citations from competitors for obvious reasons.

The structure of a contributed article follows an approach similar to that of a news release, starting with the essential information in the title and short abstract, then elaborating to explain the topic in more detail in body paragraphs with supporting visual elements while keeping promotional content to a minimum.

Looking at an example contributed article that appeared in March 2020 in *Design World* magazine (Figure 6.4), the first elements listed are:

- **Section or category**: Molding technology
- **Title**: Micro molding – The need for collaboration and DfM
- **Short abstract**: There are a certain set of rules and understandings of the molding process at the macro level that simply don't work at the micro level. The flow of molten plastic, its cooling, warpage, necessary venting and gating are all different when molding at the micro scale, and to a greater or lesser extent the process needs to be relearned.
- **Author name, title, and company name**: Roger Hargens, CEO/President, Accumold

In this contributed article example, the author begins by stating there are different rules for the molding process at the macro level than at the micro level and sets the stage with relevant, technical references to persuade the reader to relearn molding at the micro scale.

With this introductory thesis statement, the article follows with a two-paragraph introduction that leads to the main body of the article subtitled, "The product development process." The article concludes in the second to last paragraph, which begins, "Producing a plastic product with . . ." by assertively stating that the alternative "over the wall approach has to be abandoned" and outlines the important aspects of successful micro molding.

For contributed articles, mentioning company products or using content considered promotional is not just minimized; often, it is not allowed by the editor reviewing and approving the contributed content. The reason is simple – readers expect a third-party publication to provide trustworthy, unbiased information to educate them and help them do their jobs. If their articles are biased or promotional, the reader will begin to distrust the publication (Magno & Cassia, 2019). For publications, bloggers, and influencers, their readers and followers are their lifeblood – the larger their audience, the higher the value they are to advertisers, who buy ad space to secure paid access to their audience. Therefore, high-quality, trustworthy, unbiased content builds readership, which, in turn, makes their publication or outlet more valuable and influential.

One way CMs can more subtly incorporate mention of relevant products is through the supporting visual content used to illustrate points made in the main body text. For instance, in explaining the trade-offs of replacing a critical sub-system of an aging manufacturing machine versus replacing the entire machine, an author from a company that produces those critical sub-systems may include an image of one of their products as supporting visual content to their contributed article with a caption that summarizes the benefits of replacing parts instead of the entire machine.

When you secure an opportunity to submit a contributed article, the editor will provide a deadline, target word count, and the number of images to include. The CM will often serve as the content developer, working with a subject matter expert (SME) who will actually be publicly named as the author of the article. This is a practice called ghostwriting.

Micro molding – The need for collaboration and DfM

By **Roger Hargens, CEO/President, Accumold** | March 23, 2020

There are a certain set of rules and understandings of the molding process at the macro level that simply don't work at the micro level. The flow of molten plastic, it's cooling, warpage, necessary venting and gating ... are all different when molding at the micro scale, and to a greater or lesser extent the process needs to be relearned.

Companies may recognize the business need to produce smaller and smaller and often more complex and innovative products and components, but cannot see an obvious route to attain these goals.

In general, companies understand that micro molding is not just "macro molding but smaller." There comes a point, though, when making things smaller that the process to achieve this needs to change, and here the analogy of folding paper is often used. When you fold paper in half, you have a piece of paper half the size of the original. Fold it again, it is a quarter the size. However, when you get to the 7th fold, it is impossible to achieve, so to reduce the surface area the process (folding) has to change.

Many designers undertaking micro molding at scale outsource their production, so the "way" that micro

molding works, while relevant, should not be seen as a barrier. Choosing the micro molding expert takes away the need to understand the vagaries of the characteristics

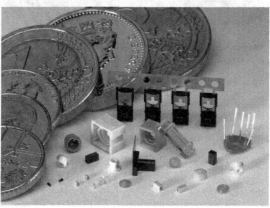

of thermoplastics when molding small. However, there are a number of other areas that any designer must focus on beyond the micro molding process.

Micro molding is one part of the overall product development process. Various groups should be involved early, at the initial product design level, to ensure mold success.

FIGURE 6.4 A contributed article, such as this one from Accumold, serves as a trusted, valuable form of earned media that a reputable third-party publication, *Design World*, published in its March 2020 issue. Contributed articles can be hundreds or thousands of words, focus on a specific topic, and follow an approach similar to that of a news release, starting with the essential information in the title and short abstract, then elaborating to explain the topic in more detail in the body paragraphs using supporting visual elements while keeping promotional content to a minimum.

The differences between macro molding and micro molding are stark. Every stage of the product development process in a micro-manufacturing scenario is motivated to attain micron and sub-micron tolerances.

design of a micro product can be influenced and adjusted to optimize manufacturing outcomes, the better in terms of cost and timeliness of production.

Essentially, DfM ensures that not only will the end product be fit-for-purpose but that it is also optimized for the production processes that will be used to manufacture it, in this case, micro molding and automated assembly. The micro-molding team that you work with should be able to advise on such issues as material choice, draft angles and undercuts, part lines, ejector pin locations, gate locations, the likely flow of material in the mold, wall thicknesses, and so on.

Perhaps the key enabling technology when it comes to micro molding is micro tooling. Tooling in any manufacturing scenario is always the most costly and time-consuming part of the product development process, but when looking at micro molding, the tolerances and complexity often required in micro molds make it especially critical.

Micro tooling is an art in itself, thus, designers should work with micro molders that can design, build, and maintain molds in house, and also have the expertise and experience to optimize tool fabrication.

One size does not fit all when looking at micro tooling. Micro molders can drill down into the specifics of a particular application, understand the effects of a certain

The product development process

Micro molding is only one part of the overall product development process, and it is important for designers to appreciate that various "departments" involved in a micro-manufacturing project should be engaged at product design inception.

Critical to success is reassessing the nature of the relationship between customer and molder in a micro-molding scenario. When dealing with contract manufacturers on the macro level, the relationship can quite acceptably be that of a job shop. The design is presented, the quote is secured, and the parts are delivered. Job done.

This cannot and will not work when undertaking a micro molding project, which necessitates that the OEM and the chosen micro molding company enter a fully collaborative partnership relationship.

The reasons for this are many, but begin with the fact that just as micro molding and macro molding are completely different processes, the design for manufacture (DfM) rules are also entirely different.

DfM for micro molding is important, and the expert in the room to offer advice and counseling is the expert micro molder, your product development partner. Often, the less baked an idea is when the micro molder is engaged the better, as the earlier that the

FIGURE 6.4 (Continued)

material, cycle time expectations, part criteria, and expected volumes before beginning to cut steel.

In house tool fabrication — in fact, vertical integration, in general, ensuring that design, molding, metrology and validation, and automated micro assembly are all undertaken in the same facility with departments working collaboratively — is important in a micro-manufacturing scenario where tolerances are tight. The probability for successful outcomes increases exponentially when the responsibility for project and production, timeline, and execution are controlled within a single entity.

The differences between macro molding and micro molding are stark when it comes to the molding process. Every stage of the product development process in a micro-manufacturing scenario is motivated to attain micron and sub-micron tolerances.

Finally, when dealing with miniaturized plastic parts and components, the assembly part of the product development process must be discussed and considered early in the design cycle. When dealing with micro-scale parts and components, the cost of manual assembly is prohibitive, and often requires levels of preciseness for sub-micron tolerances that are impossible to achieve. Automated assembly is, therefore, a must in most micro-molding scenarios.

Collaboration and transparency are not just required between the micro

molder and the customer, but also between the different teams within the micro-molding facility.

To a greater or lesser extent, designers rely on the micro molder to guide them in appropriate design choices. Transparency is absolutely important, ensuring that the customer is on the same page, understands the decision-making process, and works with the micro molder to problem solve and optimize outcomes while always ultimately being in control.

Producing a plastic product with micron or sub-micron features, repeatably, economically, and on time means that the "over the wall" approach has to be abandoned. Success in micro molding requires an inter-disciplinary approach, as it

is only in this way that the ultimate goal — an optimized product made to specification repeatably — can be guaranteed.

Success in micro molding is predicated on the forging of a truly collaborative and transparent relationship between micro molder and client. Decisions made at the early design stage will have effects when it comes to micro tool fabrication, micro molding, and micro assembly. Because of this — and the need to have an unswerving focus on the achievement of extremely tight tolerances and to validate design intent — all departments involved in the product development process must work together from the inception of a product design to ensure successful outcomes. MPF

FIGURE 6.4 (Continued)

To do this, the CM should act as an internal journalist, interviewing the SME(s) to gather the needed data and develop a well-structured and persuasive article that provides valuable information for the reader and establishes the author and company as trusted resources.

Once a draft is complete, several internal reviews from the intended author and other SMEs ensure accuracy and quality. Once it is shared with the editor and any feedback is resolved, the editor approves and accepts the article; a few weeks or even months may pass before the article appears online or in print.

Thought Leadership Articles

Most often, contributed articles in B2B markets are technical in nature or focus on a specific application or use case. However, respected senior-level executives may be invited to contribute a thought leadership article based on their unique credentials, such as their years of experience or their company's proven or disruptive success.

CMs who are asked to help with or even ghostwrite a thought leadership article should take extra care to ensure the message and story the executive seeks to tell is accurately and effectively created. To do this requires a two-pronged approach of research and interviewing the executive. To effectively prepare a thought leadership article, the CM should research:

- Thought leadership articles their company, as well as competitors, have published previously in the publication or outlet
- Thought leadership messaging and content from other paid, shared, or owned channels
- Leading competitors' thought leadership articles published on their websites or in third-party publications

Based on this research as well as the publication's format guidelines, a CM should prepare interview questions that refer to the five Ws of journalism noted earlier. Of particular note, focus on *who* the content most affects, *why* the company's position is important to the audience/industry at large, and *why* readers should understand and support the executive's point of view. During the interview, you want to gather all the information needed to develop an outline and full draft of the article. It's helpful to use some prompt questions to check that you fully understand the importance of key points and their priority, such as:

- "What is the most important message you want readers to understand?"
- "Why should readers care about this topic?"
- "How does your perspective on the issue help potential customers or the industry?"

After data is gathered through research and the executive interview, the process for writing the thought leadership article follows a similar approach to that of writing a white paper, starting with documenting the core elements discussed in Chapter 8 (i.e., topic, objective, audience, working title(s), estimated word count, timeline, abstract, and outline). The thought leadership article then goes through multiple internal reviews before the PR team coordinates publication with the editor.

Once the article is published, the resulting coverage is considered a very valuable achievement since third-party publication demonstrates the credibility and importance of the company's position to the market.

What a CM should know: Thought leadership articles are a great way to expand the top of the funnel. Authors will share these pieces on social media. Outlets will share on websites and in email marketing efforts. Links within the pieces help with search when important key terms and visuals are added.

Speaker and Awards Applications

Publishers and companies, among other types of organizations, regularly host events such as industry trade shows and conferences and invite third-party thought leaders and SMEs to submit applications to serve as a speakers. Being selected to speak at an event lends credibility to the person and, by association, the company.

Similar organizations will also host awards programs either annually or as part of their event and request that companies submit an application to nominate their product or solution in designated categories. Panels of respected judges review awards applications and select winners. Award winners are announced by the organization, which brings credibility to the company since an unbiased third party chose them among competitors as the best in their category. Once selected as a speaker or award winner, the company can then promote these honors on their owned media channels (explained in detail in Chapters 7 and 8).

Just as a job application requires both factual (contact details, years of experience, etc.) and persuasive (why the employer should consider your application, relevant work experience) information, the content development process for speaking and awards applications follows a similar approach. As illustrated in the speaking application for a content marketing industry event, Content Marketing World, shown in Figure 6.5, the CM must complete both factual and persuasive information:

- Factual information

  - Proposed session title
  - Track
  - Format
  - Audience level
  - Theme
  - Have you spoken at CMWorld before?
  - Speaking example video URL
  - Speaker info

- Persuasive information

  - Proposed session description
  - Three to five takeaways for participants
  - Why should the selection team choose you to speak at CMWorld?
  - Bio
  - Relevant speaking experience

CONTENT MARKETING INSTITUTE®

Proposed Session Title

Practical Guide to Content Marketing for the Next Generation

Track

Content Creation and Development

Format

Three-hour workshop

Audience Level

Beginner

Theme

B2B

Proposed Session Description

As the authors of the first research-based university textbook on content marketing, *Strategic Content Marketing: Creating Effective Content in Practice* (published by Routledge), Rebecca Geier and Dan Farkas will present the fundamentals of content marketing for the next generation of professionals and college students who are new to the field. The workshop will provide a comprehensive summary of research-based principles and insights from expert interviews in the field. Specifically, attendees will learn critical and strategic foundational marketing concepts that impact content marketing, which include: the myths of content marketing; product positioning and differentiation using the Four Ws for product positioning; buyer personas and the stages of the buying journey; marketing planning; and an overview of content planning, the use of buying stages, and steps to create a content calendar. Beginner content marketing practitioners will leave with a comprehensive understanding of how content marketing fits into the bigger context of marketing and business development, and they will be provided with tools, examples, and instruction on executing an effective content marketing program.

Three to Five Takeaways for Participants

1. A comprehensive overview of marketing fundamentals that new content marketing professionals, primarily in B2B markets, need to understand as they join and become valued members of a larger marketing team
2. New tools developed by the authors and introduced in the textbook that give content marketers structure for otherwise confusing and, at times, overwhelming concepts, such as the Four Ws for product positioning and content planning systems
3. Real-world examples and templates attendees can use in their jobs for specific content formats
4. Insights from content marketing experts on core aspects of successful content marketing programs, such as Robert Rose's thoughts on the role of storytelling in content marketing and Adele Revela's guidance on creating and effectively using buyer personas
5. The future of content marketing and the most critical skills new practitioners need to be effective and successful in content roles

Why Should the Selection Team Choose You to Speak at CMWorld? (Please Feel Free to Be Creative)

With thirty years as a content marketing practitioner, B2B marketing leader, author of 5-star-rated *Smart Marketing for Engineers: An Inbound Marketing Guide to Reaching Technical Audiences*, I have devoted the last three years to researching and writing the first research-based content marketing university textbook to inspire and successfully educate the next generation of practitioners about content marketing. Me and my co-author, Dan Farkas, have joined forces to ensure the textbook meets rigorous university-level standards for providing research-based principles while ensuring real-world practitioner standards and practices are incorporated to make it a useful reference in the workplace. We have spent hours interviewing company leaders and industry experts to complement our shared experience and research in order to provide real-world examples, templates, and tools to arm the beginner practitioner. With the textbook going into production in late 2023, I am so excited to finally bring what we have created to venues where CM practitioners, professors, and students gather to learn about the basics of content marketing. In particular, I hope to provide the fundamentals of content marketing to new practitioners and college students at Content Marketing World (CMW) so they have the knowledge to get the most from the other, more advanced sessions. Through a fun, engaging, and hands-on style, we look forward to educating and inspiring the next generation of practitioners and teaching critical concepts covered in depth in the textbook in a condensed, action-packed workshop.

Have You Spoken at CMW Before?

Yes

Speaking Example Video URL

Rebecca Geier, speaking at CMI's Intelligent Content Conference: https://youtu.be/X4cOCemFQDg

Speaker Info

Rebecca Geier
Austin, TX
Job title: Chief Marketing Officer
Company: Monolith

Bio

Named by *The Wall Street Journal* among the ten Most Innovative Entrepreneurs in America, Rebecca is a business leadership and marketing consultant, teacher, author, and speaker. She currently serves on the executive team of Monolith, an AI SaaS startup in the engineering industry. As Chief Marketing Officer, Geier is responsible for all aspects of marketing from brand voice to lead gen, and content marketing sits at the center as one of the most critical components of her strategy. Geier also leads her own strategic marketing consulting business, RIVE Advisors, working with B2B company leaders to grow the business and personal potential. Prior to RIVE, Geier was CEO and Co-founder of TREW Marketing, an inbound marketing agency uniquely serving engineering and scientific companies targeting technical audiences and Platinum HubSpot agency. Geier is author of *Smart Marketing for Engineers: An Inbound Marketing Guide to Reaching Technical Audiences* and is co-author of the forthcoming research-based university textbook on content marketing, *Content Marketing for Engineers, Scientists and*

Technical Communicators published by IGI Global. Geier is a regular blogger, highly rated speaker, and podcast guest.

Relevant Speaking Experience

Content Marketing World, September 2016–2018, Cleveland

Role: Industrial Marketing Workshop Instructor
Title: Content Marketing for Thomas Edison (2016), Reaching Technical Audiences with Content That Sticks (2017), Industrial Marketing – Changes Are Coming (2018)

Keysight Technologies Global Partner Conference, September 2018, Santa Rosa

Role: Presenter, Book Signing
Title: Grand Challenges Marketing to Engineers

The Transformers Association Annual Global Conference, April 2018, Ft. Worth

Role: Keynote Speaker
Title: Grand Challenges Marketing to Engineers

Intelligent Content Conference, March 2018, Las Vegas

Role: Keynote Speaker
Title: Say No to Grow

FirePro Global Partners Conference, October 2017, Limassol, Cyprus

Role: Keynote Speaker
Title: Grand Challenges Marketing to Engineers

Embedded World Trade Conference, March 2017, Nuremberg, Germany

Role: Theatre Presenter, Elektor Booth
Title: 10 Tips to Market to Engineers

American Marketing Association, November 2017, Austin

Role: Keynote Speaker
Title: How Marketing to Engineers – and Everyone Else – Has Transformed

University of Texas Executive MBA Lecture Series, September 2016, Austin

Role: Guest Lecturer
Title: Whale in a Pond, Minnow in an Ocean – A Contrast in Experiences

US Census Bureau Marketing Workshop, July 2016, Washington DC

Role: Guest Speaker
Title: Smart Marketing for Engineers

Texas A&M Mays School of Business, March 2016, College Station

Role: Guest Lecturer, Executive Professor Don Lewis's entrepreneurship class
Title: Prepare to Go to Market

FIGURE 6.5 In the speaker application for a content marketing industry event, Content Marketing World 2020, both factual (speaker information, title, speaking video example URL) and persuasive (three to five takeaways and why the selection committee team should choose you to speak) information are required. The CM's goal is to write compelling responses to position the application against competing speakers and persuade judges and selection committee members to choose their speaker.

The persuasive content elements in Figure 6.5 include questions such as a proposed session description, three to five takeaways for participants, and why the selection team should choose the applicant to speak at CMWorld. The CM's goal is to write compelling responses to each of these to directly position their application against competing speaker applications and influence and persuade judges and selection committee members to choose their speaker over other submissions. Moreover, these questions may include limitations of length or word count (such as the three to five takeaways question), making it even more difficult to persuade judges in fewer words.

To create high-quality, persuasive speaker and awards applications, a CM needs to once again put on their proverbial journalist hat and interview internal SMEs to gather the most important facts, unique strengths or value, and supporting data. Additionally, the writer should research past speakers and award winners to pinpoint the perceived unique aspects that led to their selection. When conducting this research, you should research the event or awards promotional materials to identify selling points that describe past speakers and award winners.

Applications for speaking and awards programs are deadline driven, so it's important that you plan ahead for two or more internal reviews before submitting the final application.

CONCLUSION

Until the beginning of the 21st century, the two primary channels marketers used to grow awareness and generate demand for their products were paid and earned media. With the advent of the internet, the growth of search engines and company websites, and the introduction and mass adoption of social media sites like YouTube and LinkedIn, two new media channels – owned and shared media – and content marketing as a discipline were born.

Since 2000, marketing budgets have been reallocated in part from paid media into these new channels, and traditional publishers have shuttered as more and more companies invest in building their own audiences through owned media channels and developing direct relationships with prospective and current customers with the goal of strengthening brand awareness and customer loyalty.

Earned media still matters, and the validation of reporters and third-party sources is crucial for brands to further strengthen their reputations. A CM will likely repurpose content created specifically for media into content that is more B2B friendly. A CM will also likely take B2B content marketing clusters, look for relevant story ideas, and repurpose this content into something more viable for journalists and online influencers.

Interview with the Experts: Q&A with Veteran Trade Journalist, Aimee Kalnoskas, Editor of EEWorldOnline.com and contributing editor of DesignWorldOnline.com

1. **What makes a high-quality news release?**

   a. Product or service is *newsworthy*.
   b. Release and image attached with minimal introductory text in the email (text of release also fine embedded in the email).
   c. Detailed product information (e.g., specs, applications, etc.).
   d. First paragraph contains most important information.
   e. Makes clear what it offers the reader. They don't care about *your* product; they care about their challenge or problem and if a product (hopefully, *your* product) can help them solve it.
   f. Short and to the point.
   g. Contact information for media inquiries.

2. **What are the common mistakes or elements that make a news release poor quality?**

   a. No images or low-res images.
   b. Images embedded in text as opposed to being attached as separate files.
   c. No links to more detailed information or datasheet.
   d. Content or an image presented or saved as a PDF. Much of a new product announcement is cut and pasted into publishing platforms, and attempting to cut and paste PDF text results in huge formatting issues and wasted time. Word docs are much easier and require less steps.
   e. Excessive number of quotes. One quote is enough. People don't want to read the marketing fluff normally contained in quotes.
   f. Company name in all caps, even if the name is not an acronym.
   g. Typos or grammatical errors. (It happens more often than you would think – or should tolerate.)
   h. PR jargon: phrases like *industry leader* or *solution. Solution* is a non-word used instead of a real word. If it is a data converter, it is a data

converter and not a *solution*. *Solution* should be used either following the word *aqueous* or as an answer to a problem.

i. Superlatives such as *biggest* and *fastest*.

j. Abuse of percentages when talking about performance improvements and comparisons to competitors. For example: "The processor is ten times as fast as previous processors." It is simply "ten times as fast." Period.

3. **As a journalist, how do you decide if a release is newsworthy or not?**

    a. Not touting minor product improvements – a "hero" product.
    b. It is specifically targeted to the publication's audience.
    c. Hits hot topics, markets, applications.

4. **Do you trust some companies more than others? If so, what leads companies to lose your trust in their news and/or content?**

    a. Yes. They follow question #1 and avoid mistakes in question #2, and they understand what I need and want because we have an established relationship (or we are establishing one).
    b. I will lose trust if they don't deliver or stop delivering straightforward press releases.
    c. They are strategic in what they send.

5. **What three to five characteristics and/or skills do you believe make a high performing PR writer or content producer?**

    a. Clear and concise writing.
    b. Basic understanding of technology with easy access to an SME.
    c. Understanding of a publication's audience, format (print or solely online, etc.), and type of content (new product announcements vs. new hires or promotions).

6. **How many news releases do you receive (or have to look through) in a week (or month)? How has this volume changed over the last decade?**

    a. ~200/month.
    b. The volume of releases appropriate to my audience has dropped. The number of releases that are highly irrelevant has increased. So . . . more junk.

7. **How have the publishing industry and technology trade journalism changed with the wide adoption of the internet and search engines like Google?**

    a. The size of print publications has shrunk, primarily due to decreased print advertising, but opportunities have opened up for more online content.
    b. Shrinking editorial staffs mean there is a heavier reliance on relevant, con-tributed content that suppliers can help supply via contributed articles.

The supplier is close to the customer and hears about their challenges, which makes their experiences valuable to [the] publication and its reader.

8. **Is the editorial calendar still a primary tool used to plan topics the publication will cover?**

   a. It is less and less of a tool, particularly in a time when technology changes so rapidly. However, many print trade publications in particular adhere to an editorial calendar, and they are still worth referencing with the understanding that other relevant, off-calendar articles may also be considered for online publication.

9. **Are contributed articles still a valued form of content companies can provide, and if so, what three to five aspects make them trusted and high quality?**

   a. Yes, they are.
   b. Tutorial or educational – not marketing speak.
   c. They need to address common challenges/problems and then explain the solution or likely solutions.
   d. Good graphics such schematics, tables, and relevant figures (not product-advertising shots).
   e. Exclusive to my publication.

10. **When you interview a subject matter expert for a story you're writing, what is required of them to make it valuable for you?**

    a. Understanding of the publication and its audience – and technical level of editor.
    b. Provide specific, real-world examples.
    c. Offer of additional resources to complement topic.

CITATIONS

Abdow, M. "All things media: Paid, earned, owned, and shared." *Podiatry Management.* January 2020.

Bejerman, I. *Turning the Inverted Pyramid Inside-Out: Professional Ideology, Professionalization, and Education of Journalists Reconsidered.* Montreal: McGill University Libraries. 2011.

Kulkarni, S., Thomas, R., Komorowski, M., & Lewis, J. "Innovating online journalism: New ways of storytelling." *Journalism Practice.* 2022. Taylor & Francis. January 10, 2022.

Magno, F., & Cassia, F. "Establishing thought leadership through social media in B2B settings: Effects on customer relationship performance." *Journal of Business & Industrial Marketing.* September 19, 2019.

No Author. "Meta Description." *Moz.com.* Cited January 12, 2023. Retrieved from: https://moz.com/learn/seo/meta-description#:~:text=Meta%20descriptions%20can%20technically%20be,between%2050%20and%20160%20characters

Treadwell, D., & Treadwell, J. *Public Relations Writing: Principles in Practice.* SAGE. April 19, 2005.

Walker, M. "U.S. Newsroom employment has fallen 26% since 2008." *Pew Research Center.* July 13, 2021. Retrieved from: www.pewresearch.org/fact-tank/2021/07/13/u-s-newsroom-employment-has-fallen-26-since-2008/

CHAPTER 7

Owned Media (Part 1) – Websites, Blogs, and Branded Publications

---

LEARNING OBJECTIVES

1. An overview of the owned-media channel and its growing role and importance in content marketing
2. A brief history of the shift from publisher-controlled to brand-controlled audience building
3. The role of a company website and how to effectively create content for the most prominent sections
4. Advantages of a company blog and best practices for blog writing
5. Introduction to branded digital publications and the tone and approach to article development

---

INTRODUCTION

In 1995, Rebecca was working in marketing at a growing high-tech company when we began hearing that a few employees were working on a project referred to as the World Wide Web. Those of us in marketing communications had little understanding of what "the Web," as it was referred to in its abbreviated form, was, and our perception was that this project we were hearing about was a sort of file-sharing tool this group was exploring as a quicker means to provide support to savvy customers adept at accessing it.

At the time we were hearing about this rogue project, two of the more progressive and impactful product collateral types used by our marcom team to drive demand with potential customers were a compact disc (CD) of interactive software toolkits and demos and a 600-plus-page print catalog detailing the company's thousands of products. Both the CD and print catalog took nearly a year to create and design; cost millions of dollars to print and distribute; and, like other promotional materials such as product brochures, were sent to customers around the world via mail. Not email, but rather traditional mail such as the US Postal Service in the United States. As soon as the CDs and catalogs were mailed, the team started work on the next

DOI: 10.4324/9781003369103-09

year's versions, and in about 12 months, new and improved editions were again mailed out at a cost of millions more.

That feels like a lifetime ago.

As companies began producing websites using their own domain names, they essentially became their own publishers. As a result, marketing teams began investing in the development of corporate websites. Over time, the control of when, where, and how a company's news and content was published began shifting from traditional earned and paid media channels primarily through advertising and public relations to a third approach known as owned media (the "O" in PESO, a framework introduced in Chapter 4).

As a testament to the growth in owned and shared media, according to a report by the Vox news site, 2017 marked the first time that digital ad spending surpassed spending on traditional TV (Kafka & Molla, 2017).

With owned media, just as the name implies, the company owns the channels used to publish information. Therefore, it controls when, where, and how that information is shared, as well as what type of content to produce.

As Joe Pulizzi explains in *Corona Marketing: What Marketing Professionals Need to Do Now to Survive the Crisis* (Pulizzi & May, 2020), "2010 brought a complete shift and realignment of marketing budgets. In many cases, the large advertising cuts in budget were reallocated to other activities, including social media, video marketing, podcasting, event marketing, webcasting and more."

In the beginning of this era of owned media and website creation, most companies created what were called "brochure websites" that simply looked like a company's corporate brochure online and provided a basic overview of the brand's history, mission, primary product lines, and contact information. These first websites were not interactive, rarely updated, and served the sole purpose of being a static digital presence for the company online.

With the founding of Google's first search engine, BackRub, in the late 1990s, the web changed. BackRub assigned value to web pages based on how often the page was referenced (i.e., backlinks) across the web. The engine considered websites with a high number of back-links to be of higher quality and more valuable to readers. As a result, those pages ranked higher on Google's search results page.

Marketers saw this as a way to reach prospective buyers through a completely new channel; as a result, static self-serving brochure websites quickly became insufficient. Website development as a discipline of marketing exploded as the need to improve site value to humans and Google grew. As consumers increasingly came to expect a company's website to serve as a one-stop destination for information, power shifted toward consumers who suddenly had the ability to quickly find specific information in a single search or click.

THE NEW MEDIA CHANNEL: OWNED MEDIA

In the 20th century, paid and earned media were the two main media channels companies used to reach their audiences.

Then the internet and search engines happened.

Now, a fundamental shift in control has occurred away from publishers serving as the primary media channel to companies themselves becoming publishers of their own media to build their own audiences. Companies do this by publishing content through a variety of media channels they own and control. By publishing content through their own media channels, companies control the message, the frequency, the form, and all other aspects of the content produced with the intent of growing their own audiences (Majodouba, 2016).

It's not coincidental that with the advent of owned media, the discipline that's come to be known as content marketing began to take hold. Today, creating content for the owned media channel represents a significant portion of a CM's writing load. There are two categories of content that are published on the owned media channel: digital and audio and video. This chapter will cover content marketing for three common digital types of owned media, and Chapter 8 explains two common broadcast types:

- Digital

  - Website
  - Blog
  - Print and digital publications

- Audio and video

  - Webinars
  - Podcasts
  - Videos

HUB OF OWNED MEDIA: THE WEBSITE

The most important owned media channel – and one could argue the most important of any of the PESO channels – is a company's website. The website serves many roles, from online store to customer support portal and employee recruiting engine. For the purposes of marketing, the website is the hub of all online and offline activities and the primary vehicle to generate leads and create your brand online (Geier, 2016). As ranking on Google became a greater priority, many forward-thinking marketing teams used talent, time, and financial currency to develop content their target audiences and Google could easily find.

The brand voice, tone, and writing style of websites vary widely. Similarly, the structure and depth of websites can range from a few sections with fewer than 50 total pages for startups or small organizations to hundreds of sections and millions of pages for global enterprises.

What a CM should know: As a result, a CM may be asked to create content across many different sections of a website. While not an exhaustive list, the four areas of a website that often require the most extensive CM involvement and creativity include:

- Home page
- Products, services, or solutions pages (explained in detail in Chapter 9)

- About page
- Industry or segment page

Home Page

This is the first page of a company's website that loads when you visit the address in a browser, such as Google Chrome. For example, when you visit www.Routledge.com, the publisher of this book, the page that loads is the site's home page, where you see a short description of the company, an area to search for books, and a listing at the top for quick links to key pages on the website, referred to as the global navigation.

Copy on the home page should be short so visitors can quickly scroll down through the page to learn about the company. For this reason, as you see in Figure 7.1 showing the home page of Monolith, an AI software company for engineering teams, the content elements on the home page are primarily limited to three-to-six-word headlines, 50-to-100-word descriptions, bulleted lists, short call to action text, and high-quality imagery to break up the page and keep it visually appealing. The purpose is to tell visitors clearly and succinctly what the company uniquely offers and inspire them to stay on the site and click through to learn more.

Referring to Figure 7.1, the common elements on a home page include:

- Global navigational elements that serve as a table of contents to the site

  - "Monolith platform"
  - "AI solutions"
  - "Resources"
  - "About"
  - "Contact us"

- Value proposition or tagline

  - "With Monolith's AI Software, test less and learn more."
  - "Spend less time running expensive, repetitive tests and more time learning from your engineering data to predict the exact tests to run."

- Unique product features and benefits

  - Features

    - "No-code AI software built for engineers"
    - "Monolith Software is a machine learning AI platform built by engineers, for engineers. No coding or Ph.D. in statistics is required – just your engineering expertise and test data."

  - Benefits

    - "Trusted by top engineering teams to cut product development time."

- • "Build accurate self-learning and machine learning models."
  - • "Named by Gartner as a Cool Vendor in AI for automotive."

- • Specific industries or segments served:

  - • Segments: "Discover our top data-driven business applications and engineering use cases for aerospace and defense, automotive, and industrial customers."

    - • "Vehicle dynamics"
    - • "Smart meters"
    - • "Wind-tunnel testing"

  - • "Featured industries"

    - • "Automotive"
    - • "Industrial"
    - • "Aerospace and defense"

- • Social proof through testimonials, quotes, and customer logos:

  - • Logos from customers including Kautex, Michelin, Aptar, JOTA, and BMW below the value proposition
  - • Logo and quote from Honeywell between the segment and industry sections

- • Calls to action to give visitors additional content to explore:

  - • "Request a demo" in the global navigation, below the value proposition and at the end of the page
  - • "Speak to our team" button below the value proposition and at the end of the page
  - • "Learn more" links used throughout the page
  - • "Get started" and "Read more" buttons
  - • "Read the case study" button to access the JOTA case study
  - • "Submit" button at the end of the page to "Subscribe to our monthly newsletter"

- • Awards and industry recognition to inspire further credibility:

  - • "Named by Gartner as a Cool Vendor in AI for automotive" in the features and benefits section

- • Recent news announcements

  - • "News Center: Find out how we empower engineers to use AI Software"
  - • "Improve smart meter system performance using AI"
  - • "Self-learning models: The key to unlocking engineering potential"
  - • "Engineering data quality and availability in artificial intelligence"

FIGURE 7.1 Monolith's home page demonstrates the use of short content snippets that allow visitors to quickly scroll down through the page to learn about the company. Content elements are primarily limited to three-to-six-word headlines, 50-to-100-word descriptions, bulleted lists, short CTA text, and high-quality imagery to break up the page and keep it visually appealing. The purpose is to tell visitors clearly and succinctly what the company uniquely offers and inspire them to stay on the site and click in to learn more. Common elements on a home page include the company's value proposition or tagline; specific industries or segments served; social proof through testimonials, quotes, and customer logos; and calls to action to give visitors additional content to explore.

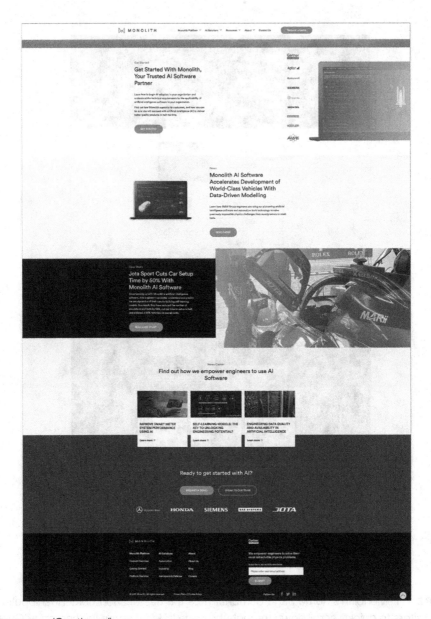

FIGURE 7.1 (Continued)

About Page

This section of the website gives visitors a view into the company's history, why it was founded, who leads it, and what it's like to work there.

Staying with the same website, Figure 7.2 shows content on Monolith's About page. The content varies in length, and since it is an area that brings the company to life through its history and employees, often takes on more of a storytelling tone than other pages on the site.

Referring to Figure 7.2, the common content elements on an About page include but are not limited to:

- Mission and vision

  - "We empower engineers to use AI to solve even their most intractable physics problems."
  - "Our vision: By 2026, we will empower 100,000 visionary engineers to use AI to cut their product development cycle in half."

- Company culture, core values

  - "Our core values"

    - "Bring yourself to work."
    - "Always be curious and open."
    - "Think like an engineer."
    - "Work smart, not hard."
    - "Be in this together."

  - "Working at Monolith: Our company culture" below the leadership team

    - "We are genuine."
    - "We have a culture of learning."
    - "We are all human, and sometimes we make mistakes."

  - Founding story as well as historical milestones and achievements

    - 2016–2022 timeline
    - "AI leaders in theory and practice"
    - "Monolith: Our startup story"

  - Leadership team pictures and biographies

    - "The Monolith AI leadership team"
    - Portraits of each leader with their biographies follow, such as "Dr. Richard Ahlfeld, CEO" shown in the expanded area

- Current job openings and how to apply (not included in this example)
- Geographic locations (not included in this example)★
- Information on how to contact the company (included on the Contact Us page of the site)★

(★These two content elements may also be housed together on a single Contact Us page.)

Industry or Segment Page

This area of a company's website helps educate and persuade a specific target audience, which can be defined by industry (e.g., automotive, telecommunications), geographic region (e.g.,

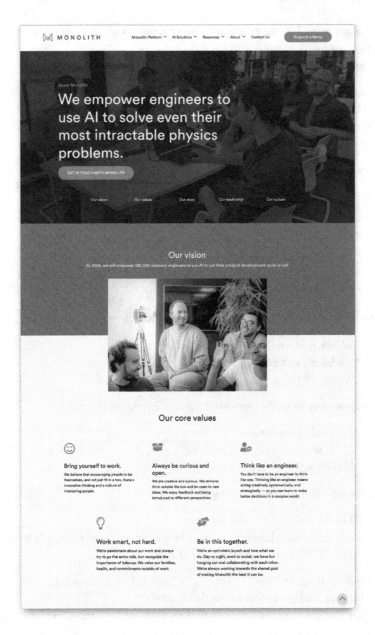

FIGURE 7.2 This About section of a company's website gives visitors a view into the company's history, why it was founded, who leads it, and what it's like to work there. Content varies in length, and since it is an area that brings the company to life through its history and employees, often takes on more of a storytelling tone than other pages on the site. Common elements on an About page include the company's mission and vision statements, core values, founding story and key achievements, leadership team pictures and biographies, and current job openings and how to apply.

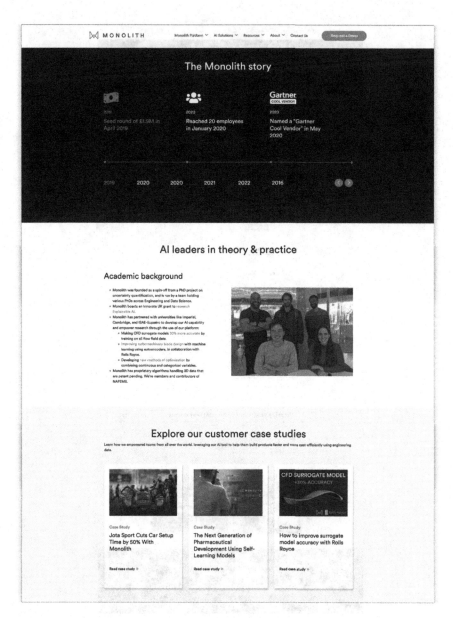

FIGURE 7.2 (Continued)

United States, Africa), or the nature of the application (e.g., wind-tunnel testing, automated manufacturing).

Common content elements on industry or segment pages are similar to those listed for the home page but with customized terminology, examples, and imagery relevant to the target segment. For instance, on the Monolith website, a web page dedicated to the automotive industry

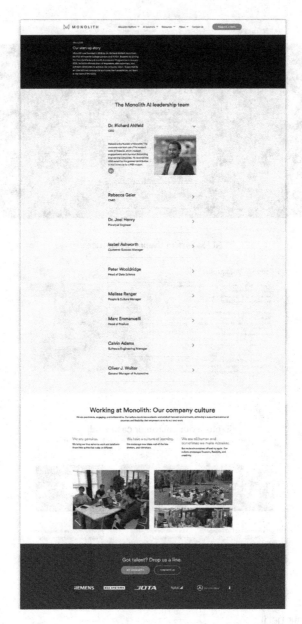

FIGURE 7.2 (Continued)

(Figure 7.3) lists content much like the home page but tailored to the industry through the use of automotive-specific terms and imagery. For instance, the headline at the top of the page is "AI Automotive engineering optimization with Monolith," which is followed by the value proposition "Monolith Software empowers engineering domain experts across all facets of the Automotive industry with AI and machine learning."

The social proof includes logos of well-known global brands in the automotive industry, including Honda, BMW, and Mercedes-Benz, and a quote from an engineering leader at a global automotive supplier, Kautex-Textron (Figure 7.3).

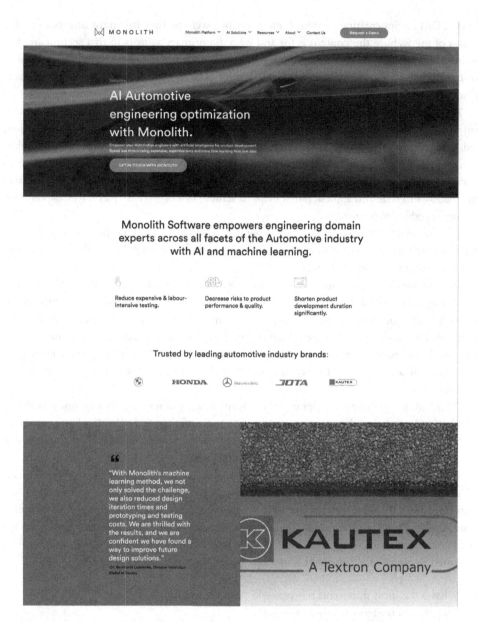

FIGURE 7.3 An Industry or Segment section of a company's website is dedicated to educating and persuading a specific target audience, like this Monolith web page that targets the automotive industry. Content on this page is similar to that found on the home page but tailored to this specific audience through use of automotive-specific terms such as the headline at the top of the page "AI Automotive engineering optimization with Monolith" and the value proposition "Monolith Software empowers engineering domain experts across all facets of the Automotive industry with AI and machine learning." Social proof includes logos of well-known global automotive brands, including Honda, BMW, and Mercedes-Benz, and a quote from an engineering leader at a global automotive supplier, Kautex-Textron.

When a CM begins creating content for a company's website, they first must understand what section of the website the content is for and who the primary visitors to that section are. For instance, the primary audience for content in the product and support sections is customers. For the About section, the primary audience is most likely potential customers, employee candidates, and investors.

A CM should then understand the objective of the page. For example, in the product section of the website, the objective is most often to motivate the visitor to stay in the section, read more content about the product, and eventually connect with the company by completing a form to receive gated information (explained in Chapter 4), such as a white paper, or to speak to a salesperson. In this instance, therefore, the CM should focus on providing valuable information in a style and approach that helps to achieve this objective. (Refer to Chapter 9 for writing a product web page.)

In contrast to the lead- and demand-generation objectives for product web pages, the objectives for the About section of the website focus more on introducing the visitor to the company's values, culture, and vision.

Each of the aforementioned sections of a website can be one long page you scroll down to read through (ideal for users accessing the site on mobile devices where clicking on links is not as user friendly), or the front page of the section can serve as a sort of table of contents linking to subsections that go into more detail about specific audience-related topics. For instance, from the About page, there may be a link to a subsection devoted to prospective employees where they can access information on the company's benefits and how to apply for current job openings.

There are many different styles of design, formatting, and writing for a company website. Even having knowledge about the section is often not sufficient to begin developing content. A CM should understand the subsection that will house the content and whether the audience and objective for this subsection match the overall section.

Once the section, subsection, audience, and objectives are defined for the website content, a CM can start by researching other similar pages in the same web section and interviewing knowledgeable stakeholders about the topic, following the best-practices approach to writing a white paper explained in Chapter 10 (i.e., documenting the topic, objective, audience, working title(s), estimated word count, timeline, abstract, and outline) and asking questions similar to those used to prepare for a thought leadership article (explained in Chapter 6):

- What is the most important message you want readers to understand?
- Why should readers care about this topic?
- How does your perspective on the issue help potential customers or the industry?

What a CM should know: Word counts and writing style for web pages are often predetermined by the page template and design. Asking a lot of questions before you get started writing a web page and documenting this key information before beginning helps ensure the first draft conforms to the design of the page it will call home and meets the visitors' needs, which is measured by growing web traffic to the page and the amount of time visitors stay on the page.

THE COMPANY'S ONLINE JOURNAL: THE BLOG

The blog is a popular and widely adopted owned media channel for B2B and B2C communication. In the simplest terms, a blog is an online diary or journal that is used for the corporate expression of ideas. Blog articles can vary greatly in the topics they cover, from news announcements, employee and company culture stories to customer testimonials, technology trends, and in-depth product or application descriptions.

The proliferation of blogs followed the large investment by companies in their websites, as Mr. Pulizzi further explained in his eBook *Corona Marketing*:

> The economic adjustment that took place after 9/11 became the first stage of content marketing. As enterprises saw their marketing budget reduced in 2002, and then subsequently returning in 2003, marketers were free to reallocate some of the budget away from what used to be an advertising line item. At the same time, Google was exploding, and global marketers started sinking large amounts of time and resources into "being found" online. Enter blogging.
> (Pulizzi, 2020)

A company's blog is a section of the company's website that is updated weekly, daily, and even multiple times per day, depending on the company's size and marketing needs.

Given how frequently they are updated with new articles, blogs play a valuable role in a company's search engine optimization efforts. Some companies may have multiple blog websites, each with a specific technical focus, such as on a segment, industry, or product line, with articles authored by subject matter experts in that field. Similarly, specific departments such as HR may have a blog devoted to articles on the company culture, employee life, and career opportunities.

Maintaining a high-quality corporate blog can be time consuming since it requires consistent posting and strong written communication skills. However, the few challenges of blogging are far outweighed by the many advantages a company blog provides, including the following:

1. Increased online traffic and leads when high-quality articles are posted regularly
2. Simplicity in quickly and efficiently sharing information, such as during a crisis
3. Ability to directly interact and share ideas with stakeholder audiences (employees, partners, investors, potential customers, existing customers)
4. Fostering creativity and information sharing among company departments and geographies
5. Keeping customers engaged by revisiting the blog to read new articles they find valuable
6. Differentiating your company through articles that highlight competitive advantages and unique expertise
7. Timely way to showcase customer successes and news announcements
8. Low cost to produce a blog, which primarily consists of the time required for writing
9. Ability to humanize the company through direct employee authorship, including company leaders
10. Outlet to publish articles by subject matter experts in the company that elevate their stature and following in relevant communities

11. Ease of sharing blog articles on shared media channels to expand the company's reach and awareness
12. Improved domain authority and SEO from backlinks created when others find the content valuable and link to a blog post
13. Establishing the company as an authority with consistent information that helps people learn and solve problems

The writing style of most company blogs is often more informal in nature and shorter than lengthier, more formal content, such as four-color designed brochures or in-depth technical white papers. Multiple authors can contribute to a blog and can write in the first person on certain topics relevant to the blog's focus.

What a CM should know: The blog calendar, which includes planning details such as article topic, author, editor, and publish date, is developed as part of the larger content marketing plan (explained in Chapter 4), and a CM is often responsible for keeping the calendar current, maintaining the schedule, and ensuring the writing quality and tone align with the blog's style guide. The blog manager also serves as a final approver of all articles before they're posted to filter out any personal bias, controversial statements, poor-quality or copyrighted imagery, or unproven claims that may diminish the brand's position as a trusted voice in the industry.

Writing Blog Posts for Different Audiences

Let's look at a few examples by the Greater Columbus Sports Commission (GCSC), which is an organization responsible for bringing world-class sporting events to the city of Columbus, Ohio. The blog appeals to several different audiences and potential buyers:

*   Buying committees from sports associations hoping to host regional or national championships. For instance, the National Collegiate Athletic Association (NCAA) has its own committee that hosts hundreds of events per year and evaluates proposals on a constant basis. These committees want to make sure there is enough infrastructure – including hotels, restaurants, and facilities – to host the event and the people staying in town. These committees also want to see the community's commitment to sports in relation to other community events and camps. This is much more of a B2B experience with technical specifications focused on travel and tourism.
*   Teams, athletes, and fans are a B2C audience. For every athlete who participates, two to four people travel with them. In many cases, these potential customers are interested in things to do around the city before and after the competition. Part of that journey is convincing people who have never been to Columbus, Ohio, why the city is and should be a destination location.
*   Businesses in and around Columbus also access the blog to better understand events occurring around town and how those businesses can sponsor or support the sports commission to ensure a world-class experience.

Sporty Things to Do in Columbus

By <u>Steve Wartenberg</u> on **Aug. 30, 2022**

Labor Day in Columbus, Ohio is always a great time. Who doesn't love a long weekend of summer sun before the clock turns to fall and foliage? This year is especially exciting in Ohio's capital city, as Airbnb listed Columbus as one of the <u>**top trending cities**</u> for Labor Day Weekend. We have a hunch the No. 2 Ohio State Buckeyes hosting the No. 5 Notre Dame Fighting Irish has something to do with that! If you're here for a game this fall, here's a list of things to do in Columbus when you're not cheering on the team.

Paddle the Scioto
Columbus has a vibrant downtown, and one of the best ways to take in the sights is from a kayak or stand-up paddleboard. You'll glide along the Scioto River, past <u>**Bicentennial Park**</u>, the <u>**COSI**</u> science museum, the <u>**National Veterans Memorial and Museum**</u>, the historic <u>**LeVeque Tower**</u> and then onto the <u>**Scioto Mile**</u>. Two companies offer water adventures: <u>**Windrose Outdoor**</u> for on-your-own rentals, and <u>**Olentangy Paddle**</u> for guided tours.

Run or Walk the Scioto
If you're not a paddler (yet), a walk, jog or run along the city's downtown riverfront is another fun way to see the city. From downtown, head toward the river (the eastern bank) and start walking or running. If you head north, you'll eventually come to the spot where the Olentangy River runs into the Scioto. From here, it's a quick jog over to <u>**Lower.com Field**</u>, home of the Columbus Crew. If you head south from downtown, you'll eventually reach <u>**Scioto Audubon Metro Park**</u>, where's there's the <u>**Grange Insurance Audubon Center**</u>, outdoor climbing wall, obstacle park and dog park.

Go the distance
If you're in the city at the right time (by coincidence or plan), Columbus hosts two large, well-organized and popular long-distance running events: the <u>**OhioHealth Capital City Half & Quarter Marathon**</u> (in April every year) and the <u>**Nationwide Children's Hospital Columbus Marathon**</u> (every October).

Cycle the city
Biking is another great way to travel along the river, or elsewhere in Columbus. There are more than 80 <u>CoGo</u> bike-share stations located throughout the city. It costs $2.25 for a 30-minute rental, and $8 for the day. You can get a bike at one station (let's say downtown) and then drop it off somewhere else (let's say Scioto Audubon Metro Park). <u>**German Village**</u>, the <u>**Short North**</u> and the Ohio State campus are other nearby, fun destinations.

FIGURE 7.4 The Greater Columbus Sports Commission has helped bring in events that have generated more than $625 million in visitor spending since 2002. Its blog showcases key themes that event organizers seek when planning major competitions.

According to Jesse Ghiorzi, who oversees communications for the sports commission, the blog allows them to reinforce the idea that "Columbus never has an off-season" and that sports are the core fiber that brings the Columbus community together. Its blog showcases this for B2B and B2C buyers.

In the first example, for B2B readers, the post "Sporty Things to Do in Columbus" addresses items that are of importance to people planning summer events. Figure 7.4 shows how the author highlights several ways active people can pursue their passion when visiting the city. It also highlights the city's biking infrastructure and alternative transportation, something Ghiorzi said is appealing to event organizers who always seek ease of use in transportation.

More than two dozen external links validate the notion that Columbus has something to offer for everyone. They also showcase the public and private partnerships event organizers seek when looking for host cities. There's even a link to an Airbnb listing about Columbus being one of the five best places to visit over Labor Day weekend.

The blog ends with a call to action to learn more about the sports commission's work in and around Columbus.

The second blog example from GCSC, targeting B2C readers – "Five Reasons to Go to a Sports Camp this Summer" – features several key elements that reinforce the sports commission's core messaging to diverse audiences.

The post discusses universal solutions on a theme of particular importance to parents. Summer camps help students achieve higher test scores, learn problem-solving skills, and improve self-esteem. External links to secondary sources like National Public Radio and the Aspen Institute validate these claims and improve the blog's search engine optimization. Internal links allow interested participants to learn more and register. There are also calls to action at the post's beginning and end. These engage people who just skim the beginning to stay involved. Those reading the entire post are likely interested in learning more and can easily register with a single click.

The post concludes with general information about the sports commission and how it tries to create world-class events and opportunities for everyone in Columbus.

The third example from GCSC demonstrates how blogs can also afford a chance to tell personal stories that can have an impact in B2B and B2C situations. In the post "A Brief History of Women's Basketball in Columbus, Ohio," the blog leads with examples of ratings success with both the Women's National Basketball Association (WNBA) and the NCAA (Figure 7.6).

The blog then informs readers of the sport's 100-year history in Columbus and reminds them of the city's commitment to diverse sporting opportunities for all. Highlighting regional and national champions reinforces the sports commission's message that Columbus has no off-season and reminds readers of the city's willingness to host future events. This kind of storytelling is an effective way to reinforce key points, especially to younger people (Emde et al., 2016).

The post concludes with a recap of the NCAA Women's Final Four hosted in Columbus in 2018. The series of games broke NCAA attendance records and earned *SportsTravel* magazine's Sports Event of the Year, beating out the Super Bowl and the Olympics. The 2018 event brought $21.7 million in direct visitor spending to the region. More than 80% of visitors were from outside Ohio, with 60% making their first trip to Columbus.

Five Reasons to Go to a Sports Camp this Summer

By Jesse Ghiorzi on Feb. 06, 2023

Though it's still chilly in Columbus, summer will be here before you know it. For parents with kids - that means one thing....
IT'S CAMP SEASON.

We partner with The Columbus Foundation to run Community Youth Camp for 6 to 12-year-olds in central Ohio. Kids play up to four sports a day for four days, learning new skills and building confidence. Registration for Youth Camp is open now right here. For 2023, we offer two sessions, both at KIPP Columbus - June 20-23 and June 26-29.

Summer is the best time for kids to play outside and make new friends. It's also the perfect time to try new sports. Here are five reasons why your kids should go to a camp this summer.

5. HIGHER TEST SCORES

Playing sports can make you smarter? Believe it or not, active kids have up to 40% higher test scores. That's according to the Aspen Institute, which has done lots of research on the benefits of youth sports. A sports camp, especially one that allows your child to try more than one sport, gives them the opportunity to learn a sport in a fun and inclusive environment. At camp, the focus is on learning and improving, not winning and losing.

4. LEARN TEAMWORK AND PROBLEM-SOLVING SKILLS

We're all on one team or another. Sometimes it's a work project, sometimes it's a family or a community or volunteer group. If you break it down, a team is just a group of people working together to achieve a common goal. The most obvious teams are sports teams! Playing sports together gives children a chance to learn their role, how that interacts with other roles and what they need to do to succeed.

Additionally, we'll all face problems at some point. Sport camps are great places to learn how to solve them. "We want to score a touchdown, but the other team wants to stop us. How can we get past them into the end zone?"

3. HIGHER SELF-ESTEEM

Back with another one from the Aspen Institute. Countless studies show the link between playing sports and higher self-esteem in young children. A sports camp gives kids a chance to learn, try, fail, tweak, try again and succeed. The lessons picked up at play will build confidence and self-esteem that extend beyond the field and into the classroom and other parts of life.

2. LIFELONG PARTICIPATION

Adults who play sports are just grown up versions of kids who play sports! According to an NPR study, 73% of adults who play sports played when they were kids. If you enjoyed playing sports as a kid, it's the best thing you can do for your child to introduce them to sports at a camp this summer. Maybe they'll gravitate towards one or more sport and you can explore a full season this school year.

1. IT'S FUN

And the number one reason kids play sports - fun! Sports camps teach the fundamentals in a fun way. They get to run, jump and make new friends. We can't think of a better thing to do this summer.

We hope you make it to a field, court, pool, rink, track or somewhere else you can play this summer. Maybe we'll see you at Community Youth Camp!

FIGURE 7.5 The Greater Columbus Sports Commission believes that there is no off-season in Columbus. It uses its blog to remind residents about the value of sports on and off the field. This is a subtle reminder to consider sports camps, something the Sports Commission values as a key community driver.

Blog posts can be created from repurposed content of other types, such as case studies or news releases. For instance, the original content type for the blog post in Figure 7.6 was a news release, which was featured as an example of this type of earned media in Chapter 6. After the news release was distributed to the media, the content was repurposed from this earned media format ideally suited to journalists into a blog post tailored to other stakeholders, such as prospective customers.

Just as blog posts can be derived from other content, a blog post is easy to repurpose for earned, social, and other owned media. The sports commission uses blog content when

FIGURE 7.6 The Greater Columbus Sports Commission takes pride in being a leader in the hosting of events for women and girls. Its blog highlights this passion for equity in sports and has helped it secure major sporting events like the NCAA Women's Final Four Tournament.

writing proposals and pitching event organizers. The blogs enable journalists and social media partners to easily share accurate information. The blog incorporates core messaging, key terms, and links that create digital currency for relevant target audiences and search algorithms, and reinforces key branding elements, helping potential buyers better recall key differentiators of a business or non-profit (Zaichkowsky, 2010). The blog also forces content marketers and others in the organization to seek good story ideas; this cultivates a creative culture that impacts a brand throughout its work.

Blogging Timelines

While short deadlines may sometimes be expected, CMs will usually have several weeks or longer to prepare a blog article, including developing an outline, researching relevant articles and supporting data, identifying helpful images to aid in the storytelling, creating drafts, and revising to finalize. Ideally, the final blog article is fully complete a week before the publish date. This provides the blog manager with the time needed to set up the blog for posting, including posting images, adding calls to action, and editing for areas of the post that are most critical to search engine optimization, such as the title tag, meta description, headings and subheadings, image alternate text fields, introductory sentence, and concluding paragraph.

What a CM should know: Blog posts are a well-established and growing owned media channel. For a CM, it is a critically important format that is also fun and leaves a great deal of room for creativity in article titles, images, captions, and calls to action.

OWNED MEDIA: BRANDED DIGITAL PUBLICATIONS

The value of a brand helps drive business goals (Leek & Christodoulides, 2012). A symbolic example of how far owned media has come is the broad use of brand publications, most commonly in the form of digital magazines. While brand publications are not necessarily new, historically, only companies that could afford the high cost of printing and mailing them used this media. Moreover, the reach of a company's publication was traditionally limited to their existing database of contacts unless they paid publishers to distribute to their circulation.

However, the growing investment in websites, content marketing, and shared media channels fueled the shift to marketing teams building their own audiences, rather than paying to gain access to traditional publishers' audiences through purchased lists. As companies began to build audiences that valued their content and directly visited and interacted with them via their owned and shared media channels, and digital publishing removed the prohibitively high cost of printing and mailing, the conditions were ripe to fuel an expansion in the use of the branded publications that today serve to strengthen a company's relationship with prospective customers and other stakeholders as well as building loyalty with current ones.

Brand publications are most often published either monthly or quarterly, although sometimes the frequency may be less often, even bimonthly or semi-annually. The types of content included in brand digital publications can vary based on whether it is written in a formal tone or it follows a more conversational, informal design and language. This tone is set by the overall brand strategy and is consistent across content channels and types. Most often, however, content in brand publications takes the form of traditional magazine articles that range from longer features to shorter announcements and human interest stories. Article topics vary from in-depth new product coverage and major industry trends to customer case studies, technology developments, and company news, such as patent awards, upcoming events, and partnership announcements. For example, Figure 7.7 shows the May 2020 issue of *tED Magazine*, a monthly publication by the National Association of Electrical Distributors (NAED) that was awarded the top honor of Best B2B Magazine of the Year in May 2019 by the American Society of Business Publication Editors (ASBPE, 2019). In this May issue, the cover story provides

CURRENT / COVID-19 UPDATE

In It Together

by Joe Nowlan

N MARCH, IN THE EARLY DAYS OF THE CORONAVIRUS pandemic, many companies and businesses were just beginning to arrange for their employees to work from home. Shortly after, once state and local governments issued stay-at-home/shelter-in-place edicts, that became the new reality.

At the NAED offices in St. Louis, the work-from-home decision was made fairly early on—and it soon became apparent that the arrangement was going to be the norm for quite some time. "We started having daily Zoom meetings with the management team," explained Ed Orlet, senior vice president of government affairs and strategic projects. "Also, our members look to us to bring people together, to provide networking and best practices. Tom Naber [NAED president and CEO] said, 'We need to move networking online and we need to do it now because now is when people need information.'"

Since then, NAED has been able to keep members informed on the fast-moving changes throughout the electrical industry, including legislation passed by Congress that could help business owners.

In addition, webinars and online networking sessions have enabled members to engage in frequent water-cooler talk—albeit via the Internet and Zoom meetings, among other means of communication.

For Kelly Jones, NAED director of learning and program content, it meant more work had to be completed faster than usual by her and her department. "We tried to shift very quickly and become more agile so that we could respond in real time to get out the critical information that people needed as quickly as possible," she explained. "Our member companies have had to adjust to having a lot of people working from home. We had to figure out how to get them the information that they need."

As more and more companies had their employees working remotely, NAED's webinars and online networking sessions became more essential. "We adjusted our process so that we could move quickly to offer webinars on immediate topics and get networking groups together so people can talk about immediate issues, such as the cleaning, sterilization, and safety policies they're putting in place," Jones said. "Other webinars have been about how to sell when working in a remote environment and what this crisis means for sales teams, SBA loan updates, new legislation, and COVID-19 economic considerations."

Jones explained that online courses and webinars covering new and important topics about COVID-19 and the best safety precautions and guidelines became essential. "The human side of this is very real," she said. "And it became real for everybody at the same time."

The pandemic also forced the Association to cancel its annual National Meeting, which had been scheduled to take place in May in Philadelphia. As a result, NAED decided to hold a virtual conference on its website.

"We shifted to offer a virtual national conference and will make that available to everyone free of charge," Jones said. "All of our members will have access to high-quality, immediate information that everyone needs right now."

The NAED National Virtual Meeting will be held May 7 from 10 a.m. to 2 p.m. CST, with the information remaining on NAED's website (naed.org) for follow-up viewing.

Essential Needs
Along with the human side was the immediate threat to livelihoods, jobs, and income. Very early on the definition of just what was an "essential" business came to the forefront because for the most part, only "essential" businesses could remain open during the quarantine.

"There was a lot of uncertainty. Members asked, 'Are we essential? How do we become essential? How is this done?'"

FIGURE 7.7 In the May 2020 issue of *tED Magazine*, a monthly publication by the National Association of Electrical Distributors (NAED), the cover story provides a multi-page in-depth look at how the organization is helping the electrical industry through the COVID-19 pandemic. The article looks and feels much like one in a traditional publisher's magazine, with a formal tone, professional two- and three-column design, and a journalistic writing style.

So we got to work helping our members operate and navigate the uncertainty," Orlet said.

Federal guidelines were issued but weren't binding. They were more like advisories rather than steadfast rules, let alone laws. What was "essential" in one state would not necessarily be the case in another state.

"No state, county, or municipality had any legal obligation to follow the federal guidelines, and many of them were putting very different guidelines in place," Orlet explained. "So we saw the need to help our members and policymakers understand the implications of policy decisions."

NAED works closely with the Family Business Coalition (FBC), based in Washington, D.C., to coordinate information at NAED members' local level. Alex Ayers, executive director of the FBC, weighed in on the "essential" discussion.

"Guidelines are state by state if not county by county or city by city," Ayers said. "One of the things we saw in Washington, while they were going through the peak in coronavirus cases, was that they shut down a lot of nonessential construction, or what they considered nonessential."

While the importance of social distancing wasn't being questioned, immediate construction stoppage put many distributors in a bind. "If contractors can't work at installing the electrical and the lighting, there's not much purpose in having that electrical distributor open," Ayers said. "You're going to be much more limited."

> We adjusted our process so that we could move quickly to offer webinars on immediate topics and get networking groups together so people can talk about immediate issues.
>
> —KELLY JONES, NAED

So while some states, such as Illinois, deemed most distributors as still "essential," it didn't always mean that distributor would be operating at full capacity. Getting the word out—and exchanging views and experiences via their webinars and networking sessions—was paramount at the NAED offices.

"People were trying to figure out what construction sites were open or were shut down," Orlet said. "Distributors would ask, 'Am I going to have a big order delivered to a jobsite? What if there's nobody there to get it and the material is lost and I'm responsible for it?' That was a big deal."

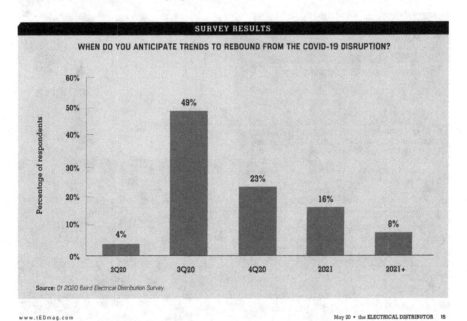

SURVEY RESULTS

WHEN DO YOU ANTICIPATE TRENDS TO REBOUND FROM THE COVID-19 DISRUPTION?

Percentage of respondents

- 2Q20: 4%
- 3Q20: 49%
- 4Q20: 23%
- 2021: 16%
- 2021+: 8%

Source: Q1 2020 Baird Electrical Distribution Survey

FIGURE 7.7 (Continued)

a multi-page, in-depth look at how the organization helped the electrical industry through the COVID-19 pandemic. The article looks and feels much like one you would read in a traditional magazine, with a formal tone, professional two- and three-column design, and a journalistic writing style that follows the inverted pyramid described in Chapter 6.

For the CM responsible for developing a full-length article such as this one, the process is quite similar to that used to create contributed or thought leadership articles, with the caveat that since this is the company's own publication, it is acceptable to include direct references to company products and services and opinions about trends or current events in the markets it serves.

With the different regulations and definitions of what was "essential," it became crucial to get clarifying information out to NAED members.

"It was easy for distributors to be confused. That was why speed and getting a lot of information out quickly was very important," Orlet explained. "There are so many details in these programs that you have to keep track of. That's been our biggest challenge. It doesn't help anybody to get information out quickly if it's inaccurate or lacks context."

As an example, Congress passed the *Families First Coronavirus Response Act* on March 18 and the *Coronavirus Aid, Relief and Economic Security Act (CARES Act)* on March 27. The legislation included some almost subtle modifications to the tax laws that were easy to miss.

Palmer Schoening, chair of the FBC, pointed out an important change to the *Quality Improvement Property Tax*—a change that corrected something that had been inadvertently overlooked in the *Tax Cuts and Jobs*

Act that had been passed in 2017.

"There are a couple of different ways that the *Tax Cuts and Jobs Act* changed expensing of electrical equipment. One is *Sec. 179* and that tends to be for purchases under a $2.5 million total threshold. But with bonus depreciation, the larger of the two expensing provisions, there was a technical correction that needed to be done because Congress literally wrote four words wrong in the *Tax Cuts and Jobs Act*," Schoening noted.

"They made it harder to expense

Strange Days
Controlling what we can helps to keep it all from spinning out of control.

FIGURE 7.7 (Continued)

In developing articles for brand publications, the CM will need to understand the purpose of the article, the target reader, the word count, and/or the format guidelines. With this information defined, the CM then documents the core elements discussed in Chapter 6 (i.e., topic, objective, audience, working title(s), timeline, abstract and, outline) and prepares to interview the subject matter expert(s) using questions based on the five Ws of journalism in some improvements to buildings, including electrical equipment, he continued. "So some of the electrical equipment that NAED members distribute still had a 39-year depreciation schedule before passage of the *CARES Act*. The bill narrowly fixed that problem, allowing for immediate expensing of that equipment if it is an improvement to an existing nonresidential commercial building. Fixing the qualified improvement property glitch was one of NAED's main legislative priorities that we can now check off the list."

As the pandemic has brought out the best in some, the opposite has also occurred, at least occasionally. Ayers cautions businesses against responding too quickly to emails or texts guaranteeing quick sources of funding.

"Many businesses are hurrying to get funding whether it's through the Small Business Association (SBA) or their bank. But there are a lot of scams out there," Ayers said. "It could be via email with a link saying, 'Apply here' and then asking for your personal information. All of that is going to continue for the next several months. It's very important for NAED members to be on the lookout. It's just very important to be extra vigilant because these predators are out there."

As of this writing, there seemed to be no end in sight for the quarantine or any time when even some areas of the country might get back to normal. Still, while hectic at times, Jones explained that the challenges seem to be something people are responding well to. "Seeing the resilience of the industry and the leadership that is coming out of this is heartening," she noted. "People will continue to learn from that when they have time to stop and reflect. There will be real opportunities here for learning how to do lots of things differently and better." ∎

Nowlan is a Boston-based freelance writer/editor and author. He can be reached at jcnowlan@msn.com.

CONTRACTOR Q+A

To better help electrical distributors respond to the needs of electrical contractors, "Contractor Q&A" features remarks from real contractors from around the country. Responding are David Jones, owner of David Jones Electric in Chattanooga, Tenn., and Electrotek in Sylva, N.C., and Deb McGowan, owner of Veritas Electric in Seattle. This month we asked:

WHAT PROBLEMS ARE YOU EXPERIENCING IN YOUR BUSINESS DUE TO THE COVID-19 OUTBREAK AND WHAT STEPS ARE YOU TAKING TO CURB THE EFFECTS?

Jones: North Carolina issued a stay-at-home order stating that if your residence is outside the state, you cannot enter unless you have been quarantined for two weeks, so I have shut down operations there right now. Chattanooga does not have a high infection rate and I am observing all the precautions—maintaining space, washing hands, etc.—so I can carry on business in a straightforward manner: We talk, agree on a price, and then move on. I might see five new customers a day. Business is not quite as usual, but the virus has not destroyed it yet.

My distributors are trying to be helpful. I spoke with several that have been very understanding; for example, if I'm going to make a late payment, they just want me to let them know. For orders...they'll prepare [it] and bring it out.

McGowan: Once the number of confirmed COVID-19 cases started to grow in this area, the phone calls and requests for work and estimates slowed significantly. There were a few emergency service calls, which I declined due to a full schedule, but as more cases were reported, I chose to cancel all appointments. I felt I needed to have a protocol in place to keep my employees and customers safe. In Seattle, electrical contractors have been deemed an essential service for emergency service calls and construction dealing with hospitals and low-income housing only. For my company, it will be on a case-by-case basis whether I go out on a call. I'm happy to do virtual estimates and was able to help a client troubleshoot an issue he was having through email.

My distributor is taking steps to keep everybody safe. If I need anything, the order will be put inside a locker outside. ∎

Send your questions to "tED" Editor Misty Byers at mbyers@naed.org.

FIGURE 7.7 (Continued)

order to gather all the information needed to develop an outline and full draft of the article. Following multiple drafts and reviews, when the article and all other content for the magazine is approved, design of the issue begins in earnest. Final publication on the company's website follows some weeks later, and the article is live on the company website for years to come, not only providing a historical perspective and reference but also strengthening search engine optimization as other sites find the articles valuable and link to them from their websites.

What a CM should know: With the freedom of format and tone that comes with the modern, online design of brand publications, the fundamentals of good writing practices and storytelling are more important than ever. No matter the format, you should always ask and document "Who is the primary reader of this content?"; "What is the most important message readers need to understand from this content?"; and "Why should readers care about this topic?"

CONCLUSION

Until the beginning of the 21st century, the two primary channels marketers used to grow awareness and generate demand for their products were paid and earned media. With the advent of the internet, the growth of search engines and company websites, and the introduction and mass adoption of social media sites like YouTube and LinkedIn, two new media channels – owned and shared media – and content marketing as a discipline were born. In the 20 years since the turn of the century, B2B marketing budgets have been reallocated from paid media to these new channels, and traditional publishers have shuttered as more and more companies invest in building their own audiences through owned media channels and developing direct relationships with prospective and current customers with the goal of strengthening brand awareness and customer loyalty. The digital channels of owned media – the website, blog, and branded publications – are at the core of good content marketing, and a robust and organized owned media plan will make it easier for a CM to create diverse content that meets consumer needs. In the next chapter, we'll continue our focus on owned media by explaining content marketing for audio and video formats, including podcasts.

CITATIONS

ASBPE Staff. "Professional Builder, *tED Magazine*, American Banker, and architect win top 2019 ASBPE Azbee Award Honors." May 10, 2019. Retrieved from: https://asbpe.org/news/2019/05/10/professional-builder-ted-magazine-american-banker-and-architect-win-top-2019-asbpe-honors-kevin-davis-of-aba-journal-receives-its-stephen-barr-award/

Emde, K., Klimm, C., & Schluetz, D. "Does storytelling help adolescents to process the news?" *Journalism Studies*. 2016.

Geier, R. *Smart Marketing for Engineers: An Inbound Marketing Guide to Reaching Technical Audiences*. Rockbench. January 2016.

Kafka, P., & Molla, R. "2017 was the year digital ad spending finally beat TV." *Vox*. December 4, 2017. Retrieved from: www.vox.com/2017/12/4/16733460/2017-digital-ad-spend-advertising-beat-tv

Leek, S., & Christodoulides, G. "A framework of brand value in B2B markets: The contributing role of functional and emotional components." *Industrial Marketing Management*. 2012.

Majodouba, B. "Designing a B2B digital communication marketing strategy in a consultancy context." *University Do Porto*. July 1, 2016. Retrieved from: https://repositorio-aberto.up.pt/bitstream/10216/112305/2/269242.pdf

Pulizzi, J. *Corona Marketing: What Marketing Professionals Need to Do Now to Survive the Crisis*. May 2020.

Zaichkowsky, J.L. "Strategies for distinctive brands." *Journal of Brand Management*. 2010.

CHAPTER 8

Owned Media (Part 2) – Podcasts, Videos, and Webinars and Their Role in Content Marketing

---

LEARNING OBJECTIVES

1. How to apply the attention, interest, desire, action (AIDA) model to multimedia content development
2. Getting started on developing multimedia content and unique elements to consider
3. How to choose a format for a good podcast
4. The process and best practices to develop podcast content
5. The process and best practices to develop video content
6. The process and best practices to develop webinar content
7. The best practices leading experts use to develop successful multimedia content marketing and storytelling

---

INTRODUCTION

On August 1, 1981, a new television channel began broadcasting on cable. Music Television (MTV) aimed to change the way people thought about music, adding visual storytelling and live performances as a way to connect people with their favorite bands in a way radio couldn't. Fittingly, the first video was from a band called The Buggles. The title . . .

"Video Killed the Radio Star."

A CM doesn't need to play a guitar or have a 1980s haircut to see the power that video can have in storytelling. This journey has gone on for centuries:

- In 1436, Johannes Gutenberg invented the printing press. The first books were just words.
- In 1874, Julia Margaret Cameron created the first photo book.

DOI: 10.4324/9781003369103-10

- In 1895, Gugliemo Marconi created the first radio.
- In 1927, Philo Taylor Farnsworth invented the television.
- In 1956, Charles Ginsburg invented the VCR to make all video on demand.

THE HISTORY OF COMMUNICATION FROM TEXT TO ON-DEMAND CONTENT FIRST TOOK MORE THAN 500 YEARS.
WITH THE INTERNET, THE SAME TIMELINE TOOK JUST 14 YEARS.

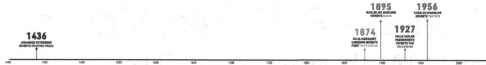

FIGURE 8.1 The development of communication from text to on-demand video took more than 500 years. With the internet, from the first website to the creation of YouTube, the timeline for all content to become on-demand took just 14 years.

In the internet age, this same journey from words to on-demand video followed a similar path, but it happened much faster. From the first website in 1991 to YouTube in 2005, all content became on demand in a span of less than 15 years.

Social media first started in 1997 with Six Degrees. Two years later, you could share videos with Friendster.

The speed of the adoption of technology and the expansion of new media channels has greatly accelerated over time. Just look at ChatGPT (discussed in more detail in Chapter 12). It is the fastest-growing application in history, with more than 100 million users just two months after its launch.

Today, multimedia content is a critical component of a CM's content plan. If it's not, a competitor's video will very likely kill the content star in your brand.

This chapter will look at three main formats a CM can use to create multimedia content:

- Podcast
- Video
- Webinar

Before describing each of these in more detail, it's important to first translate the content marketing journey for modern audiences. The good news is there's a tool to do that, and it's even older than MTV.

APPLYING THE AIDA MODEL TO MULTIMEDIA

St. Elmo Lewis developed the AIDA model in 1898 to explain personal selling and how a customer goes from having no clue your brand exists to exalting its value to anyone who will listen (Sellers, 2022). As a refresher to what we covered in Chapter 4, the four stages of the model are:

- Attention
- Interest
- Desire
- Action

THE AIDA MODEL

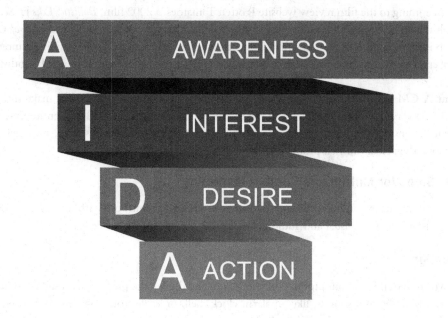

FIGURE 8.2 The AIDA model is common in all forms of marketing and strategic communication. When it comes to video and audio, content marketers will find a more condensed timeline to work through the AIDA process.

For the CM thinking about multimedia content, the four stages – attention, interest, desire, and action – are a checklist for effective multimedia. We are a mobile society of skimmers whose attention spans are getting shorter and shorter, from 150 seconds in 2004 to just 47 on average today (Mark, 2023). How many of us, for instance, have tried to watch a video online only to be annoyed by the ad that plays for a few seconds beforehand? We wait impatiently – for less than five seconds – ready to click to "Skip Ads" at the first possible opportunity.

A CM can bemoan this short viewer attention span or, worse, ignore it. Or they can acknowledge the fact that their video content has to grab their viewer's attention within five seconds and accept the challenge. That means thinking about the basics of AIDA in the span of five seconds. Difficult? Yes. Possible? Yes, with the proper planning.

The AIDA model reflects the three-act play structure described in Chapter 5.

- Characters grab attention.
- Conflict creates interest and desire for a conclusion.
- Action allows for the protagonist to win.

How long should multimedia content be? It's impossible to answer. The average time someone watches a video is 2.7 minutes (Zauderer, 2023). Some people watch for three seconds and lose interest. Some people binge watch shows for three hours and barely blink. In B2B content marketing, among the content assets used, 66% of B2B marketers indicated they use videos, the second-highest content type among 13 listed (Beets et al., 2022).

According to the film review website Rotten Tomatoes, a 2002 film, *Ballistic: Ecks vs. Sever*, which is one hour and 31 minutes, is the worst-ranked movie of all time. *The Wizard of Oz*, which is 21 minutes longer, ranks first. If length was the only criterion for watching a movie, the average person today would have heard more of Ecks and Sever than Toto and Dorothy.

What A CM should know: Whatever type of multimedia content you create, make sure to check off every step of the AIDA list in the first five seconds and again with the entire finished product. Consider that every piece of multimedia content is five seconds long, regardless of how long the actual finished product is.

AIDA Steps for Multimedia Content Marketing

The content journey outlined throughout this book is easy to repurpose with the AIDA model. This will only look at visual and audio elements that accentuate the process.

Attention

A CM needs to think about product differentiation and display the product with sights, sounds, and words. Sights and sounds, like an alarm clock, bell, or sizzle from a grill, create an emotional reaction. Appropriate words and adjectives help connect those sights and sounds to concepts. Writer Alex Snovio aggregated a list of power words, shown in Figure 8.3, that elicit positive reaction. They were proven to show higher open rates and clickthroughs in email marketing and can work in other forms of communication (Snovio, 2019).

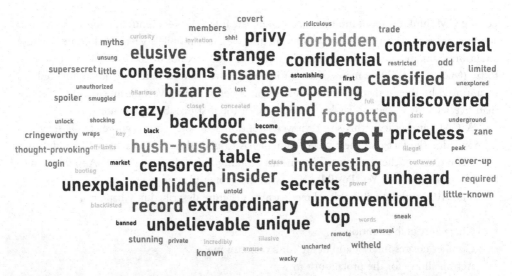

FIGURE 8.3 Power words are crucial in multimedia content because the viewer or listener is often multitasking. Finding ethical ways to incorporate these words can force a busy person to slow down and pay attention to a content marketing message.

Interest and Desire

It makes sense to merge these two steps because a good CM will establish the conflict at the heart of any good story. The conflict creates interest and a desire. If those are compelling, the viewer or listener will want to see how the conflict resolves.

From a copy standpoint, using the word *you* helps create a connection to make people believe the scenario they are watching or hearing is something they could also experience. It's one way to create connections between products and people.

Think of a foosball table. Why would someone want to buy a foosball table? A good CM will have research, for instance, that explains how parents want to spend time with their kids away from screens. Seeing a video with a family spending quality time together creates interest from a parent viewer who wants to do activities with their kids that don't involve being on a phone. The visuals and sounds that show and tell the product in action create interest and directly lead to desire.

- The sound of spinning the foosball player for a hard shot
- The foosball going into the goal
- The excited child defeating a parent
- The sound of laughter

Is a CM selling a foosball table? Technically, yes, but a creative CM understands they are also selling what the product or service offering affords the buyer in an accessible way. By connecting the notion of people wanting to spend time with their family and showing through video and sound how a foosball table makes it happen, you create desire.

Action

Make it easy for people to buy or learn more. If someone can buy the foosball table online, have sounds of the person typing on a keyboard as they visit the website. Show the table being ordered with easy installation. With video, several brands will put a QR code on the corner of the screen for the entire ad. This way, if someone is interested in buying, they can do so immediately. In situations in which a video may only appear for five seconds, this is a great way to make the most of a small touchpoint with a potential buyer.

What a CM should know: Your content research journey and buyer persona work align with AIDA. The idea is to have sound and video that validates each step of the customer journey.

DEVELOPING MULTIMEDIA CONTENT: GETTING STARTED

Chapter 5 explains different ways to develop compelling content ideas persuasively. For a CM, this means writing words, but it also means developing appropriate images. With video and audio, there are added elements that make the process a bit more cumbersome, but often, you don't have to start from scratch. As you get started, use existing resources within organizations to help you speed up the process of creating compelling multimedia content.

Repurpose Existing Assets

Think about photos. Many brands host events, pay a photographer to take 200 photos, use four of those photos for social media, and let the other 196 collect dust in the cloud. Which are the highest-performing pages on your website that you could repurpose into multimedia formats? A brief content audit of internal communication will likely point you to either unused digital assets or those that only exist in one format and can be repurposed in video or audio.

Access Advocates and Experts

Think of people who want your brand or product to succeed. Those can be people in different departments, current successful customers who are advocates of your company or product, or business partners who helped bring the concept to life. Using those people as potential interview subjects or guests allows for easier buy-in to get started and uses motivated partners to bring energy and enthusiasm to a CM plan.

Other resources for CMs are the key leaders and respected subject matter experts (SMEs) inside their company. For instance, a CM working for a hospital system may interview one of the medical team's renowned surgeons; another working in the legal field may meet with a leading attorney at the firm; yet another CM may speak to a partner in their accounting practice. All these experts have amazing stories to tell but limited time to tell them because of their pressing work responsibilities.

In Chapter 11, we share a story of a PR leader, Stu Opperman, whose team worked with healthcare clients during the COVID-19 pandemic. Here's how he leveraged his client's SMEs:

> We just tried to stay with the facts and position our health experts who have been in the field for 30, 40, 50 years. We leaned on them, put them out there to the world, and had them share information and not buy into the politics, of which we wanted no part. We just presented facts.

With even a short 15- or 30-minute interview, the CM can create podcast, video, and photo content that harnesses their expertise, reputation, and credibility. Here are just two ways:

- A CM can interview a key leader as part of research for a marketing campaign. Using the audio or video from the interview, they can repurpose the useful information and integrate it into blog posts or, if it's recorded, use it as a standalone podcast.
- A CM can arrange time once a month, a quarter, or a year to interview a key leader and repurpose smaller clips into blog posts or other social media.

This way, whenever a prospective buyer is interested in hearing from an expert, they are only a click away because a CM thought ahead and made the most of their moments with that SME.

Build a Business Case

Just as effective written content marketing creates positive business outcomes, effective multimedia content resonates with audiences who prefer to consume information in audio and video formats. For example, consider these statistics from recent studies by Edison Research (Edison Research, 2023) and the Interactive Advertising Bureau (IAB, 2022) on the rising popularity of online audio, including podcasts, in the US:

- 75% of Americans age 12+ have listened to online audio in the last month, and 42% have listened specifically to a podcast in the last month.
- US podcast advertising revenue is expected to grow 200% to $4 billion by 2024 from $2 billion in 2022.
- Among US adults age 18+ who have ridden in a car in the last month, 37% were listening to online audio.
- Weekly podcast listeners listened to an average of nine podcast episodes in the last week.

Video has seen a similar explosion in popularity over the last decade.

- In 2022, 3.37 billion internet users watched online video content (No Author, 2021, *Statista*).
- A 2021 report found video to be popular content among B2B companies, with a mix of product, training, how-to, and social advertising videos among the most popular types of content (No Author, 2023, *Statista*).
- More than 90% of businesses will use video as a marketing tactic (Wyzowl Research, 2023).

What a CM should know: Podcasts and videos have seen tremendous growth over the last ten years and are a preferred content type across markets.

Now let's take a closer look at how CMs develop content for each of these three formats, starting with an exploding multimedia content type – podcasts.

DEVELOPING PODCAST CONTENT

When thinking back to the history of communication, words were first. Audio arrived second. Video came third. Most content marketers will begin their journey with the written word. Using the past history of communication, let's proceed with thoughts on effective audio and then add video when thinking about multimedia content creation.

This is certainly the experience Dan had at WOUB Public Media in Athens, Ohio, more than two decades ago. The E.W. Scripps School of Journalism at Ohio University is among the top-ranked journalism schools in the world, and WOUB was the training ground many used to hone their skills. At WOUB, the process for moving up the ladder was clear:

- Report for radio first
- Broadcast live on AM
- Broadcast live on FM
- Report for television
- Anchor television

There was no skipping around or cutting corners. As one of Dan's first news managers would say, "If you can't tell the story, the visuals won't matter." At the time, getting camera time was *the* goal, and audio was a stepping stone or checkpoint. Podcasting has changed everything.

Podcast Formatting

There are many steps required in creating podcast content, from properly opening and closing the episode to integrating snippets of content, such as rolls and branded segments, throughout (Figure 8.5). To comprehensively explain the steps, best practices, tools, and technologies required to professionally produce, host, and edit a podcast would require an entire book.

The following is an introduction to the basic concepts CMs should be comfortable applying to podcast development.

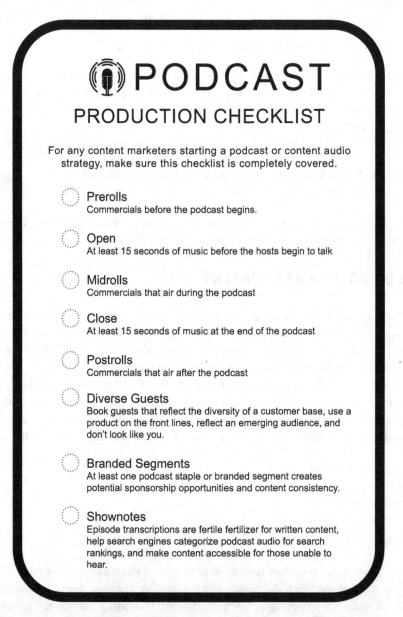

PODCAST
PRODUCTION CHECKLIST

For any content marketers starting a podcast or content audio strategy, make sure this checklist is completely covered.

- **Prerolls**
  Commercials before the podcast begins.

- **Open**
  At least 15 seconds of music before the hosts begin to talk

- **Midrolls**
  Commercials that air during the podcast

- **Close**
  At least 15 seconds of music at the end of the podcast

- **Postrolls**
  Commercials that air after the podcast

- **Diverse Guests**
  Book guests that reflect the diversity of a customer base, use a product on the front lines, reflect an emerging audience, and don't look like you.

- **Branded Segments**
  At least one podcast staple or branded segment creates potential sponsorship opportunities and content consistency.

- **Shownotes**
  Episode transcriptions are fertile fertilizer for written content, help search engines categorize podcast audio for search rankings, and make content accessible for those unable to hear.

FIGURE 8.4 There are many steps required in creating podcast content, from properly opening to closing the episode and integrating snippets of content, such as rolls and branded segments, throughout. For content marketing, the following is an introduction to the basic concepts CMs should be comfortable applying to podcast development.

Chapters

When you watch a television show or listen to an entire radio program, there are segments or chapters that are usually divided by commercials. That kind of flow also works for content marketers creating a podcast. Let's say your brand has developed five stages in a buyer's journey. A podcast could have five different chapters that address each stage of the buyer's journey. The concept mirrors the idea of having an outline of main points that many learned in early education.

Rolls

Most podcasts have a preroll, midroll, and postroll (Figure 8.5):

• The preroll is commercials that air before the podcast begins.
• The midroll is commercials that air during the podcast.
• The postroll is commercials that air after the podcast.

Even if there are no commercials to be sold, a CM should add rolls for the beginning, middle, and end. The rolls create vocal variety, which is key to audio pacing and allows for longer-form content to be more easily digestible. When podcast editors create a deliberate pace, they increase the likelihood listeners will stay tuned.

Having rolls also allows a CM to showcase other opportunities within a business, such as promoting upcoming events or the next episode. They could also include announcements related to charitable causes the brand partners with or ESG achievements (i.e., environmental, social and governance).

Manage Ad Locations
Mark preroll, midroll and postroll ad markers to ensure targeted ads and promos insert into your episode.

YOUR EPISODE CONTAINS THE FOLLOWING AD MARKERS
♀ **Hint:**
   Most episodes need at least 1 preroll, 1 midroll and 1 postroll marked. Check with your internal adops team for specific information.

| 2 PRE | 2 MID | 1 POST |

Click the button below to mark additional ad locations in your episode

MARK AD LOCATIONS

FIGURE 8.5 An example of managing advertisement locations in a podcast at preroll, midroll, and postroll. In addition to inserting commercials, there's usually 10 to 15 seconds of music, which a podcaster can find online for a small fee (often under $100).

Open and Close

There needs to be at least 15 seconds of music before the hosts begin to talk. If a listener fast forwards past the preroll, the music lets the listener know where the show begins and ends. This also creates vocal variety and pacing.

Figure 8.6 shows an example of how a show open or close would look in the editing process. There's usually 10 to 15 seconds of music, which a podcaster can find online for a small fee (often under $100). The music fades down as the host starts the show. The opposite happens at the end of the show.

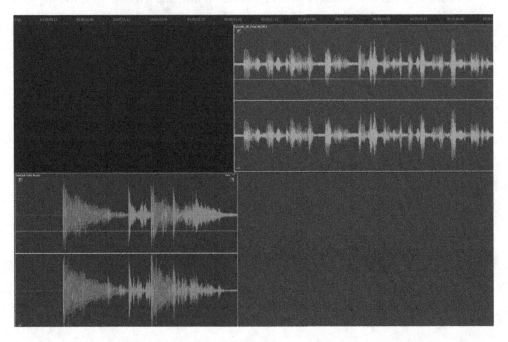

FIGURE 8.6 The use of 10 to 15 seconds of music at the open and close of a podcast episode lets the listener know where the show begins and ends. In the open, the music fades down as the host starts the show, and the opposite happens at the end of the show. The image shows a visual example of an open when editing a podcast.

Branded Segments

Content consumers crave consistency. Every episode doesn't have to follow the exact same formula, but the idea of having something people can anticipate gives them a reason to stay tuned. They know what to expect.

Bill Simmons is one of the most downloaded podcasters in history. In a weekly NFL segment that Simmons does with friend and comedian "Cousin" Sal Iacono, the two close every podcast with a segment called "Parent Corner," in which the focus shifts from football to family.

The idea of at least one podcast staple or branded segment creates potential sponsorship opportunities for the brand and content consistency for the listener. Dan ends every podcast with the same five questions he asks every guest:

1. What book do you wish everyone would read?
2. What is your go-to cocktail/mocktail?

3. What is your favorite restaurant in the town where you live?

4. Who is the funniest person you know?

5. What do you wish you would have known when you graduated that you know now?

Show Notes

This is digital currency for a CM. Using tools like Otter.ai and Descript, a CM can transcribe the entire recorded podcast. This serves as fertilizer for written content, and it also helps search engines categorize podcast audio for search rankings. For people unable to hear, it also makes content accessible.

Abbreviated show notes also allow listeners to find specific segments of interest and immediately go to that part of the podcast. This takes a single piece of content and makes it more specific for people in their respective buyer journeys.

Figure 8.7 shows a basic example of show notes. This allows the podcast host to introduce the guest and offer a general sense of the conversation that takes place.

The times at the end of the show notes correspond to different segments or chapters within the podcast. This way, if a listener wants to go directly to the chapter on working with young reporters, they can immediately advance to four minutes and 30 seconds into the episode to listen to that section.

Jenna Cooper, APR, is a seasoned strategic communications professional, executive coach, and frequent speaker on crisis communications, strategic planning, and public speaking. Her nose for news transplanted her in television broadcast markets across the country including Boise, Austin, Atlanta, and Seattle.

In this episode, Jenna discusses how journalism skills can empower high-profile leaders to better convey their messages in good times and bad. She also offers insights on the best way to work with reporters under deadline and how to build relationships that prevent problems from morphing into a crisis. We close out with a conversation about books, infused cocktails, and getting kids to do the dishes.

1:00 Considering proactive crisis communication

4:30 Working with young reporters

8:00 How to build relationships with reporters

12:00 Getting leaders to take time to develop messaging

18:00 Five Questions

https://www.linkedin.com/in/jennacooperapr/

https://c3-collective.com/

One Small Step Can Change Your Life: The Kaizen Way

https://passpr.com/

FIGURE 8.7 Show notes, like this example from *The Strategic Communicator* with Dan Farkas, allow the podcast host to introduce the guest and offer a general sense of the conversation that takes place. The times at the end of the show notes correspond to different segments or chapters within the podcast. For instance, if a listener wants to go directly to the chapter on working with young reporters, they can advance to four minutes and 30 seconds into the episode to listen to that section.

Diverse Guests

It's important to have key thought leaders as guests. It's also important to have guests who reflect the diversity of your customer base.

- Find product users on the front lines.
- Find people who reflect an emerging audience.
- Find people who reflect the diversity of your brand's customer base and world.

Using diversity, equity, and inclusion (DEI) as part of the guest-booking process will amplify the podcast's voice and reach. It also can reduce barriers to entry and increase product humanization.

Why? There is grace in effort.

Nobody expects a healthcare worker on the front line or a factory worker on the third shift to be an audio engineer. When a CM lets those people tell their stories with core messaging (discussed in Chapter 5) as a guide, listeners get more memorable and diverse content that verifies the corporate story. Podcast guests will share their stories with your audience, and the audio reaches new listeners who otherwise may not know your brand exists. If the audio is a bit hollow, listeners will find grace in the effort.

What a CM should know: A CM already knows most content is too long, didn't read (TLDR). Podcasts are likely too long, didn't listen (TLDL). When a CM uses the AIDA concept to summarize key podcast themes off the top with their guests and then expands on those during the show, it creates long-form and short-form information that can help potential buyers.

Note to reader: Reference the Q&A with Douglas Burdett, host of the highly acclaimed Marketing Book Podcast, *at the end of the chapter to learn the processes and best practices he uses to produce his show.*

DEVELOPING VIDEO CONTENT

Once a content marketer feels comfortable with words and sound, video becomes an added layer to accentuate the story. Nuances in video are constantly evolving, but there are several constants that ensure a viewer stays tuned to your video content.

Ease Eye Pressure

Corey Adkins is the content/communications director at the Great Lakes Shipwreck Historical Society. Before he took this role, Adkins worked for 23 years at a CBS affiliate in Northern Michigan. He has won dozens of awards, including 13 Emmys. When thinking of shot composition, Adkins thinks of what the human eye does, which boils down to four things:

- Wide (Here's a room full of people.)
- Medium (Here's the right side of the room.)
- Tight (Here is one person taking notes.)
- Super Tight (Here's the person's pen.)

The eye then bounces from one shot (medium) to anything other than another medium shot. Any editing that goes against what the human eye does creates a fight-or-flight moment. Keeping a viewer engaged in your short brand video is totally different from keeping them engaged in a movie on the big screen. When watching cinematic pans and zooms in theaters, viewers are invested. They spent money on the ticket and three times that much on the popcorn. The chairs are super comfortable. They aren't moving. When someone sees those kinds of sweeping movements on a phone or tablet, it's a different story.

When filming, move the camera with your feet, not a tripod. When filming an object that shouldn't be moving, use a tripod. Shaky video creates fight-or-flight moments. If there is no tripod, the closer to the action someone gets, the less shaky the video will be.

Create Pace

Moving from broadcasting to communications has been an eye-opening experience for Adkins. In one year, his press releases have garnered international attention, including CBS, NBC, ABC, FOX, and *The New York Times*. Compelling video has been a key driver in the historical society's earned media efforts, according to executive director Bruce Lynn:

> *Having video is extremely important for the success of these releases. We provided video for dozens (if not hundreds) of TV and internet earned media outlets. It allows the journalist to put their own little twist on the story while we still control it.*

Adkins is passionate about pace. There are times when it's important to edit clips every two-to-three seconds to create immediacy. There are also times when it's key to step back and let the story tell itself, allowing shots to linger for 10 to 15 seconds.

"You must be patient. Successful video production takes time," Adkins said. "When done right, it gets into your customer's psyche and lives 'rent free' in their minds. I have found bringing personality to press releases has made them extremely successful; people are attracted to stories."

Lisa Arledge spent more than a decade working as a news reporter and anchor before opening MediaSource, a communications agency that relies on video to tell client stories. Arledge said meeting with video crews prior to filming is essential in getting the right pace and purpose for good video storytelling (Figure 8.8).

Arledge said,

> "The best thing a marketing or communications pro can do when working with a video production team is communicate the why; why are you choosing to produce a video and what do you want to happen once the video is produced. While it is tempting to go full speed ahead into the shoot, you're missing an important step that can make or break your video project."

That step is to communicate the *why*.

VIDEO STORYTELLING PROCESS

The MediaSource 4 step process sets up communicators for success when producing video content

FIGURE 8.8 This video storytelling framework by MediaSource uses a four-step process to guide CMs in the creation of video content, from strategy and creation to marketing through outreach and measurement at the end.

Foreshadow Audio to See and Say

Think of how often you are at a restaurant or event where there are multiple video screens with no audio. A 2019 study from Verizon found 69% of people often watch video with no sound (McCue, 2019). Then think of how often a viewer might be listening to a video but distracted with cooking, cleaning, and other daily chores.

It's highly likely a content consumer will only see or hear your video. That means a CM needs to think about how to seamlessly use both audio and video to meet the needs of someone only listening or someone only watching. Meshing audio and video creates a continuity that increases the likelihood a message gets consumed and understood.

When editing a video, Adkins will use the natural sound of an object before introducing a visual of it. For example, Adkins will use the sound of waves splashing before showing video of those waves crashing into a pier.

"People can forgive bad video but *never* bad audio," Adkins said.

Adkins and Arledge agree that the use of audio and video together helps slow down an audience that often suffers from content overload.

"Video can capture your audience's attention and make them stop scrolling in ways that words cannot. You can communicate your message in fewer words and less time because the visuals work with your words to tell the story," Arledge said.

Have a Plan

Adkins and Arledge both believe it's important to have a plan or checklist of what a video shoot should look like before sending crews into the field or a studio. A common approach to building this plan is to have a storyboard.

Figure 8.9 shows a storyboard template. A storyboard helps CMs and videographers have a full picture of each scene, including the scripted copy and image description. The scene/image

STORYBOARD TEMPLATE

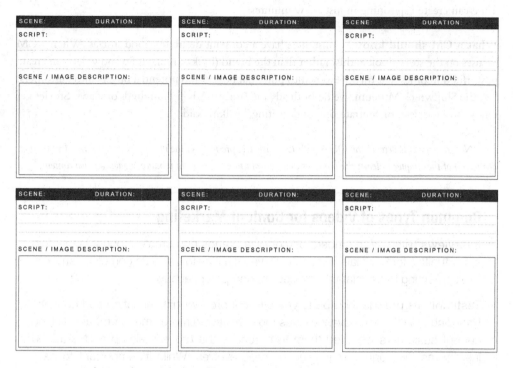

FIGURE 8.9 A storyboard helps CMs and videographers have a full picture of each scene, including the scripted copy and image description. The scene/image description can be written to explain the visual goals and include illustration or a photo from a pre-production shoot. A storyboard also includes a section to define the time duration of each shot.

description can be written to explain the visual goals and include an illustration or a photo from a pre-production shoot. A storyboard also includes a section to define the time duration of each shot.

What a CM should know: While having a plan ensures core video concepts get recorded, it's also important to realize that some of the best video moments are extemporaneous or in the moment. Content marketers should have a plan but be open to ideas that might appear in the moment on a video shoot.

Add Captions

Recent studies found that 80% of people who use captions do not have a hearing impairment (Klimes, 2021). Videos with captions also get better metrics in terms of views, completions, clickthroughs, and conversions. Captions also help brands meet website disability standards, and the text can help with search engine optimization.

What a CM should know: Automated tools like otter.ai, Descript, Amara, and even You-Tube can create captioning in just a few minutes.

What a CM should know: Consumers have a constant desire for good stories. When a CM focuses on the story (look at this) rather than the brand (look at me), audio and video can create powerful outcomes that turn viewers into potential buyers and potential buyers into customers. "At the Shipwreck Museum, we do both ads and stories. Ads get hundreds of views. Stories get tens of thousands. Concentrate on good writing," Adkins said.

Note to reader: Reference the Q&A with Lisa Arledge, president of the video production firm MediaSource, at the end of the chapter to learn the processes and best practices she uses to produce engaging video content.

Common Types of Videos for Content Marketing

Interviews with staff members personalize brands and create thought leadership opportunities for key staff. They also serve as a way to translate complex concepts into something more relatable for viewers and potential buyers.

Testimonials provide third-party validation of product differentiation and benefits. Providing questions in advance gives the interviewee more time to prepare. Asking current customers what led them to purchase the product also provides added insights as the content marketing process evolves. While it's important to have questions set in stone, follow-up questions based on interviewee answers can create powerful moments.

Product overviews and demonstrations expand on something most content marketers have done since childhood: show and tell. Figure 8.11 serves as both a testimonial and a demonstration, as Volk showed students how using free graphic design tools like Canva can create quality graphics without previous design experience.

Demonstrations are a visual way to showcase a product's key features and benefits. Some demonstrations may use animation to visualize items that are difficult or impossible to physically see in a demonstration. Whiteboard videos can help a subject matter expert outline the creative process in an animated and personal way.

Product overviews and demonstrations are also easy for a content marketer to repurpose. For example, one comprehensive video could highlight four product features, from which a CM could create four separate shorter videos that each highlight a different feature.

How-to videos help people solve problems with a step-by-step approach. Most homeowners will access how-to videos to solve common problems around the house. For a content marketer, specific how-to videos are powerful search engine optimization tools as potential buyers search for highly technical and specific language. For instance, hardware and software vendors can create videos that use their brand's service offerings to improve a consumer's business process or prevent a malfunction.

Additionally, creating videos to show customers how to troubleshoot common issues saves your support team time and allows them to focus on the more challenging issues not easily solved in a short how-to video.

DEVELOPING WEBINAR CONTENT

Merriam-Webster defines *webinar* as "a live online educational presentation during which participating viewers can submit questions and comments." This only captures half, if not less, of the value of a webinar. In reality, a webinar can be live, but its long-term value is as a recorded video that drives lead generation and SEO for the CM while providing valuable on-demand content for your audience.

When a prospective buyer registers for a webinar, live or on demand, they are inherently expressing genuine interest and consideration, given the time commitment required to watch (anywhere from 20 to 60 minutes). That's why a CM should have a plan to engage webinar attendees before, during, and after the event.

Producing and marketing an effective webinar on top of the complexity involved in its creation can take up a large portion of a CM's time or even be a full-time role on a larger marketing team. The following is a synopsis of the main components of developing webinar content and the impact on a CM program.

Title Slide

Most webinars begin with a title slide that includes the brand logo and presentation title. Many webinars will also include a photo of the presenter in the title slide itself or the slide immediately thereafter.

Tom Martin, owner of Converse Digital, is an author and internationally recognized social selling speaker who uses webinars as part of his business marketing, such as one he hosted titled "Turning Conversations into Clients." Figure 8.10 shows Martin's title slide, which includes the presentation title and his professional photo and alerts attendees there will be a chance for questions during the webinar.

The Rundown

In the world of broadcast news and live television, a rundown is the sequence of events that will occur in a given broadcast. The rundown is a way to prioritize what the speaker will say and how much time they will have to present their information (Figure 8.11). The rundown offers a degree of structure for presenters in live or recorded situations.

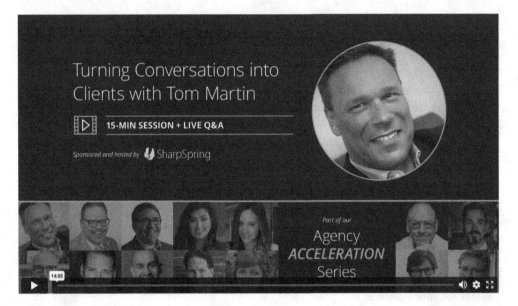

FIGURE 8.10 Webinars begin with a title slide that includes the brand logo and presentation title. As shown in this example from a webinar hosted by author and internationally recognized social selling speaker Tom Martin, the title slide can also include the speaker's professional photo.

ITEM	START	DURATION
Recording begins—clock starts	00:00	0
Welcome and recap of recent events	00:00	01:30
Introduction of guest speakers	01:30	0:45
Discuss special offers for webinar attendees	2:15	0:45
Give attendees schedule of the rest of the event	3:00	0:30
Guest speaker #1 begins their portion of the event	3:30	15:00

FIGURE 8.11 The rundown is a way to prioritize what the speaker will say and how much time they will have to present their information. The rundown offers a degree of structure for presenters in live or recorded situations.

Goals

This is a brief slide to outline what attendees will learn from the webinar, much like an agenda. This establishes realistic expectations for those choosing to consume the content and also frames the flow of the presentation and who will speak on which specific topic. If those goals don't align with customer needs, it's an easy way to filter out an unqualified connection or lead.

Speaker Introduction

The moderator introduces the speaker or speakers with a 30-to-45-second biography that highlights their key areas of expertise. During this brief introduction, a slide is shown that includes the speaker title, company, and a link to learn more about and connect with them, such as a link to their profile on LinkedIn or company website.

Key Takeaways

In a 30- or 60-minute webinar, it's impossible for a viewer to remember everything. An effective webinar will list three to five key audience takeaways and what they learn (Figure 8.12). There's a difference between key takeaways and goals. Goals are the topics that will be covered during the webinar; key takeaways reflect the main points listeners will learn and, where applicable, how your product or service makes the goals achievable.

Martin's webinar outlines the five challenges people face when trying to sell in person or on social media, shared in a creative and memorable way using alliteration. Highlighting these

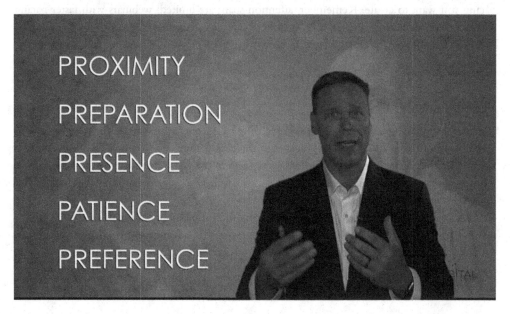

FIGURE 8.12 In a 30- or 60-minute webinar, it's impossible for a viewer to remember everything. An effective webinar lists three to five key audience takeaways and what they learn. Martin's webinar outlines the five challenges people face when trying to sell in person or on social media, shared in a creative and memorable way using alliteration. Highlighting these five key messages at the beginning and end of a webinar reminds the attendee what they need to know when the session is complete.

five key messages at the beginning and end of a webinar reminds the attendee what they need to know when the session is complete.

Key takeaways can further serve as section breaks during the webinar to help set pace and remind the viewer what will be discussed next. Often, section slides are inserted in the presentation for each key takeaway to cue the moderator to segue to the next one.

Body Content

This is a chance to convey the key takeaways in more detail. Successful webinars will often use poll questions, chat features, and breakout rooms to help ensure attendees stay active and engaged during the presentation. While the COVID pandemic forced many to become quickly familiar with these now-common features, there are ways to extend interactive elements even in a recorded webinar.

Ideally, every slide should have a mix of copy and visuals to engage diverse learners. This means graphics instead of bullets and videos instead of photos. Copy should also be minimal and in a font that's easy to read. Webinar slides should also feature company branding.

Focus on keeping words per slide minimal, ideally ten or fewer words per bullet point, and a font size of 18 or larger.

Each slide may take from 30 seconds to five minutes, depending on the content and the pacing you want to create. Remember, attention spans are limited; webinars with faster pacing and incentives or breaks, such as polls, help keep attendees engaged. Incentives could include a contest, free offering, or an additional piece of content the webinar host highlights during the presentation.

Questions and Answers

It's critical to make sure attendees have ample time to ask questions. Often, the moderator will verbally ask questions that attendees answer in the chat feature. For example, as the webinar is beginning, the moderator may ask attendees to state in the chat where they're attending from. This not only engages attendees but also serves to familiarize viewers with the chat feature and creates a sense of community.

During the dedicated Q&A section following the formal presentation, it's always good for a webinar host to have two or three questions prepared in advance to break the ice and give time for attendees to get their confidence to ask questions. In a live setting, leaving 10–20% of the total webinar length for questions and answers is common. Recorded webinars should have a way for attendees to email questions to the presenter.

Call to Action

An effective webinar should not just end when the event is over but initiate further conversation with potential leads after the event. Brands can offer calls to action such as free or discounted services, appointment forms for further meetings, or brief surveys to continue attendee

FIGURE 8.13 Ideally, a webinar is not the conclusion of an interaction with a potential buyer. Webinars should spark further engagement with attendees that occur in more custom and personal settings using calls to action, such as free or discounted services, appointment forms for further meetings, or brief surveys to continue attendee engagement after the event.

engagement after the event (Figure 8.13). It's also important for webinar hosts to be polite and thank people for their time and attention.

Martin's webinars usually end with three potential action steps. Someone can buy a copy of his book, register for a personal consultation, or access the dedicated link for coaching opportunities.

What a CM should know: Webinars are a significant time investment. An astute CM will optimize the shelf life of a webinar with content that promotes the webinar in other forms of communication. When following up with attendees, a CM can gain information on which learning goals were of most interest and adapt further content to expand upon goals that resonated the most with attendees.

CONCLUSION

It's impossible to reflect the diversity of your audience without having a diverse offering of content. While audio and video are more accessible than ever, time-tested audio and video production fundamentals are still necessary to create a meaningful product that engages potential customers. A CM may never pick up a camera or microphone, but they must be able to have conversations with production teams, clients, and coworkers on how to create and distribute appropriate multimedia content for appropriate audiences. Video may not have killed the radio star, but the combination of audio and video in a content marketing campaign will help a CM's effort one sound and second at a time.

Interview with the Experts: Q&A with Douglas Burdett, Host of The Marketing Book Podcast

Douglas Burdett is a marketing consultant, former US Army field artillery officer, Madison Avenue ad man, and stand-up comedian. Every Friday since January 2015, he has published an interview with the author of a new marketing or sales book. He has read every one of the hundreds of books featured on the show. *The Marketing Book Podcast* has been named as one of the top marketing podcasts by *Forbes* and LinkedIn, among others, and has millions of downloads and listeners in over 160 countries.

1. ***Why do you think podcasts succeed or fail?***
   Podcast industry experts have indicated that the majority of podcasts don't make it to episode 8. The biggest reason podcasts fail is because of a lack of focus on who the listener is and what they want. Sadly, this results in a show that is often not interesting, helpful, or entertaining (and not listened to) and a discouraged podcaster. Also, producing a quality podcast episode takes more time than new podcasters realize, and building an audience can take years.

2. ***Why did you pick weekly episodes? What would you recommend?***
   Consistency is more important than frequency in building an audience, and I felt that I could not produce more than one good episode a week. Many new podcasters start out with great enthusiasm, initially producing more episodes at a pace than they can ultimately sustain. This signals to the audience a lack of commitment. It's better to start out slow and add more regular episodes than to cut back the frequency.

3. ***What is your workflow to create and publish the podcast?***
   The Marketing Book Podcast is a weekly interview show, so I try to make the experience as easy and convenient for the authors I interview. Invited guests are sent a link to a private page on my website where they learn about the benefits of being a guest on the podcast and what they can expect in an interview. On that same page, they schedule their interview (using OnceHub) and later receive automated follow-up emails to prepare them for the interview.

   I record just one interview per week on Fridays as that is the most convenient day for authors. I currently record the interview on Cleanfeed, an audio-only platform.

After each episode, I follow a 60-point checklist on teamwork that I continuously refine to streamline the process. I edit together the audio using Audacity software and then run the completed audio file through Auphonic to enhance the final audio. I then upload the audio file to Libsyn, which distributes the episode to all the major podcast platforms such as Spotify and Apple Podcasts at 3:00 a.m. Eastern time every Friday. I edit my own audio because it makes me a better interviewer.

Each episode gets a website page at MarketingBookPodcast.com. That page includes a picture of the author and their book, a description of the book, the author's bio, links to books and other things mentioned in the interview, the audio from the episode, and a form to sign up for email updates about future episodes.

4. *What have you found to be the most effective marketing tactics for your podcast?*

The most important marketing tactic is to do your best to produce a quality episode consistently. One of the benefits of an interview show is that the guest can share the interview with their followers. Beyond that, it is a lot of small things, including building a listener email list, sharing each episode on social media, public speaking, getting publicity about the show, and being a guest on other shows.

Interview with the Experts: Q&A with Lisa Arledge, President of Communications at Video Production Agency, MediaSource

Lisa Arledge is the president and co-founder of MediaSource. Under Lisa's leadership, MediaSource has become one of the most respected names in content marketing, video production, and public relations.

1. *What is the best thing a CM can do when working with a video production team?*

The best thing a marketing or communication pro can do when working with a video production team is communicate the *why* – why are you as a marketer choosing to produce a video, and what do you want to happen once the video is produced?

Clearly communicate your vision but be willing to hear ideas from the video production team. If there's a video style that is inspiring the project, share it as a jumping off point for a brainstorm but be open to the magic of the creative process.

2. *What is the worst thing a CM can do when working with a video production team?*

The worst thing you can do is to jump right to the video production stage. While it is tempting to go full speed ahead into the shoot, you're missing an important step that can make or break your video project. Creating a video strategy to define why you're producing a video and what you ultimately want to happen once it's finished is the key to video success. At Media-Source we developed a four-step storytelling with purpose process that we use for video content creation:

Step 1: Dream big.
Step 2: Create your masterpiece.
Step 3: Command the spotlight.
Step 4: Toast your success!

3. *What does video do to improve communication that other forms of media simply can't replicate?*

In today's world of content overload, video can capture your audience's attention and make them stop scrolling in ways that words cannot. You can communicate your message in fewer words and less time because the visuals work with your words to tell the story. Video has the power to spark emotion and create memorable moments for your audience.

4. *When a client says, "Just use your phone to film this," how do you respond?*

Yes, we can just use the phone, but the question is "Should we?" There is definitely a place today for videography that is shot on a phone. Social media content created on phones is a great example. However, there are situations when a CM should weigh the pros and cons of shooting on a phone versus shooting with a professional crew. Today's phones can produce a quality look, but the final output is only going to be as good as the person operating the phone or running the professional camera.

5. *How do you define shot composition to people who aren't trained videographers?*

Composition is how things are arranged on screen in your video. For example, if you're interviewing a person, composition is where you place them on screen in relation to the background and other things around them. It's important to pay attention to composition because how the shot is composed helps tell the story.

6. ***If someone were launching a video strategy from scratch, what advice would you give them?***

When launching a video strategy from scratch, make sure you don't forget the business strategy. Understand what you're producing, why you're producing it, and how the videos will work with other content in your communications program.

Also, start slow – a pitfall in launching a video program is biting off more content than you can chew, especially if you don't have a large team. Be realistic in the amount of content you can produce and always pick quality over quantity.

Finally, just like other forms of communication, it's important to set up a way to measure your video program so that you understand the value it brings. If you can show return on investment (ROI), you will likely get more resources for your video program.

CITATIONS

Beets, L.M., Handley, A., & Stahl, S., et al. "12th Annual B2B content marketing: Benchmarks, budgets and trends." 2022. Retrieved from: https://contentmarketinginstitute.com/wp-content/uploads/2021/10/B2B_2022_Research.pdf

Edison Research. "The podcast consumer 2019." The infinite dial study 2023. *Edison Research.* March 2, 2023. Study retrieved from: www.edisonresearch.com/wp-content/uploads/2019/04/Edison-Research-Podcast-Consumer-2019.pdf

Interactive Advertising Bureau (IAB). "Sixth Annual U.S. podcast advertising revenue report: FY 2021 results & 2022–2024 growth projections." Prepared for IAB by PricewaterhouseCoopers LLP (PwC). May 9, 2022.

Klimes, O. "Captions increase viewership, accessibility and reach." February 10, 2021. Retrieved from: www.newtontech.net/en/blog/23083-captions-increase-viewership-accessibility-and-reach/

Mark, G. "Attention span: A groundbreaking way to restore balance, happiness and productivity." *Hanover Square Press.* January 10, 2023.

McCue, T.J. "Verizon media says 69 percent of consumers watching video with sound off." July 31, 2019. Retrieved from: www.forbes.com/sites/tjmccue/2019/07/31/verizon-media-says-69-percent-of-consumers-watching-video-with-sound-off/?sh=6aba393835d8

No Author. "Number of digital video viewers worldwide, 2019–2023." *Statista.* October 12, 2021. Retrieved from: www.statista.com/statistics/1061017/digital-video-viewers-number-worldwide/

No Author. "Leading types of video used in marketing worldwide, 2019–2023." *Statista.* January 10, 2023. Retrieved from: www.statista.com/statistics/622023/leading-types-of-videos-used-b2b-marketers-worldwide/

Sellers, A. "The AIDA model: A proven framework for converting strangers into customers." *HubSpot Blog.* February 4, 2022. Retrieved from: https://blog.hubspot.com/marketing/aida-model

Snovio, A. "How to increase email open rate through power words." *Medium.com*. July 15, 2019. Retrieved from: https://medium.com/snov-io/how-to-increase-email-open-rate-through-power-words-43167204fb08

Wyzowl Research. "The state of video marketing." 2023. Retrieved from: https://wyzowl.s3.eu-west-2. amazonaws.com/pdfs/Wyzowl-Video-Survey-2023.pdf

Zauderer, S. "Average Human Attention Span By Age: 47 Statistics." May 19, 2023. Retrieved from https://www.crossrivertherapy.com/average-human-attention-span

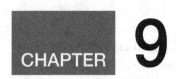

Product Collateral and Its Role in Content Marketing

INTRODUCTION

When potential customers begin the process of purchasing a new product – let's say a Bluetooth speaker – one of the first things they will likely do is search for information about competing products to compare features such as weight, water resistance, portability, and price. Successful brands and CMs organize this information into product collateral, a critical genre of content that CMs use to communicate the value proposition, user benefits, and technical features of a product to potential consumers. As product collateral is consumed in the early stages of the purchase journey, it is most often considered top-of-the-funnel content and is ungated (i.e., does not require a form fill to access).

Product collateral pieces are most often developed and published in digital format as well as print, following a similar structure that answers the following questions for the user:

- Who is the product for?
- What value does the product deliver?
- What is the differentiated product messaging?
- What are the technical specifications?

DOI: 10.4324/9781003369103-11

A 2022 TrustRadius study looked at top criteria for making purchasing decisions for business technology (Headley, 2022). The group surveyed more than 1,000 buyers. The top three responses:

- Product demonstration (see the product in action as it relates to specific customer needs)
- Product or vendor website (learn about the product collateral)
- User reviews (others talking about the product collateral)

Given the importance of product collateral in the buying process, the CM must understand how to develop effective collateral, how potential buyers use the most valued forms of collateral, and how the content varies across digital, print, and multimedia.

This chapter will explain the organization and development of content for several of the most popular forms of collateral as well as how each format of collateral aids consumers in the buying process. With the best practices in creating content for a few of these types of collateral described in detail, other types of product collateral will become easier for CMs to create.

THREE CRITICAL ELEMENTS OF PRODUCT COLLATERAL

There are many ways potential buyers can research product information and a myriad of factors that can influence their decision. So much information, from how the product compares to competing options to specific features, can exhaust a CM who's trying to organize and prioritize all the possible types of information marketing, sales, and development colleagues may want to include. After all, a product flier, for instance, is only two pages; with such limited space, a lot of information will have to be left out. While in theory there's unlimited space on a web page, it's a terrible idea to include all information just because you can or, worse, bury the most important information at the bottom.

To emphasize the most important elements in both content and design and considering the behaviors and needs of the potential buyer, a CM should ensure that the product's value proposition and a clear description and benefits are prioritized in any collateral piece. Doing this well simultaneously allows a CM to highlight a product's features or specifications. Let's look at each of these in a bit more detail.

Product Value Proposition

Since potential buyers often have so many choices when making their purchase decision, the product collateral must quickly and simply explain your product and inspire the buyer to consider it over your competitors'.

The value proposition is a critical first step to doing this. A good value proposition explains what the product promises to deliver that makes the customer's life better, and it does so in the customer's own language (Cespedes & Narayandas, 2019). Moreover, a value proposition can speak to both tangible and intangible value.

Let's consider a Bluetooth speaker. One value the product offers could be tangible (e.g., a physical or objective feature, such as it will work at the bottom of a pool) while others could be intangible (e.g., subjective and beneficial aspects, such as that it empowers you to bring friends together for summer memories) (Lefkoff-Hagius & Mason, 1990).

The most effective product value propositions are easy to understand, use simple language, and grab the reader with wording that emphasizes a key differentiating aspect of the product, such as the leading benefit the product delivers that no other competing product offers. A great value proposition is memorable, speaks directly to your target audience segment, and is a single sentence or even a headline phrase.

What a CM should know: The value proposition is a short phrase whose sole purpose is to grab the reader's attention using memorable language that's easy to understand.

For example, the value proposition for FreshBooks accounting software is "accounting software built for business owners and accountants." This value proposition effectively achieves two critical aspects of communicating the product's value and differentiation to prospective buyers:

1.   It simply and clearly states what the product is: accounting software.
2.   It explains the target segment the software is for: small business owners and accountants.

To develop a strong value proposition, start with your product positioning statement, the Four Ws (explained in Chapter 2), and buyer personas (covered in Chapter 3.) When developing the product's value proposition, reference content from the final product positioning explained in the Four Ws regarding the customer's need or the *why* (the challenge the customer is facing), what the product is, and how it uniquely appeals to your buyer, called the *what*.

Additionally, as we explained in Chapter 3, having the buyer persona(s) developed brings clarity to whom the value proposition should address. The *why*, the *what*, and the *who* are all key ingredients that must be defined before creating an effective and compelling value proposition. Often, you can benefit from creating a variety of different versions of the value proposition in the process of finding the right words, order, and length. It helps to share your best ideas with trusted colleagues and subject matter experts who understand prospective customers' needs, their language, and how they think about the problem your product solves to get valuable feedback in narrowing down and selecting the final version.

Product Description and Benefits

While the value proposition is one of the most critical pieces of content in product collateral, it is just the beginning of what's needed to convince a potential buyer to keep reading and learning more about your product. To complement the value proposition, brief descriptions that elaborate on the value and differentiators of the product are vital to keeping the buyer interested and engaged in the content.

After potential buyers read your value proposition, a product description in the form of a few short sentences draws them in even further by explaining the product's key benefits. In marketing, the features are the characteristics or qualities of a product (such as a self-setting clock). In contrast, benefits communicate the value of the feature for consumers (such as convenience or accuracy for the self-setting clock). Benefit statements answer the customer question: "What's in it for me?"

(WIIFM) or "Why does the feature or characteristic matter to me?" (Douglas, 2000). For instance, the following is the product description for Squarespace (No Author, LinkedIn), a company that makes software to build websites (No Author, LinkedIn), from the company's LinkedIn page:

> "*Squarespace is the all-in-one platform to build a beautiful online presence. Look like an expert right from the start. Our award-winning templates are the most beautiful way to present your ideas online. Stand out with a professional website, portfolio, or online store.*"

This description further explains the unique aspects of the software platform and emphasizes the product's all-in-one platform to build a beautiful website (one customer benefit), empowering users to create websites that look like an expert created them (second customer benefit), and access to award-winning templates (third customer benefit).

Along with this short product description, three or four key statements of benefits that most set the product apart from competing products and define the value the product delivers are important to further aid and persuade a potential buyer.

Referring back to the Freshbooks accounting software, the top benefits statements for their accountants target segment are:

1. Easy-to-use interface for your clients: According to 95% of small business owners, Fresh-Books is easier to use than other platforms. When it's easy for your clients to manage their books, your job is that much more efficient – whether you support them 365 days a year or just at tax time.
2. Optimize client workflows: Freshbooks makes it easy for your clients to complete part of their workflow. That means you can focus on taking a more advisory role and developing deeper client relationships.
3. Grow your practice: Do you want to collaborate better with clients? Spend less time on their books and more on growing your firm? Build a more virtual practice? This program was made for you.

What a CM should know: The most effective product collateral pieces will begin with the product value proposition, differentiated product description, and benefits statements. This content serves a critical role in attracting the short attention span of the potential buyer, and when done effectively, it quickly answers the question "Why would I buy this product over the other options?" and draws the reader in to learn more.

Product Features and Technical Specifications

For potential buyers of feature-rich products like appliances or cars, the product's tangible features, attributes, and technical specifications can be as or more important than the value proposition or benefits. These explicit details about the product's material, design, or function empower potential customers to see how unique product features or potential upgrades can help them enhance their work or life experience more than alternative options.

For more technical purchases such as these, accurate and thorough product information is necessary for the buyer to understand whether the product can meet their requirements

(Perez Zamora, 2019). For instance, an engineer designing a medical device who is seeking a component with a high operating temperature range would benefit from learning the technical specification "operates up to 125° Fahrenheit." In the case of a medical device, this specification can be the difference between the end customer's life and death.

For incremental upgrades to existing products, unique product features are paramount in attracting the buyer to learn more about the product's enhanced capabilities over alternative options.

Often, new products have a multitude of features and specifications to promote: performance, speed, ruggedness, software compatibility, intuitive user design, and ease of programming to start.

While there is a place in certain product collateral to eventually list all features and specifications, it behooves the CM to prioritize all product features, specifications, and corresponding benefits.

Through the process of prioritization, as explained in Chapter 2, an internal list of features, benefits, and specifications is a valuable reference for a CM as they develop product collateral. The top features will likely become a source of differentiators.

With that, let's now take a look at the three most common types of product collateral – the web page, the brochure, and the flier.

What a CM should know: Product features and technical specifications can play a critical role in the buying process and are also valuable as search engine optimizers. Therefore, it's important for the CM to organize the collateral piece to prioritize features and specifications from most to least important.

PRODUCT COLLATERAL FORMAT: PRODUCT WEB PAGE

Google was founded in 1997 and today is the most popular search engine in the world, with 88% market share (No Author, 2022, *Statcounter*). Data analyzed by Smart Insights found that the number of daily searches on Google as of January 2022 was 3.5 billion, which equates to 1.2 trillion searches per year worldwide (Chaffey, 2022). Further, data by Statista on internet penetration shows that in 2017, 46.8% of the global population accessed the internet, and by July 2022, that number had risen to 63.1% (No Author, 2022, *Statista*). It's not surprising then to imagine that Google would be a highly valued source in the buying process for new products. In one survey of technical B2B buyers, the top three most valued sources for content when combining responses for "very valuable" and "moderately valuable" were all digital platforms: 85% for supplier/vendor websites and 81% for search engines (Geier & Uslaner, 2017).

With these insights on buyer behavior, we can deduce that one of the most valued and important types of product collateral is the product web page, which serves as the primary online home for all information about the product (Roto, no date). The product web page will often be the first content an interested buyer will experience as they begin their research about the product. Whether visitors to the product web page are brand new to the product or have some familiarity with it, they will use its content to understand how the product compares to competitive offerings and to find further in-depth information, such as technical specifications, as well as customer product testimonials, videos, and images of the product in use.

An effective product web page is easy to update and inexpensive to publish. A product web page is often the first in a group of web pages, or sections of a website, dedicated to promoting and explaining the product. Content on a web page is inherently very easy to maintain, given its digital nature and the fact that it is housed in a content management system (CMS), a software system used to display, update, and manage content on a website.

What a CM should know: A CM with editing access can log into a CMS to access sections of the website and make modifications to product messaging, update technical specifications, or add new collateral. Compared to reprinting brochures and other printed collateral each time a new version of the product is launched, a product web page can be updated on the fly and is lower in cost than printed publishing. Moreover, the CM can access the web page from anywhere in the world 24/7/365, making it easy to collaboratively maintain and update on the go.

The primary disadvantage of the product web page relates to layout. Every company designs websites differently, and visitors must orient themselves to the design and layout of each company's product pages as they search for information. A buyer must often visit multiple pages to get all the product information needed to become sufficiently informed to make a buying decision.

This disadvantage, however, is a great opportunity for a CM to be an advocate for the prospective buyer and provide constructive user experience (UX) feedback on a page's design to ensure the content is easily discoverable and accessible. An effective product web page includes the following content elements, appearing on the web page in the order listed:

- Web page headline
- Feature image and value proposition
- Short product description
- Top differentiators with benefits statements
- Supporting content, such as product features, customer logos and testimonials; product videos; add-on products or compatible third-party tools; media coverage and awards; specification tables; and pricing and purchasing information
- Images and links to related product collateral
- Calls to action

The first three content elements of a product web page – the web page headline, feature image, and value proposition – serve a critical role given their location at the very top of the web page. The web page headline is usually just a few words that appear in the largest size font at the very top of the page and contains the first words the visitor will likely read when they reach the web page. A product web page headline anchors the reader with what the product is and what value it provides.

Appearing just below or next to the web page headline is the feature image of the page (sometimes called the "hero" image) and the value proposition. These visual and contextual details grab the reader's attention and inspire them to stay on the page to learn more and scroll for further information.

For example, in reference to the product web page for HubSpot customer relationship management (CRM) software, you first see the page headline "Grow Better with HubSpot," followed immediately by the value proposition: "Software that's powerful, not overpowering. Seamlessly connect your data, teams, and customers on one CRM platform that grows with your business." To the right is a feature image with a product screenshot of the HubSpot software dashboard (Figure 9.1).

Following these first content elements, the product description and benefits expand on the product's unique value and how it works. Figure 9.2 shows the sub-headline "What Is HubSpot?" along with a product description:

> *"HubSpot is a CRM platform with all the software, integrations, and resources you need to connect marketing, sales, content management, and customer service. Each product is powerful on its own, but the real magic happens when you use them all together."*

Following this product platform overview and two calls to action – demo premium CRM and get free CRM – is a listing of three unique platform offerings, each with corresponding benefits:

- Marketing Hub: Marketing software to help you grow traffic, convert more visitors, and run complete inbound marketing campaigns at scale

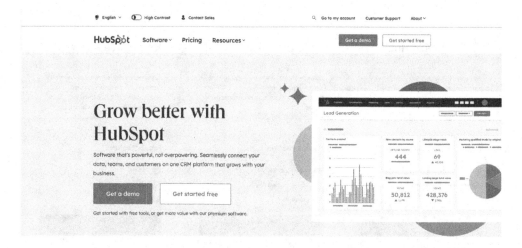

FIGURE 9.1 The first three content elements of a product web page – the web page headline, feature image, and value proposition – serve a critical role given their location at the very top of the web page. The top of the HubSpot customer relationship management (CRM) software web page starts with the page headline "Grow Better with HubSpot," followed immediately by the value proposition: "Software that's powerful, not overpowering. Seamlessly connect your data, teams, and customers on one CRM platform that grows with your business." To the right is a feature image with a product screenshot of the HubSpot software dashboard. These visual and contextual details grab the reader's attention and inspire them to stay on the page to learn more and scroll for further information.

- Sales Hub: Sales CRM software to help you get deeper insights into prospects, automate the tasks you hate, and close more deals faster
- Service Hub: Customer service software to help you connect with customers, exceed expectations, and turn them into promoters who grow your business

Following these most important top-level content elements, supplemental content is often next and can vary in order, such as more in-depth product features, customer logos, testimonials, product videos, add-on products, compatible third-party tools, media coverage, awards, specification tables, pricing, and purchasing information.

HubSpot chooses to emphasize the large community of users, breadth of resources, and events they provide to ensure the user knows they are not alone and will be well-supported, as shown in Figure 9.3.

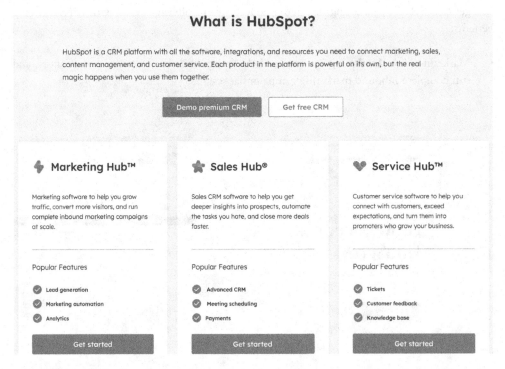

FIGURE 9.2 Following the page headline, feature image, and value proposition, the product description and benefits expand on the product's unique value and how it works. This figure shows the sub-headline "What is HubSpot?" along with a product description, "HubSpot is a CRM platform with all the software, integrations, and resources you need to connect marketing, sales, content management, and customer service. Each product is powerful on its own, but the real magic happens when you use them all together." Following this product platform overview and two calls to action – demo premium CRM and get free CRM – the unique platform offerings Marketing Hub, Sales Hub, and Service Hub are listed, each with corresponding benefits statements.

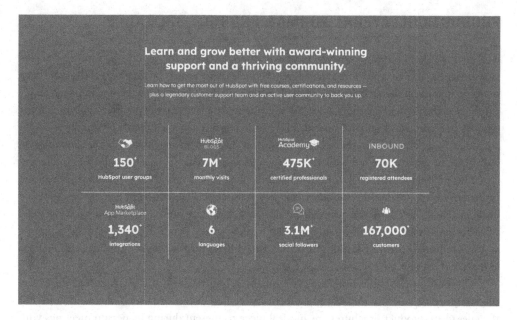

FIGURE 9.3 Following the top-level web page headline, feature image, and value proposition, supplemental content is next and can vary in order, such as product features, customer logos, testimonials, product videos, add-on products, compatible third-party tools, media coverage, awards, specification tables, pricing, and purchasing information. Here, HubSpot chooses to emphasize the large community of users, breadth of resources, and events they provide to ensure the user knows they are not alone and will be well-supported.

When looking through the HubSpot product website, consumers will also see additional collateral, content offerings, and calls to action. Throughout the product web page, complementary product collateral pieces, such as downloadable versions of the product flier, relevant blog posts, case studies, and white papers encourage readers to click and read more about the product. These calls to action, or CTAs, encourage the reader to take an action by clicking on a piece of content that interests them. CTAs can take many forms, including the product collateral just mentioned, text buttons, video play buttons, and hyperlinked text.

Two CTAs on the HubSpot product web page are the two buttons – Get a demo and Get started free – the reader can click on to learn more about the software (Figure 9.1).

What a CM should know: Given how much information there can be on product web pages and how accessible they are, it's no surprise this collateral type is often the first content an interested buyer will experience and read as they begin their product research. For this reason, a CM needs consistent access to any web-related content and related pages to keep the pages as current and engaging as possible.

PRODUCT COLLATERAL FORMAT: PRODUCT BROCHURE

The second type of product collateral CMs will often develop is the product brochure – a multi-page designed piece that provides a high-level overview of the product with much of the same content that appears on the product web page. However, while the product web page is a digital-only experience, the product brochure is a stand-alone designed piece that the prospect consumes either digitally in a portable document format (PDF) or in a printed piece. Often a product brochure is a content asset promoted on the product web page, shared as an attachment in sales and marketing emails, or promoted as a downloadable piece on social media such as LinkedIn and Instagram.

The product brochure is a high-quality, well-designed collateral piece used to educate prospective buyers about the unique value, key features and benefits, and primary uses for the product (Ladd, 2010). When printed, product brochures are among the highest-quality type of collateral as they are most often printed on heavy, glossy paper in four colors (also known as 4c), a full-color form of printing that uses four different ink colors – cyan, magenta, yellow, and black (CMYK).

The product brochure both educates qualified buyers about the product and showcases the company's brand in a well-designed format potential buyers can touch, feel, and hold. For the sales team, product brochures are an ideal piece to present during in-person meetings with qualified buyers or to offer selectively at in-person events like seminars and trade shows.

A downside to the product brochure is the time required to create it and the cost to design and print it; a brochure can easily cost thousands of dollars to print. Additionally, when a product is updated with new features or an upgraded version, the brochure is no longer current and becomes a sunk cost. With a digital product web page, you avoid these costs because the format is easily updated without requiring design changes. Therefore, brochures are most often used for primary products and require extra attention to flow, formatting, and design to make the investment worth the effort.

Although the length of a product brochure varies from four to more than eight pages, the most effective ones provide a thorough overview of the product with product positioning, differentiators, important features, and technical specifications. An effective product brochure should include the following content elements:

* Cover: sets the stage with the brochure title, feature image, and company branding

    * An effective brochure has a short title with a few simple words at most, perhaps the name of the product or a value proposition.
    * In Keysight's brochure for its "Test-as-a-Service," the title includes both the product name "Keysight Test-as-a-Service" and the value proposition message "Accelerate Test. Improve Safety." (Figure 9.4).
    * The feature image brings visual appeal to the story and can take many forms, from images of the product to an application shot to user-focused images that show the product in action.
    * The cover in Figure 9.4 features an application-related image of a schematic of a car, which lets the reader know that this brochure is about products and services related to the automotive market: in this case, autonomous vehicle safety.

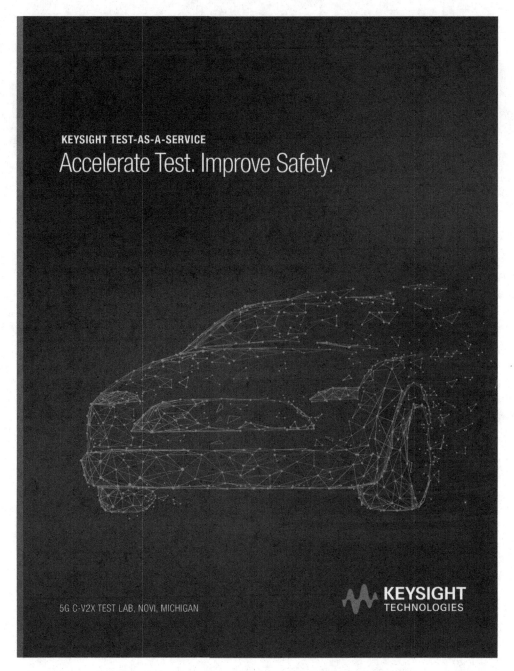

FIGURE 9.4 The title of Keysight's brochure for its Test-as-a-Service includes both the service name Keysight Test-as-a-Service and the value proposition "Accelerate test. Improve safety." The cover features an application-related image of a schematic of a car to indicate that the brochure covers information related to the automotive market. The brochure cover's design, including the use and placement of color, imagery, and the company logo, all work together to set the tone of the brochure.

- **The first two pages**: contain an introduction to the product and the problem it solves.

  - The opening pages of a brochure start with an overview of the problem the prospective customer faces (i.e., the *why* of the Four Ws). In Figure 9.5, the first paragraph begins, "The race is on to be first to market with safe autonomous driving as car manufacturers improve safety." It goes on to explain additional challenges the customer faces in meeting technical compliance requirements for third-generation partnership project (3GPP) mobile telecommunications and "vehicular to everything" (C-V2X) standards.
  - By using the customer's language, the brochure builds confidence with the reader that the company understands their problem and has a product to solve it, inspiring them to continue reading and build consideration for purchase.
  - The next paragraph introduces the product – in this case, a Test-as-a-Service lab in Michigan – and its value proposition and description by briefly describing how Keysight uniquely helps customers solve their design and test challenges "with the broadest and most reliable end-to-end hardware and software solutions."
  - Four key features and benefits are briefly explained in the buyer's language at the bottom: C-V2X application layer testing, standards-based testing, parametric testing, and custom testing.
  - A right-hand sidebar box is offset from the main text and gives the reader a scannable list of offerings (scenario testing, 3GPP standards, network emulation).

- **Interior pages**: used to provide more detail about the unique features and benefits of the product

  - The bulk of the pages inside a product brochure are used to delve deeper into a product's unique features (i.e., the *what* of the Four Ws).
  - Often, CMs will devote a whole page to a single feature and benefit or group of related features and benefits. For instance, in the Keysight brochure, each page focused on one feature, such as C-V2X application layer testing and standards-based testing (Figure 9.6), with a one-sentence overview, what the feature provides, and the benefits of the feature.
  - Each page includes an image highlighting the product in use, which brings the product to life and makes the pages more visually appealing.
  - Sidebars are also used on these feature/benefit pages to provide a quick, scannable list of more detailed specifications of the feature (Figure 9.6): "Sample list of application layer testing by category").

- **Last page/back cover**: conclusion that includes reference information and the company logo

  - The last page of the brochure may be a formally designed back cover or a more simply designed last page that serves as a reference page for more information.

5G C-V2X Test Lab

Accelerate Test. Improve Safety.

The race is on to be first to market with safe autonomous driving as car manufacturers improve safety. As new standards evolve, test accuracy, repeatability and reliability mandate the need for both application layer testing and 3GPP compliance readiness. The regulatory uncertainty for C-V2X standards is delaying investment in establishing and staffing test labs. C-V2X includes vehicle-to-vehicle (V2V), vehicle-to-infrastructure (V2I), vehicle-to-network (V2N), and vehicle-to-pedestrian (V2P).

Introducing Keysight Test-as-a-Service 5G C-V2X test lab in Novi, Michigan. Keysight, the 5G automotive industry test leader, helps customers solve design and test challenges with the broadest and most reliable end-to-end hardware and software solutions. Let our experts show you the latest automated test setups that apply Society Automotive of Engineers (SAE) protocols with Keysight PathWave software.

Keysight offers you C-V2X application layer, standards, parametric, and custom testing scenarios. Accelerate time to measurement with minimal cost. Reduce risk by performing safety scenarios testing at our lab with our experts. Contact Keysight today to delve deeply into complex measurements to rapidly uncover true insights about your design.

Sample list of TaaS offerings

Scenario testing
- Up to 20 independent on board units (OBU) with customizable trajectories and basic safety message (BSM) information
- Drive device under test (DUT) through scenario via Global Navigation Satellite System (GNSS) simulation

3GPP standards
- Receiver test
- Transmitter test
- Demodulation performance test

Network emulation
- 5G non standalone (NSA)
- 5G standalone (SA)
- LTE advanced professional

C-V2X APPLICATION LAYER TESTING

Access the latest test setups, PathWave software, and expertise for complex scenario testing of the C-V2X application layer and Intelligent Transportation Services (ITS) stack.

STANDARDS-BASED TESTING

Collaborate with 5G experts to validate your product's performance to standards-based specifications for pre-compliance and conformance tests.

PARAMETRIC TESTING

Access state-of-the-art instruments, PathWave software, and experts to help characterize the performance of your design.

CUSTOM TESTING

Partner with Keysight application consultants to design and develop test plans for your leading-edge product designs.

FIGURE 9.5 The opening pages of a brochure start with an overview of the problem the prospective customer faces (i.e., the *why* of the Four Ws), stating, "The race is on to be first to market with safe autonomous driving as car manufacturers improve safety." Using this opening page to briefly describe additional challenges the customer faces in meeting technical compliance requirements for third-generation partnership project (3GPP) mobile telecommunications and "vehicular to everything" (C-V2X) standards attempts to build confidence with the reader that the company understands their problem and has a product to solve it, inspiring them to continue reading and build consideration for purchase.

C-V2X application layer testing

Access state-of-the-art test setups, PathWave software, and expertise for congestion, day one, and complex scenario testing of the C-V2X application layer and intelligent transportation services (ITS) stack.

Keysight provides

- 5G experts who work across R&D, manufacturing, and standards boards
- Cutting-edge calibration test setups, PathWave software, and accessories
- Traffic scenario creation and monitoring in a congested environment
- Messaging that conforms to SAE protocols
- Application consultants with the domain expertise to perform measurements
- Detailed data and reporting capability

Benefits

- Ensure your device accurately allocates complex signal resources in a dynamic environment while new standards are adopted and evolve
- Quickly gain insight into critical basic safety message (BSM) interpretation such as forward collision warning, do not pass warning, intersection movement assist, and other use cases
- Make measurements now with minimal capital and operating expense while government bodies adopt regulatory standards
- Keep your teams focused on accelerating designs

Sample list of application layer testing by category

Active road safety messages
- Do not pass warning (DNPW)
- Forward collision warning (FCW)
- Emergency electronic brake lights (EEBL)
- Intersection movement assist (IMA)

Cooperative traffic efficiency
- GeoNetworking (GN)
- Basic transport protocol (BTP)
- Local dynamic map (LDM)

Cooperative local and global internet services
- Cooperative awareness message (CAM)
- Decentralized environmental notification message (DENM)
- Signal phase and timing (SPAT)
- Mapping message (MAP)
- Security (SEC)

Congestion testing
- Speeding cars in the carpool lane during heavy traffic
- Multiple use cases

FIGURE 9.6 Interior pages such as the two shown here are used to provide more detail about the unique features and benefits of the product (i.e., the *what* of the Four Ws). Each page includes a one-sentence feature description, what Keysight provides with this feature, and the benefits of the feature. Often, CMs will devote a whole page to a single feature and benefit or group of related features and benefits, such as here on the left-hand page, which focuses on the C-V2X application layer testing feature, and the right-hand page on standards-based testing.

Standards-based testing

Access the latest test setups, PathWave software, and 5G experts to validate your product performance to standards-based specifications for pre-compliance and conformance tests.

Keysight provides

- State-of-the-art equipment with traceable calibration, PathWave software, probes, fixtures, and accessories
- Tests that follow 3GPP standards and use test setups found at Plugfest, 5GAA, OmniAir, and more
- Application consultants with the domain expertise to perform measurements
- Detailed data analysis and reporting capability

Benefits

- Increase your confidence in passing future certification testing
- Validate your product performance to standards
- Save time in the development of test assets and resources
- Optimize your test investment with pay-per-use pricing

Sample list of 3GPP LTE-V2X R14 test capabilities

Transmitter tests (TS36.521-1 Clause 6)
- UE min/max output power
- Maximum power reduction (MPR)
- Additional MPR (A-MPR)
- Configured transmitted power
- Transmit off power

Receiver sensitivity and interference tests (TS36.521-1 Clause 7)
- Receiver characteristics
- Maximum input level
- Adjacent channel selectivity
- In-band blocking
- Out-of-band blocking
- Spurious response

Demodulation performance tests (TS 36.521-1 Clause 14)
- Demodulation of physical sidelink shared channel (PSSCH)
- Demodulation of physical sidelink control channel (PSCCH)
- Power imbalance performance with two links
- PSCCH/PSSCH decoding capability

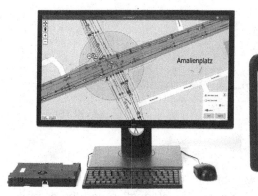

FIGURE 9.6 (Continued)

About Keysight Services

Keysight Services offers the most comprehensive array of people, processes, and tools in the industry to help you improve productivity and product quality. Our calibration, repair, asset optimization, technology refresh, education, financing, and additional services focus on lowering your risks and costs. Learn more at www.keysight.com/find/services.

Introducing PATHWAVE

Traditional product design and development workflows are full of design and test silos, unnecessary rework, and legacy manual processes. Accelerate your workflow with PathWave, the platform for agile and connected engineering workflows. Keysight's trusted design and test software is evolving to meet the ever-increasing needs of your organization. The PathWave software platform provides a consistent user experience, common data formats, and control interfaces. Find out more about the PathWave Software Platform.

Contact us today

Characterize and validate your design performance with state-of-the-art equipment and expertise located at the Keysight Novi, Michigan site. Start reducing your test cost and time-to-market today with Keysight Test-as-a-Service. Learn more at www.keysight.com/find/TestasaService

Learn more at: www.keysight.com

For more information on Keysight Technologies' products, applications or services, please contact your local Keysight office. The complete list is available at: www.keysight.com/find/contactus

This information is subject to change without notice. © Keysight Technologies, 2019. Published in USA, September 13, 2019, 5992-4250EN

FIGURE 9.7 The last page or back cover of the product brochure serves as a conclusion to the content piece and includes reference information and the company logo so it can be quickly identified as a brochure from Keysight. This section can be a formally designed back cover or a more simply designed last page, where the reader finds information on how to contact the company, how to purchase the product, post-purchase product support, and add-on products or services available to enhance the product's functionality.

- On this page, the reader finds information on how to contact the company, how to purchase the product, post-purchase product support, and add-on products or services available to enhance the product's functionality.
- The company logo is strategically placed on this back page for reference so anyone can quickly identify the brochure as being from Keysight (Figure 9.7).

What a CM should know: A brochure should include both storytelling and practical information with content elements including customer quotes, application uses, specification tables, and ordering information.

PRODUCT COLLATERAL FORMAT: PRODUCT FLIER

The product flier is a one-page, two-sided content piece that provides a brief overview of the product in a condensed format. Due to its much shorter length compared to the product brochure or web page, the product flier serves as a snapshot of the most important product aspects in a format potential buyers can consume quickly.

An effective product flier piques the prospective buyer's interest and inspires them to visit the product web page to research the product in depth. Like the product brochure, the product flier is consumed digitally as a PDF accessed from the product web page, as an attachment in sales and marketing emails, or via promotion on social media. It may also be printed and shared with customers at in-person meetings or events.

The key components of a product flier are contained on one page, front and back:

- **Front**: flier title, value proposition, product description, feature image, differentiated features, related benefit statements with supporting images
- **Back**: abbreviated specifications, product image(s), CTA, and contact information
- **Flexible secondary content**: target applications, customer quotes or logos, company boilerplate, awards

When a reader sees a product flier, they immediately see a variety of information all on one page. This is why a flier's layout and design are of the utmost importance. A flier shouldn't overwhelm the reader; content should flow in order of importance and in a visually appealing way.

The Silicon Audio flier for its optical seismometer product (Figure 9.8 – left-hand image) flows much like the product web page or brochure. However, with only two pages to describe the product, the information is kept brief and is designed for quick reading with relevant images.

GREATER PRECISION. BETTER DECISIONS.

SILICON AUDIO LOW-NOISE OPTICAL SEISMOMETER

- ✓ LOW SELF NOISE
- ✓ OMNIDIRECTIONAL
- ✓ HIGH CLIP LEVEL

Silicon Audio re-engineered the traditional geophone with an optical interferometer to create a seismic solution for land, marine and scientific applications that is particularly useful when low-frequency detection is critical for success.

APPLICATIONS FOR SEISMIC SOLUTIONS

With superior noise sensitivity, familiar form factor, and broadband response, the low-noise optical seismometer achieves performance advantages previously associated with scientific instruments in an easy to deploy, rugged design.

| FLAT RESPONSE FOR LAND SEISMIC APPLICATIONS | ULTRA LOW NOISE FOR MARINE SEISMIC APPLICATIONS | HIGH PERFORMANCE FOR SCIENTIFIC APPLICATIONS |

LAND Engineers focused on land-based resource exploration will benefit from the optical seismometer's flat response from 0.1Hz to 1kHz, low cross-axis sensitivity, and low power, which make it ideal for detecting noise in difficult terrain.

MARINE Engineers in marine applications can detect low-frequency (sub 1Hz) signals with high fidelity, translating to an additional decade of low-frequency data for deeper imaging into the seafloor.

SCIENTIFIC In other applications, scientists get scientific-grade performance with higher clip- and lower distortion-levels.

Silicon Audio delivers scientific-grade sensor performance for resource exploration and scientific discovery. By integrating the reliable mechanics of conventional geophones with innovative optical technologies, our sensors provide enhanced performance and better quality data for end users, whether at land or sea.

SIAUDIO.COM

FIGURE 9.8 In this product flier for the Silicon Audio optical seismometer, content flows much like it does on the product web page and brochure. However, with only two pages to describe the product, the information is kept brief and is designed for quick reading with relevant images. Product fliers are consumed by prospects in their early stages of learning about the product and are produced and consumed in higher volume than product brochures due to their relatively short length and brevity of information.

SILICON AUDIO LOW-NOISE OPTICAL SEISMOMETER

DYNAMIC RESPONSE MEASUREMENT

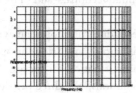

Rather than using the traditional geophone's magnetic coils for voltage output, the optical seismometer integrates an interferometer, which captures seismic data by detecting the movement of light in response to mechanical vibrations.

The result is a much better signal-to-noise ratio compared to existing technology, and the ability to record much lower frequencies.

PERFORMANCE

- Passband: 0.1Hz - 1kHz (flat to acceleration)
- Noise: below 5 ng/ √Hz from 1.0 Hz to 400 Hz
- Distortion: <0.03% at 12Hz and .7in/s p-p
- Spurious resonance: >2kHz
- Tilt tolerance: 360-degree (omnidirectional)
- Clip level: ±1.5 g pk

SENSOR NOISE FLOOR MEASUREMENT

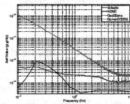

POWER

- Power: 22mW/axis
- Supply voltage: 6-17V

PHASE RESPONSE MEASUREMENT

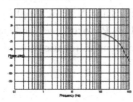

HANDLING

- Dimensions: 1.25" diameter x 1.54" (single axis)
- Transport: No mass lock required
- Mass centering: Automatic
- Shock tolerance: up to 3000g
- Operating temperature: -10C to 75C

GENERAL

- Configuration: 1-axis and 3-axis
- Feedback: Force balance with interferometric transducer

SILICON
AUDIO

Silicon Audio is actively seeking partners to customize development of the optical seismometer for diverse fields of use and applications. If you are interested in evaluating a sample optical seismometer or discussing a development partnership, contact us at sales@siaudio.com or +1 512.389.2224.

SIAUDIO.COM

FIGURE 9.8 (Continued)

- **Front**: Product introduction, benefits, and uses
- **Title**: "Silicon Audio Low-Noise Optical Seismometer"
- **Product value proposition**: "Greater Precision. Better Decisions."
- **Close-up product image**
- **Differentiated product features**: "Low Self-Noise," "Omnidirectional," and "High-Clip Level."
- **Product description**: Silicon Audio re-engineered the traditional geophone with an optical interferometer to create a seismic solution for land, marine, and scientific applications that is particularly useful when low-frequency detection is critical for success.
- **Product uses**: In the section, "Applications for Seismic Solutions," the three primary use cases for the product – land, marine, and scientific – are briefly described.
- **Company branding**: At the bottom, the brand positioning is included along with the logo and website URL offset in a blue area to distinguish them from the product-related information

Often, a flier's front page includes flexible secondary content used to communicate the most important aspects of the product, such as target applications, customer success company messaging, and industry award logos. In Figure 9.8, this includes content describing application uses of the product, starting with the section subtitled "Applications for Seismic Solutions," and a short benefits statement that aims to explain the product's unique capabilities. This is followed by information about the three primary application areas, including full-color images and benefits-oriented application headlines for each: "Flat Response for Land Seismic Applications," "Ultra Low Noise for Marine Seismic Applications," and "High Performance for Scientific Applications." One or two lines of text then explain the product benefits for use in each area.

- Back (Figure 9.8 – right image): product specifications

  - Readers can quickly skim through the four feature areas: Performance, Power, Handling, and General.
  - Under each of these headings is a bulleted list with detailed specifications the prospective buyer can skim and supporting imagery to visually explain the technical details.
  - Company branding: Offset area featuring the company name, logo mark, website, and additional company messaging.

The disadvantages of the product flier mirror those of the product brochure – the time and cost to design and print. While the flier is less costly to update than the brochure, it still requires a graphic designer to modify and a professional printer to produce.

What a CM should know: Prospects usually consume the product flier in their early stages of product learning. It is produced and consumed in higher volume than product brochures due to its relatively shorter length and brevity of information. As a result of its shorter length, a product flier advantage is that it can be more frequently and easily updated as product features and specifications change and improve.

CONCLUSION

Product collateral helps potential buyers who have very specific needs make better purchasing decisions. Product collateral is a critical content type that makes the difference between whether a buyer considers the product or not. Effective product collateral in digital and print formats work together to help consumers easily access information in their preferred style to make an informed decision. CMs will be asked to develop content for three primary types of product collateral – the web page, brochure, and flier – that are most commonly used to promote new products, and each has its own advantages and disadvantages related to length, ease of maintenance, design, and cost. A CM should keep in mind key collateral elements, including whether it is a digital or printed piece and the collateral's purpose, tone, and length. Additionally, the CM can save time and ensure consistency across collateral by repurposing many of the same content elements, such as the value proposition and benefits statements, from one collateral format to another.

CITATIONS

Cespedes, F.V., & Narayandas, D. *Business-to-Business Marketing*. Harvard Business Publishing. December 2019.

Chaffey, D. "Search engine marketing statistics 2022." *Smart Insights*. February 16, 2023. Retrieved from: www.smartinsights.com/search-engine-marketing/search-engine-statistics/

Douglas, L.C. "Marketing features vs. benefits: Learn the difference and then see the difference in your bottom line." *Entrepreneur*. December 1, 2000.

Geier, R., Uslaner, L., & Cooleen, A. "Smart marketing for engineers: 2017 research report." October 30, 2017. Retrieved from: www.slideshare.net/JenniferMayerCorcora/smart-marketing-for-engineers-ieee-globalspec-and-trew-marketing-2017-research-report-81387257

Headley, M. "2022 B2B buying disconnect: The age of the self-serve buyer." *TrustRadius*. June 14, 2022. Retrieved from: www.trustradius.com/vendor-blog/2022-b2b-buying-disconnect-the-age-of-the-self-serve-buyer

Ladd, A. "Developing effective marketing materials: Brochure design." December 2010. Retrieved from: https://utia.tennessee.edu/cpa/wp-content/uploads/sites/106/2020/10/cpa179.pdf

Lefkoff-Hagius, R., & Mason, C.H. "The role of tangible and intangible attributes in similarity and preference judgments." *Association for Consumer Research*. 1990.

No Author. "Digital population July 2022." *Statista Worldwide*. Retrieved from: www.statista.com/statistics/617136/digital-population-worldwide/#:~:text=Global%20internet%20usage&text=The%20global%20internet%20penetration%20rate,highest%20internet%20penetration%20rate%20worldwide

No Author. "Search engine market share worldwide from Dec 2012–Dec 2022." *StatCounter*. February 2023. Retrieved from: https://gs.statcounter.com/search-engine-market-share#monthly-201212-202212

No Author. "What is Squarespace?" *LinkedIn*. Retrieved from: www.linkedin.com/products/squarespace/?trk=products_details_guest_similar_products_section_similar_products_section_product_link_result-card_full-click

Perez Zamora, M. "Marketing communications plan for Jolla Oy." *Theseus*. November 2019. Retrieved from: www.theseus.fi/handle/10024/264415

Roto, V. "Trusted to deliver excellence – trust design in all touchpoints." no date. Retrieved from: https://cups.cs.cmu.edu/soups/2013/trustbusters2013/Trusted_to_Deliver_Excellence_Roto.pdf

CHAPTER 10

Two Common B2B Content Marketing Types: White Papers and Case Studies

LEARNING OBJECTIVES

1. Discover the unique aspects of content for B2B versus B2C audiences and content types that are most valued in B2B markets
2. The purpose of white papers and how to develop three common types
3. The importance of and suggested tactics for repurposing white papers to maximize content marketing reach and ROI
4. The role of customer case studies in the buyer journey and how to effectively develop them.

INTRODUCTION: B2B VS. B2C CONTENT MARKETING

As stated in the Introduction, we wrote this book to help aspiring CMs develop and execute a dynamic, integrated content marketing strategy across B2B and B2C markets. Many of the concepts explained in the text, such as product positioning and segmentation and developing buyer personas, apply across B2B and B2C markets. Moreover, the process marketers follow to create a content marketing plan and the many types of content explained in the chapters of this book are similar across both markets. Any marketer working for any organization can use these concepts to create meaningful connections with current and potential customers.

However, there are distinct challenges CMs in B2B markets in particular face that "are rooted in the nature and needs of [the] customers' buying criteria and purchasing processes, as well as in the impact of B2B marketing choices on business strategy" (Cespedes & Narayandas, 2019). Looking at two simple examples makes this distinction immediately clear:

1. B2B purchases are made for professional business purposes, such as an aerospace manufacturer purchasing a radar system to track weather or emit signals following a crash in water.
2. B2C purchases are made for personal consumption, such as a consumer buying a pair of shoes online or in a store.

DOI: 10.4324/9781003369103-12

For the CM, the difference means creating content to persuade one person to buy your product versus convincing a group of people at a business, each with different needs and buying criteria. It is because the B2B purchase is so much more complex and the role of content marketing so different that we chose to devote an entire chapter to specific B2B content types.

1. B2B purchase decisions are made by multi-person groups, with the typical buying committee consisting of six to ten decision-makers, each engaged with four to five pieces of content (No Author, 2019, Gartner).
2. The cost of B2B purchases can rise to a million- or billion-dollar price.
3. The risk of failure is much greater with B2B purchases, from negatively impacting brand reputation to threatening customer safety. Imagine if a radar system on a plane or an embedded medical device in a person malfunctioned – it could mean life or death.

With an understanding of the unique differences in B2B content marketing, you might wonder why we chose to focus on white papers and case studies. First, we chose them because they are among the content formats used most by B2B marketers. In Figure 10.1, among the content assets B2B marketers used or created most, case studies were used by 61% and e-books/white papers by 56% (Beets et al., 2022). Three of the other content types in the top spots – namely, webinars, short posts, and videos – are covered in other chapters of this book. Second, we chose to focus on the two content types that require more involved writing than short copy types, such as infographics and charts, which involve strong collaboration with designers. However, this content type is a critical one that we encourage the CM to learn.

CONTENT ASSETS B2B MARKETERS CREATED / USED IN LAST 12 MONTHS

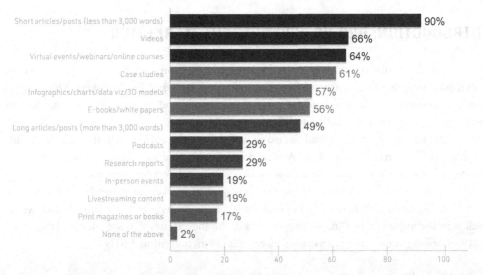

FIGURE 10.1 In the 12th Annual B2B Content Marketing Study, case studies and white papers are among the most used by B2B marketers. Case studies were used by 61% and e-books/white papers by 56%. These content types require more involved writing than infographics or charts, which involve short copy and strong collaboration with designers.

We'll now take a detailed look at both of these important B2B content types in more detail, starting with how to produce successful white papers for B2B purposes.

WHITE PAPERS

History and Purpose of White Papers

The term *white paper* is derived from *white book*, an official government publication with a white cover. The British government introduced white papers in the early 1900s, the most famous example of which was the "Churchill White Paper" in 1922. The purpose of these early white papers was to inform citizens of planned policy and legislation and to solicit opinions before the policies were voted and confirmed (Stelzner, 2006).

This content type gained popularity in B2B marketing in the late 1990s and early 2000s. As a comparison, a Google search for *white papers* would have provided one million hits in 2001; by 2006, that number had soared to 329 million (Stelzner, 2006). In a 2016 study on content preferences, 82% of B2B buyers said white papers were the content type they used most to make decisions (and 79% citing them as content they are most likely to share), followed by 78% for webinars (covered in Chapter 8) and 73% for case studies (covered later in this chapter) (Demand Gen Report, 2016). White papers can demonstrate a company's expertise, establish thought leadership, build trust, and generate demand from potential buyers. Like their intended use, modern white papers educate on a topic rather than overtly market to readers.

This use contrasts with other content types used in B2B marketing, making white papers unique and valuable to an integrated CM strategy. For instance, 88% of surveyed engineers identified value in white papers when researching the latest engineering technologies, industry trends, and products or services (IEEE Global Spec and TREW Marketing, 2021). Further, 76% of B2B buyers will willingly share personal information for access to white papers (Krol, 2017). It's no surprise then that B2B marketing teams use white papers extensively to reach and retain customers. Given their widespread use, STEM professionals and technical communicators can be expected to lead or be involved in the writing of white papers (Willerton, 2013).

The purpose of modern white papers is multifaceted. As stated earlier, the primary purpose is to educate readers, build trust with potential buyers, and generate sales leads (Stelzner, 2006; Willerton, 2007). When compared to other B2B content types, white papers are long form and range from 1,500 to 5,000 words. Due to their length and educational nature, white papers can take weeks and sometimes months to create. Given the demand on resources and time required to create a high-quality white paper, topics are strategically considered and chosen to align with the company's most important technologies and markets.

Subject matter experts (SMEs) are often the attributed authors of white papers because they can best demonstrate expertise on a topic. However, CMs play a leading role in creating white papers because they have the skills to communicate high-tech content in a clear, accessible language. Together, the SME and CM craft a narrative that demonstrates a credible understanding of a topic, cites reliable and accurate data, provides visuals that illustrate fundamental concepts, and incorporates authentic examples to translate abstract notions into concrete ideas.

This rhetorical organization of content presents the company as a trusted expert and ultimately converts prospects into buyers.

White papers also function as a valuable resource for non-buyer stakeholders, including journalists, investors, and employees. They supply new employees or stakeholders less familiar with the topic with information to help them better understand important technologies or concepts. For example, when launching a new product, PR teams will gather information into a media kit for members of the trade media who cover the relevant market space and will include a white paper that, while not specifically addressing the product being launched, touches on related technologies or market dynamics that journalists may find informative in understanding the underlying concept, current state or future projections on the topic or technology, or uses or applications of the product.

DEVELOPING WHITE PAPERS

Because white papers are a privatized content type, researchers find it difficult to access and collect a sizable, authentic sample for analysis. As a result, little evidence-based research on this topic exists. This lack of data creates more ambiguity about the conventions and style of a white paper. In fact, you may work for a company that no longer sees value in this content type for attracting prospects.

Before discussing the essential arguments and recommended structures of white papers, we want to reiterate their purpose: white papers deliver information in ways that establish trust with readers. This information should show that the company cares about its buyers by investing time to educate rather than to push a product. It has been noted that some companies loosely associate a white paper with content that is, in fact, company- or product-centric and promotional in nature (Graham, 2013). This loose attribution may be unintentional, but it still dilutes the intended purpose – and value – of the white paper. For instance, engineers have indicated they will dismiss white papers that are focused more on selling than educating (Willerton, 2008). B2B buyers are becoming more savvy in recognizing content as valuable and trustworthy compared to a straight sales pitch (Demand Gen Report, 2016) and "hate any bait-and-switch games" (Wall & Spinuzzi, 2018). The risk of a white paper being labeled as promotional content is the loss of trust of the potential buyers whose expectations were unmet and a decreased chance they will continue to engage with the company's content.

Structural Elements

Despite the lack of evidence-based research on white papers, data from the studies that have been conducted are insightful and valuable to the content creation process.

In particular, Campbell and Naidoo (2017) analyzed a dataset of high-tech marketing white papers to determine the common rhetorical moves – writing tools – in the content. Think of these rhetorical moves as the structural elements of effective white papers. These arguments can be integrated into any of the three white paper types we discuss later. The specific section in which you incorporate these elements is less important than how you integrate them throughout the white paper to structure your content and appeal to readers. Campbell and Naidoo's research revealed five structural elements they refer to as essential arguments.

1. **Identify a business problem**. Begin your white paper by introducing a specific business problem – a problem that needs solving. This identifies a gap in knowledge that the company has the expertise and credibility to address with its product or service. When establishing the business problem, identify the market drivers for the problem. This establishes urgency and signals to readers that the problem needs a solution *now* and not at a later date. This strategy focuses readers on the importance of solving the problem.

2. **Offer a solution to the problem.** After you have established a complex business problem, present possible solutions. Only present the solution *after* you have identified the problem. This essential argument accounts for the intended purpose of the white paper and the reason readers either continue to read or toss the document in the trash. Stelzner (2006) cautioned against describing the solution in the first few paragraphs (or even the first few pages) of the white paper. Instead, consider a soft-sell marketing approach, such as introducing the solution generically, including the key features of the product or services or describing the business benefits of adopting the product or service.

3. **Issue a call to action**. Even when using a soft-sell marketing approach to educate on a topic, you still want readers to act positively toward the company. Your call to action should be indirect in style and communicate in an informative style (think business proposal rather than sales brochure). For example, restate the market drivers used to describe the business problem or prompt readers to reach out to the sponsoring organization. Again, remember the purpose of the white paper: this essential argument should focus more on presenting information than on marketing to the reader.

4. **Establish the author's credibility**. White papers are valuable to B2B audiences because they appeal to their intellectual curiosity. Overall, the approach you take in delivering information on the topic should establish trust and credibility with readers. Providing information about the author organization and citing informational sources are a more explicit means of establishing credibility.

5. **Provide disclaimers or legal considerations**. Industry experts (Stelzner, 2006) have indicated that many white papers list legal considerations, such as copyright and other restrictions, at the end of the document. The related content does not need to be lengthy or prominent, but you should ensure with your legal department that the language is compliant, and the claims in your white paper protect your company from any legal action.

Three White Paper Types

There are countless recommendations for structuring white papers based on the objective, audience, and topic. For example, some industry experts have identified two unique structures for white papers while others have identified three (e.g., Stelzner, 2006; Graham, 2013). Your company could also have its own preferred structure.

Based on our combined experience in industry and academia, we recommend the following three structures. Even if other structures are preferred, many of the same best practices to approach and execution can be applied to any white paper.

1. Market or technology trends
2. Technology or application primer/explainer
3. Problem-solution

Let's take a deeper dive into each structure using real-world B2B company examples.

Type 1: Market or Technology Trends

Use the trends structure if your primary objective is to present the company as a trusted expert in a key market or to differentiate a company's product from its competitors'.

To strengthen audiences' trust and to create a positive reader experience, your white paper should use a structured approach with a well-branded design that is easy to navigate and read. Consider adding content that supports the text visually, such as graphs, charts, and application photos that further educate and inform the reader about the topic. For a trends white paper, the structure and key components often will include:

- **Cover** – serves to associate the content with the company/sponsor and includes the related logo(s), white paper title, and often a related image or illustration
- **Executive summary, table of contents, and author attribution** – lets the reader know what the white paper is about, what each section covers, and the author's expertise in the field
- **History** – provides background on what led to the trend's rise
- **Key drivers** – explains the current state of the industry, technologies, and/or consumer behaviors that are fueling momentum for the trend
- **Challenges** – discusses difficulties teams face in adapting the trend to their products and services
- **Benefits** – outlines the advantages the trend brings to companies and society at large
- **Adoption** – touches on suggestions and guidance to help the reader consider how to adopt the trend, including help by way of products and services from the company (this is the primary section where promotional information is most effectively included to maintain the reader's trust)
- **Conclusion** – briefly summarizes market conditions driving the trend and challenges readers with the importance of adoption

We model this structure in the white paper in Figures 10.2–10.4, "Autonomous Driving: An Eye on the Road Ahead" from Wind River Systems (an Intel company). As an embedded software company whose products are used in critical infrastructure of planes, automobiles, and manufacturing plants, Wind River has a vested interest in demonstrating a deep understanding of the challenges of its buyers who are designing next-generation machines. In the automotive market, the trend toward cars that drive themselves (autonomous vehicles) poses enormous opportunities, with new applications along with a significant number of threats, such as passenger and pedestrian safety. As Wind River seeks to demonstrate its expertise as a software provider that designers of next-generation autonomous vehicles can trust, the company published an in-depth white paper to explain the technological challenges car manufacturers must address to succeed.

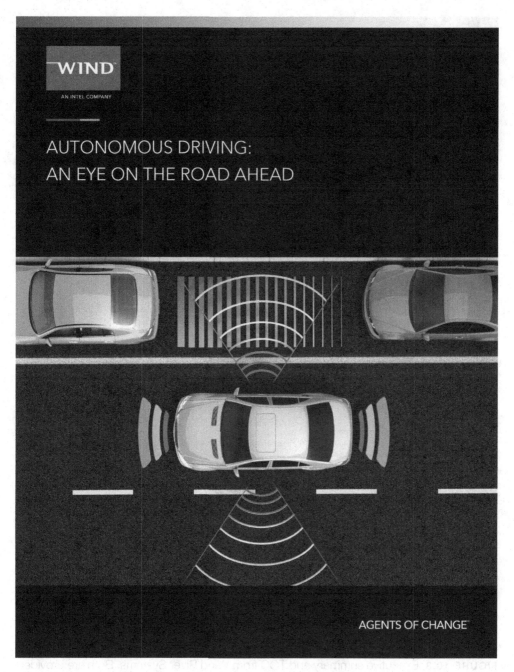

FIGURE 10.2 White paper cover from Wind River Systems. Effective covers should associate the content with the company/sponsor and include the related logo(s), title, and often a related image or illustration.

EXECUTIVE SUMMARY

The day when drivers can completely surrender control of their cars to autonomous driving systems, at any speed, for any distance, on any type of road, could arrive as early as 2020 by some projections. Many hurdles remain to be crossed between now and then: Laws and regulations must be written. Industry standards must be established. Consumers must be educated and persuaded. And marketers, who for decades have built car brands on the thrills of control, handling, and performance, will have to find new buzzwords to define a new driving—or non-driving—experience.

Technological advancement toward autonomous driving, however, is accelerating faster than the legal framework or market forces that will govern it. The hardware footprint required to house complex autonomous systems is shrinking, while processing speeds and capacity are expanding. Advanced driver assistance systems (ADAS) are already a reality, with features like pedestrian detection, adaptive cruise control, collision avoidance, lane correction, and automated parking becoming increasingly commonplace.

Still, the technology behind driverless cars is not without its challenges—increasing complexity, safety, and security chief among them. This white paper will look at the current state of autonomous driving, its various stages, and the key technological challenges car manufacturers must address to get in the game.

TABLE OF CONTENTS

FIGURE 10.3 Executive summary and TOC from Wind River Systems. Both are provided on one page, offering readers a clear snapshot of the white paper's overall objective and organization.

FROM ADAPTIVE CRUISE CONTROL TO FULL AUTOMATION: THE ROADMAP

While serious public discussion and consumer awareness of autonomous driving have increased considerably in just the past few years, automotive engineers and university scientists have been working on it for over a decade. In 2004, the U.S. Defense Advanced Research Projects Agency (DARPA) launched a series of driverless car races that enabled builders to showcase their concepts over long and arduous courses.

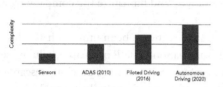

Figure 1: Key development milestones for autonomous driving technology

Over time, the technology that will eventually take autonomous driving mainstream has been continually refined and its footprint reduced, to the point that it has become commercially viable as ADAS deployed in cars on the road today. ADAS include intelligent systems aimed at proactively helping drivers avoid accidents, improve driving efficiency, and reduce driver fatigue. Figure 2 illustrates some of the currently available ADAS functions.

Longitudinal and Lateral Control	Collision Avoidance	Vehicle and Driver Monitoring
Speed control	Rear-end collision avoidance	Tachograph to record speed, distance, and driver activity
Adaptive cruise control	Obstacle and pedestrian detection	Alerting systems
Road and lane departure avoidance	Intersection collision warning	Vehicle diagnostics
Lane change and merge assistance		Driver drowsiness detection
Parking assistance		
Blind spot detection		

Figure 2: Sample ADAS functions

The sensing technologies behind ADAS include laser-based lidar, ultrasonic and motion-based sensing, cameras, and communications between vehicles and from vehicle to the Internet. Data acquired by the sensing systems are then interpreted and cross-analyzed with other pertinent data, resulting in a particular action by one or more of the respective electronic control units (ECUs), as illustrated in Figure 3.

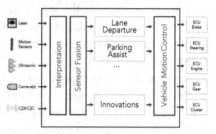

Figure 3: Conceptual design of ADAS systems

In 2013, the U.S. National Highway Transportation Safety Administration (NHTSA) issued its first policy statement on automated vehicles, in which it defined four levels of automation:

Level 1 – Function-specific automation: Specific control functions are automated, such as cruise control, lane guidance, and automated parallel parking. Drivers are fully engaged and responsible for overall vehicle control (hands on the steering wheel and foot on the pedal at all times).

Level 2 – Combined function automation: Multiple and integrated control functions are automated, such as adaptive cruise control with lane centering. Drivers are responsible for monitoring the roadway and are expected to be available for control at all times, but under certain conditions can disengage from vehicle operation (hands off the steering wheel and foot off pedal simultaneously).

Level 3 – Limited self-driving automation: Drivers can cede all safety-critical functions under certain conditions and rely on the vehicle to monitor for changes in those conditions that will require transition back to driver control. Drivers are not expected to constantly monitor the roadway.

FIGURE 10.4 This example white paper uses figures and tables to supplement the text. Consider adding content to your white paper that visually informs the reader about the topic.

This 3,000-word white paper implements the trends structure well. It establishes the reader's expectations for what is covered, providing historical context as well as current analysis; explains the market drivers, challenges, and benefits of the trend; and concludes with recommendations on how the reader can adopt the trend using a soft-sell approach that is key to effective B2B white papers. Visually, the white paper engages its readers with a well-designed cover that includes the company's logo, the title of the white paper, and an illustration of an autonomously driven car using sensor technology to park in between two other cars (see Figure 10.2). The executive summary and table of contents provide a high-level snapshot of what the reader can expect (see Figure 10.3). Missing on this page is information about the author. Often, companies will include this information at the end of the white paper. In this case, no author information is included, but when the author is an experienced and respected SME, adding this information can increase the piece's credibility and humanize the company by putting a face to the information.

The body of the white paper consists of multiple sections, beginning with the history section ("From Adaptive Cruise Control to Full Automation: The Roadmap"), which establishes the topic by outlining the history of autonomous driving, citing previous research on the topic, and acknowledging key technologies that have positively contributed to the autonomous vehicle trend (see Figure 10.4). Effective visual content is used here to support key concepts; the bar chart depicts key development milestones for autonomous driving technology, and technical imagery is shown in a chart that references the conceptual design of technology that is a building block of autonomous driving, referred to as advanced driver-assistance systems (or ADAS).

The white paper uses two sections to explain key drivers of the trend toward autonomous vehicles. The sections "What's Driving It: Safety First" and "The Connected Car: Better Safety Through Situational Analysis" discuss factors such as human error in car accidents, the growing number of cars on the road, and the enablement of vehicle-to-vehicle communication by improved use of sensor technology. In the section "Helping Car Manufacturers Get There," the authors explain the challenges automotive designers face and point to specific technologies to overcome these challenges: namely, the use of two technologies the authors refer to as virtualization technology and partitioning. While it's not important that you understand what these two technologies do, it's helpful to note how the authors kept the tone educational while subtly alluding to these two technologies used in their products. While no Wind River products are mentioned by name, the authors explain application approaches that use key features and technologies included in Wind River products. This approach illustrates the soft-sell call to action that Campbell and Naidoo (2017) found to be an approach engineers prefer (Wall & Spinuzzi, 2018; Willerton, 2008).

Benefits are briefly discussed in the section "Trains, Planes, and Automobiles," with a catchy title from popular culture that alludes to the opportunity automakers have to adopt autonomous technology thanks to industries such as aerospace and rail transportation that have paved the way. In covering the section focused on adoption, the authors here take a more direct promotional tone in the section "The Right Development Partner." It is not atypical for a white paper to end with a more direct appeal to the reader to consider the company's offerings; however, it must be done thoughtfully to be effective. By devoting the majority of the content of the white paper to this point to purely educational purposes, the company has delivered value to the reader and, in turn, developed trust. As long as this more promotional section maintains a tone of trust by focusing on how the company can help the buyer overcome challenges and become competitive using its products and services, it's an acceptable approach. Wind River does this by emphasizing the importance of selecting the right technology partner that is proven in the industry with relevant experience in safety- and security-critical applications and explaining the key technical aspects of its products that make it uniquely suited to address the needs of automotive designers wanting to adopt this trend.

The conclusion section, simply titled "Conclusion," briefly reiterates the growing trend toward autonomous driving and inspires the readers by challenging them to solve the technical hurdles and make this a competitive advantage for them in the markets they serve.

Finally, Wind River includes disclaimers and legal considerations, one of the core elements identified by Campbell and Naidoo (2017). At the end of the white paper, the following language is included: "©2015 Wind River Systems, Inc. The Wind River logo is a trademark of Wind River Systems, Inc., and Wind River and VxWorks are registered trademarks of Wind River Systems, Inc. Rev. 09/2015." As Campbell and Naidoo note, this language does not need to be lengthy.

Type 2: Technology or Application Primer/Explainer

Use a primer or explainer structure if your purpose is to educate readers about a technology or application in which the company has expertise. Using a more instructional tone, the structure of your white paper includes many of the following elements, although not every primer or how-to white paper will follow this approach exactly, and the elements may be located in different areas of the paper.

* **Cover** – serves to associate the content with the company/sponsor and includes the related logo(s), white paper title, and often a related image or illustration
* **Executive summary, table of contents, and author attribution** – lets the reader know what the white paper is about, what each section covers, and the author's expertise in the field
* **Aspect** – provides in-depth explanation of a key feature, technical aspect, or how-to step
* **Aspect 2** – provides in-depth explanation of a key feature, technical aspect, or how-to step
* **Aspect 3** – provides in-depth explanation of a key feature, technical aspect, or how-to step
* **Aspects 4+** – provide in-depth explanation of a key feature, technical aspect, or how-to step
* **Promotional section** – a brief segue into how the company's expertise and technical offerings can assist the reader with the application or technology
* **Conclusion** – briefly summarizes the history of the technology or application, highlights the aspects or how-to steps covered in the main body of the paper, and acknowledges the company's expertise for adoption

We model this structure with the white paper "Medical Grade Wi-Fi" from Silex Technology (Figure 10.5). Silex is a wireless connectivity manufacturer and service provider, and its white paper explains the use of Wi-Fi connectivity technology in medical device applications.

Medical Grade Wi-Fi

The term "Medical Grade Wi-Fi" is widely used but not well defined. It is based on a generally accepted belief that the needs of medical device manufacturers that are implementing Wi-Fi in a hospital environment differ from most other applications.

This white paper provides information on the steps required to successfully evaluate and implement Wi-Fi connectivity for your medical device.

FIGURE 10.5 From the cover, it is immediately clear to the reader that the purpose of this white paper is to serve as a primer/how-to on a specific topic: "This white paper provides information on the steps required to successfully evaluate and implement Wi-Fi connectivity for your medical device." The table of contents further explains the three most important aspects for evaluating and implementing Wi-Fi in medical device application, from understanding connectivity requirements (Part 2) to integrating connectivity into your device (Part 3) and addressing specific application requirements (Part 4). By using a structure of sections, each with visual aids, such as the illustrations and charts the Silex authors use in Exhibit 1: Wi-Fi Band Comparison, this white paper of nearly 3,500 words is easy for the reader to follow and consume.

silex
technology

Table of Contents

FIGURE 10.5 (Continued)

sīlex
technology

2.4 GHz	5 GHz
83 MHz spectrum	550 MHz spectrum (~7X more capacity)
3 non-overlapping channels	Up to 23 non-overlapping channels
More sources of interference (Bluetooth headsets, cordless phones, microwave ovens, other devices)	Fewer incumbent devices creating interference
Support for 802.11b, 802.11g and 802.11g/n devices	Support for 802.11a and 802.11a/n devices

Exhibit 1: Wi-Fi Band Comparison

Access Point Roaming

Radio chipset's built-in roaming is very simplistic and designed primarily for high-volume laptop and cell phone manufacturers. The typical usage scenario is as follows:
- User becomes stationary with device (e.g., conference room with laptop)
- User makes a wireless connection to access point #1
- User moves to another location and again becomes stationary with device (e.g.,
- office with laptop)
- User makes a wireless connection to access point #2

In the above example, the laptop is not being used while in motion. On the other hand, medical devices often transmit critical data such as ECG waveforms while the patient is in transit (e.g., on a gurney). The medical device manufacturer needs a solution that handles access point roaming seamlessly without data loss caused by wireless connectivity problems.

Providing "true" mobile connectivity requires a sophisticated management scheme including these enhancements:
- User configurable handoff threshold
- User configurable multiple SSID list
- Tracking of five or more access points

Silex Technology solutions based on the Qualcomm Atheros AR6003 chipset (with the enhanced Silex Technology driver/supplicant) are validated to roam, on average, in 100 ms or less in an open system environment.

FIGURE 10.5 (Continued)

From the cover, the purpose of the white paper as a how-to piece is immediately clear: "This white paper provides information on the steps required to successfully evaluate and implement Wi-Fi connectivity for your medical device." The Silex team chose to put this information on the cover; others may choose to place this in the table of contents or introductory section. There is no right or wrong place for these elements as long as they are clearly visible in the opening section of your paper.

The table of contents first lists the Executive Summary section and Part 1: Learn Why Wi-Fi is a Mandatory Feature for Portable Medical Devices, serving as an introduction to the use of the technology in this specific application area. The main body of the white paper then includes three main sections devoted to explaining the use of Wi-Fi in medical device applications:

Part 2: Understand Key Medical Device Connectivity Requirements
Part 3: Integrate Wireless Connectivity into Your Device
Part 4: Address Customer-Specific Application Requirements

Notice these sections begin with a command verb (e.g., *understand*, *integrate*), which further fulfills the goal of educating readers. In these three sections, the authors cover in-depth information about each aspect of the use of Wi-Fi in medical device applications, including subtopics such as Dual-Band Support, Low Power Consumption, and Non-Linux/Android RTOS Implementations. By explaining one aspect of the topic at a time, the authors can distill a technical topic into digestible subtopics for the reader to more easily understand. This is often a process that technical communicators can help SMEs accomplish more efficiently. By using a structure of sections, each with visual aids such as illustrations and charts, including the one used in Exhibit 1: Wi-Fi Band Comparison, this white paper, nearly 3,500 words in length, is easy for the reader to follow and consume.

This primer white paper structure is also used for other types of white papers, such as how-to types that describe how to implement or execute a particular process or technology. Unlike in primer white papers, the main body of a how-to white paper is devoted to an in-depth explanation of the critical steps required in the process. By simply laying out and explaining each step in sequential, logical order, an otherwise complex process is broken down into components that are explained one by one.

Type 3: Problem-Solution

Use the problem-solution structure if your purpose is to demonstrate a company's expertise by explaining a problem in the market and then educating the reader on the most effective solutions or explaining how to solve a particular challenge or application. Specifically, companies will use this approach to educate and even persuade buyers that the company understands the technical problems they face and is equipped to create innovative solutions or serve as a trusted advisor to help them overcome these challenges.

The structure of a problem-solution white paper is similar to those of the others in terms of opening and closing, but the body text is dedicated to setting up the problem and then describing the solutions.

- **Cover** – serves to associate the content with the company/sponsor and includes the related logo(s), white paper title, and often a related image or illustration
- **Executive summary and table of contents** – briefly explains what the white paper is about, lists each section
- **Introduction to the problem** – provides background on the problem
- **Challenges** – discusses difficulties the problem poses to technical teams across key application, areas such as slowing time to market, reducing performance capabilities, or increasing costs
- **Shortcomings of existing or previous solutions** – explains how the problem has been addressed by other approaches and why those have fallen short, sets up the next section with the recommended solution
- **Solution** – introduces the solution(s) and explains its advantages with sound data, logic, and relevant examples of its implementation and use
- **Conclusion** – briefly summarizes the problem and the failed or unsatisfactory attempts to solve it, then reinforces why the company's recommended solution(s) is/are the best approach and challenges the reader to rethink alternative solutions

We model this structure with the white paper "Bridging the Gap Between Engineering and Production Through Test Standardization" by G Systems, Inc. (Figure 10.6). G Systems is a test engineering services company in the aerospace and defense industries.

The first paragraph introduces the problem, an essential argument in an effective white paper:

> *"In many companies, there is little to no reuse between the engineering and production test departments. All too often, engineering and production independently create solutions that meet their department's specific needs without communicating with each other, resulting in numerous inefficiencies."*

> (page 3)

In this case, the authors cleverly suggest that an approach the reader may consider a solution – i.e., the ways individual departments solve their own specific needs – may in fact be a problem. This approach, they argue, creates silos within an organization that limit the crosstalk between departments, resulting in no consistent processes for testing production efficiency. Without mentioning it explicitly, the white paper immediately identifies any organization's pain points: the loss of time and money. A problem that exists because of one or both of these barriers makes for an effective white paper topic.

After introducing the problem, the white paper sets out three solutions that are informed by the "decades of experience" of G Systems. This presentation is a subtle, soft-sell marketing approach that builds the company's credibility as an expert on the topic. Rather than declaring "buy our product now," the white paper instead focuses on the longevity and credibility of the G Systems organization. The authors establish their company's credibility – an essential argument in an effective B2B white paper – by stating on page four in the text,

> *"This white paper pulls from G Systems' decades of experience in assisting companies with test standardization planning and execution to outline a few different methods for implementing test standardization and how your organization can approach the process in a manageable way."*

TABLE OF CONTENTS

INTRODUCTION

Most companies know that using identical test equipment and methodologies in their engineering and production test departments improves overall efficiency. However, many companies shy away from test standardization practices due to the issues created by departmental "silos."

These silos typically mean there are differing test requirements and goals between departments, resulting in huge efforts needed to gain the multidepartment consensus necessary to make changes. But, change may be easier than you think. This whitepaper outlines a few practical methods for implementing test standardization and how your organization can approach the process in a manageable way.

FIGURE 10.6 The white paper identifies three possible ways for customers to implement standardization solutions informed by the collective expertise of the G Systems team. By setting up the problem and recommending three specific solutions – software test standardization, test hardware and instrumentation standardization, and data sharing and storage standardization – they demonstrate their knowledge and expertise and, in doing so, build trust with the prospective buyer.

In many companies, there is little to no reuse between the engineering and production test departments. All too often, engineering and production independently create solutions that meet their department's specific needs without communicating with each other, resulting in numerous inefficiencies.

While top-level management usually recognizes the benefits test standardization can bring, they are often looking for a magic, and impossible to create, system that can perform every possible engineering and production test. This usually leaves mid-level management stuck with the difficult task of managing both up and down to implement a level of test standardization that meets the business goals of top management, but is also a workable solution for the engineering and production teams who are often hesitant to standardize on a system that is not their own. Sound familiar? You're not alone.

Overall, most organizations understand that not reusing equipment or tests interdepartmentally and creating similar tools and tests instead is usually highly inefficient. Most companies also know that, in theory, test standardization is a good idea. However, in practice, it's not always easy to implement.

> Not reusing equipment or tests interdepartmentally and creating similar tools instead is highly inefficient.

gsystems.com | 3

FIGURE 10.6 (Continued)

Beyond departmental "silo" mentalities, companies often get hung up on the logistics and potential costs of standardization, especially when department budgets are fragmented and funded separately. **Yet the following benefits can far outweigh the costs and hassle of** implementing a standardized test solution:

- Test results in the same format as you move from engineering to production
- Hardware, software, and database reusability
- Cost and time savings

This whitepaper pulls from G Systems' decades of experience in assisting companies with test standardization planning and execution to outline a few different methods for implementing test standardization and how your organization can approach the process in a manageable way.

DETERMINING HOW TEST STANDARDIZATIONS CAN HAVE THE GREATEST IMPACT

Test standardization doesn't always mean an expensive overhaul of your entire engineering and production test operations. Instead, a more manageable approach to test standardization is to look at the three major components of your test systems—software, hardware, and data management—to determine where the largest **potential benefits exist from standardization within your organization.** Standardization in just one of these areas can have enormous time **and cost benefits.**

Let's take a deeper look at the various options for standardization across these three components of your test systems.

SOFTWARE TEST STANDARDIZATION

When it comes to software test standardization, in a perfect world, all engineers in both the engineering and production departments would agree on a single development tool to use. Not only does this bring consistency in the development environment, but it can also help unify the amount of software needed to perform multiple operations.

For example, one G Systems' customer standardized on NI LabVIEW software because they could easily perform control, data acquisition, and vibration analysis all with the same software tool. But, getting a quick agreement on a single development platform isn't always a likely scenario.

> Test standardization doesn't always mean an expensive overhaul of your entire engineering and production test operations

FIGURE 10.6 (Continued)

The body of a problem-solution white paper further addresses the challenges, shortcomings, and proposed solutions to the defined problem. In the G Systems white paper, the body then expands on the three solutions to the test standardization problem – software, hardware, and data management – and discusses each independently in its own subsection. Independently describing each solution accomplishes two primary tasks:

1. It distills highly technical language into digestible bits. Even for trained engineers, this organization improves the overall readability and comprehension of the information.
2. It implicitly offers three discrete solutions to the problem rather than one giant "package deal" that buyers need. This implies that buyers have choices and can customize the solutions based on their specific needs.

Identifying which problems to emphasize in your white paper means understanding the challenges customers face with their existing solutions, business practices, or methodologies and the negative aspects of these solutions. Often, this data comes from lessons during the first stage of the new product development process (discussed in Chapter 2), when companies identify new product ideas, and marketing and sales departments conduct a business analysis of customer needs and competing products available on the market. This data is a treasure trove for CMs to use for problem-solution ideas that can be turned into valuable white papers to create and promote as part of the launch of a new product. Other times, data comes from hands-on experience working with customers, observing the challenges they face, and drawing on the company's expertise to explain how to solve them. Your marketing team and in-house SMEs can help you brainstorm and develop a white paper that solves a problem your customer base faces.

DEVELOPMENT PROCESS AND ROLES

Given the length, informational tone, density of content, and high quality of writing expected in a white paper, CMs should collaborate with SMEs early and often throughout the development process. Often, the CM will lead the effort of white paper content creation and even serve as a ghostwriter for the SME, who ultimately is attributed as the author. The first step in creating a white paper is developing the project elements, including the following:

- **Technical topic** – What is the subject matter the white paper aims to educate the reader about?
- **Objective** – How does the paper strengthen the company's brand position as a trusted expert?
- **Audience** – Who are the primary readers of the white paper? (Reference your buyer personas.)
- **Working title(s)** – These may change through the writing process.
- **Author(s)** – The subject matter expert is attributed as public author of the paper (even though a technical communicator is often heavily involved in or even ghostwrites the paper).
- **Estimated word count** – Typically ranges from 1,500–3,000 or more words.

- **Timeline** – From project kickoff, through writing and review, to design and publication, with reviewer(s) and final approver(s) named.
- **Abstract** – This is a 150-word paragraph that serves as an abbreviated executive summary of the topic, its importance to the reader, and the objective of the paper.
- **Outline** – This details the flow, from executive summary through the body to the conclusion, with supporting points; key technical details; and other supporting content, including images, data, customer references, etc.

Developing the Core Elements During a Project Kickoff Meeting

The CM meets with the SME(s) to discuss and agree on the core elements of a white paper. This discussion is often in the form of a project kickoff meeting, which can last two or more hours and usually includes the writer as well as the manager, the SME(s), and the product marketing manager(s) or other person(s) who serves as mentor(s) to the SME throughout the project from a technical, competitive, and customer-minded perspective.

Several of the core elements to be agreed on during project kickoff require research, brainstorming, and group input to ensure the greatest accuracy and thoroughness. For instance, some in the meeting may disagree at the outset about who the primary and secondary audiences for the white paper are, or it may take time to think through the outline and agree on the flow and key supporting elements. However, this time spent up front is well worth it to discuss and reconcile differences so the team aligns on the core elements moving forward.

The Leadership Role of the CM

Prior to the kickoff meeting, depending on previous white paper writing experience and knowledge of the company and its products and technologies, ideally, the CM drafts some or all of the core elements, which are presented to the project team during kickoff. This not only increases efficiency in the kickoff meeting but can also elevate the value of the CM as someone who is prepared and knowledgeable about the subject matter. To lead in this way – with prepared drafts and serving as facilitator during the meeting – requires experience, confidence, and strong interpersonal skills. These qualities are critical to your CM career and becoming a respected leader; moreover, possessing these content marketing and leadership qualities often leads CMs to be given greater responsibility, promotion to higher levels of management, and increased compensation.

Your leadership role as CM before and during the project kickoff meeting is to:

- Schedule the meeting
- Set the agenda and share with the team ahead of time
- Facilitate discussion throughout
- Document what was agreed on
- Monitor discussion time to ensure core elements are all defined and the meeting ends on time

If all core elements are not agreed on before the kickoff meeting ends, or there is an impasse on any of the core elements, the CM schedules a follow-up meeting with the relevant people to discuss and reach agreement on all the core elements.

The Writing and Review Process

Once the core elements are defined, the writing can begin. Writing a white paper can take several weeks or even months to complete, and the timeline defined during project kickoff serves as a valuable reference to keep the team on track. Additionally, other teams in product marketing and marcom are affected by the timeline as they may be depending on the white paper to use in their campaign, product launch, or lead generation plans, so it's important the white paper project adheres to the agreed-upon timeline. Using the outline as a guide, the CM follows an iterative draft and review process to create the white paper.

Draft and Review #1

The CM develops a first full draft of the white paper. In this draft, visual content may be included, or there may simply be reference to visual content that will be added in the second draft. Once the first full draft is completed, it goes into the first round of review. During project kickoff, as part of defining the timeline, the team should agree on who will serve as reviewers at each stage of development. There are usually three rounds of review of the white paper, and each should include input and commentary from both the SME and content editor(s).

The CM may consult individual reviewers to discuss their input and get clarification as needed on any comments or edits. In some instances, if there is conflicting feedback from reviewers, the CM may call a group meeting to reconcile contradicting edits and agree as a group on corrective actions. The first round of review may take one to three weeks, based on reviewer availability, the length of the content, and the amount of input.

Draft and Review #2

The CM next creates a second draft, incorporating reviewer edits and referencing their compiled feedback to strengthen the next version of the white paper. In this second draft, all visual content elements as well as associated text, such as image captions, titles, and labels, should be added. Often, creating the visual content elements requires assistance from graphic designers or even R&D teams, who may be asked to provide technical data, such as supporting functional or operational charts or graphs. The CM is responsible for ensuring these related content pieces are completed on time so they can be included in the second draft and not delay the white paper.

With all text and visual elements included, the second draft of the white paper is complete and ready for the second round of review. The same approach to review is followed for the second review as was followed in the first round, with the CM giving one to two weeks for a thorough review and to reconcile any conflicting feedback.

Draft and Review #3

The third draft of the white paper should be considered final from a technical and content perspective and ready to move to the third round of review. There are two objectives for the third round of review:

1. Editing followed by layout
2. Designing the white paper

For the first editing step, a professional editor is brought into the process to check for spelling and grammatical accuracy. This could be the original CM, someone else from the content team, or an independent editor hired for this specific purpose. Once all editing errors are corrected, the white paper moves into the second step of design, which requires a professional graphic designer. The design should match the tone of the content piece and use colors from the brand style guide to direct the reader through the paper. The area of the white paper where more creativity and bursts of color are commonly used is on the cover, where graphic elements such as illustrations and photography can help set a professional tone and draw the reader in with visual appeal. For companies that have an existing library of white papers, the design should follow a template so each matches the look and feel of other white papers the company has published. If the company does not have a template and this is the first white paper the company has produced, this design should serve as the template for other white papers that follow.

Once the white paper is fully designed, it is ready for a final review. In this review, only minor text edits are made, and the focus is on finalizing the design. Finally, the white paper can be published, marketed, and repurposed.

MARKETING AND REPURPOSING WHITE PAPERS

Because B2B audiences value white papers, marketing teams rely on them as a critical mechanism to drive website traffic, build trust, and generate leads. For this reason, white papers serve as a core content piece for major marketing initiatives, such as marcom campaigns and product launches. White papers are marketed and repurposed in a variety of ways, such as those described in Chapter 4, including:

* Part of a media kit prepared and distributed to trade editors for a product launch
* A call to action on relevant product web pages
* A blog series in which sections of the white paper are turned into separate blog posts that inspire readers to download the entire white paper
* A call to action in email marketing used by sales or event follow-up
* A call to action for advertisements from print to digital and search
* Used as a basis for a webinar on the same topic
* Used as source material for a video script

When repurposed into other formats, such as webinars or blog posts, these new content pieces can, in turn, be marketed in the same channels.

White papers can have a long shelf life, often serving as a critical content marketing piece for two or more years and, even then, often require only minor updating to extend their life several more years. Additionally, as the popularity of a white paper and all its derivative content forms grows, its related web pages can rise in search ranking and, as a result, grow as a leading source of organic traffic to the company's website.

Among the many types of content CMs create to build trust and generate interest in their brands, white papers are among the most valued by B2B audiences, given their in-depth and educational approach. Because white papers are considered long-copy content, with lengths ranging from 2,000 to 5,000 words or more and reader expectations for high quality and a non-promotional tone, this content type requires a great deal of time and project organization to effectively develop. It is for these reasons that many companies fall short of producing high-quality white papers and why the role of the CM is so valuable in taking on the lion's share of the writing and project management from the subject matter expert. In this way, the SME can provide the needed technical guidance and input while not being burdened with the time required to organize, outline, write, and launch the white paper. By leading white paper projects, CMs have the opportunity to build needed organizational and leadership skills that, in turn, can lead to greater responsibility, promotion, and an increase in compensation.

AN INTRODUCTION TO CASE STUDIES AND THEIR ROLE IN THE BUYER JOURNEY

As far back as the 1800s, case studies were established ways to showcase knowledge in a tangible and applied circumstance (Joseph, 2019). The opportunity for a CM is to reduce prospective buyers' fear or hesitation in their purchase consideration by demonstrating that others have had a successful experience. This is done by telling success stories of your existing customers and humanizing the experience with your product and company. The idea of humanizing relief, gratitude, security, and joy morphs products into connected protagonists that empower people to be the hero of their story.

Buyers don't want to just take your word for it – they want to hear how others have benefited from using your products and services. Seeing examples of pain points alleviated, stresses reduced, and milestones achieved serves to connect emotional satisfaction with a brand's product or service. That connection often sparks further conversation and engagement. Case studies not only improve the sales process by reducing perceived risk but also allow customers to help tell your story (Geier, 2016).

The use of online reviews demonstrates the growing expectation buyers have of accessing the opinions of others who have used the product or service. For instance, the research team at Statistica found that US digital shoppers in the 18-to-24 age group expected more than 200 reviews per product, and the average number of expected reviews across all ages was 112 (Chevalier, 2022).

In an analysis of more than 300 case studies over ten years, researchers found "great differences in the structure division and the integrity of different divisions of case studies" (Wang et al., 2022). Where they did find consensus was in the profound impact case studies had on managers and practitioners making strategic decisions.

Effective case studies showcase customer success stories and build on the concept of third-party validation. When case studies offer primary sources and ways for consumers to find those sources, they empower the reader to fact-check. This transparency helps validate the case study's claims (Hammill, 2021). Just as a journalist works to tell a story for readers, CMs must put on their journalism hats to tell informative and relevant customer success stories that align with the marcom and content marketing plan while making the customer the hero of the story.

DEVELOPING A CUSTOMER CASE STUDY

At its core, a customer case study is a story about your customer's success with the intent of building trust with your target audience. Therein lies a key challenge for the CM tasked with writing a case study – how do you tell a story about a customer's success while subtly proving that your product provided value and was instrumental in the achievement?

The answer lies in three fundamental best practices for the CM to follow:

1. Adhere to proven storytelling best practices described in Chapter 5: namely, following the three-act arc structure and incorporating ethos, pathos, and logos.
2. Be curious to understand the challenge your customer faced and what the impact of not solving the challenge would have meant personally and to the business.
3. Keep your reader in mind by creating a story that is, first and foremost, helpful.

With these three tenets of effective case study writing, here are four steps to follow to secure and effectively develop and market your customer case studies (Geier, 2016).

1. Focus on quality over quantity.

Developing case studies can be a significant time investment – for you and your customers. The first step is working with sales and customer success teams to identify potential customers who have had a positive experience and are likely to want to advocate for your company and product. Once a list of customers has been developed internally, it takes time to make contact with a customer and go through the process of securing an agreement to the project.

Once a customer agrees, weeks and sometimes months are required to collaborate with them to develop the case study, conduct reviews, and obtain approval, which may involve the customer's legal or PR teams.

With this time investment, one CM may only have the capacity to write a few case studies in a year. Therefore, prioritize those case studies that will have the biggest influence on your target audience. The criteria for prioritization varies by company and may include the familiarity with the customer's brand (if it's a well-known, respected company), industry, use of specific products or services, application, or geography.

2. Take the lead on writing to make it easy on your customer and to control the story.

To save your customer time, and to control the narrative of the story, the CM should draft the case study based on internal research and at least one in-depth interview with the customer. Case studies also allow a CM and potential buyer to have an open-ended conversation about how the case study might apply to a specific buyer situation. Questions to ask during a customer interview can include the following:

- How would you describe your application or project?
- What problem were you trying to solve?
- Why was this important for you and your company to solve?

- What were alternative solutions you considered or even tried? Why did you choose our company/product over these alternatives to solve this challenge?
- Using our products or services, what are you able to do that you could not do before?
- What was the process of using the product, including the training and support you received?
- What are the primary benefits you have realized from using our product in this application?
- How has this success impacted you in your job (saved me time, allowed me to be more creative, etc.)?
- Can you quantify the time or cost savings you and your company are realizing as a result of this success?

Combine information gathered during your customer interview (or email questionnaire) with input from your peers in sales and customer success to get a full picture of the customer challenge and product value. You then have the information you need to create a draft of the case study for internal review. While a case study can vary in length, most are fewer than 1,000 words total and follow a straightforward structure that makes it easy for the reader to follow and find relevant information including:

- The customer: Introduce the company, the markets it serves, and the team or individual customer who is the main character of the story.
- The challenge: Describe the problem the customer was trying to solve and why it was important to solve it.
- The current situation: Explain how the customer was trying to solve the problem using existing tools or approaches and why they fell short.
- The results: What was the customer able to achieve with your product? (Include specific quantitative data.)
- The visual proof: Include real-world application photos of your customer using the product as well as compelling charts or graphs to visually communicate ROI.

With feedback from relevant internal reviewers, you can then share a draft with the customer that can be modified as needed. Most of the time, assuming your draft is accurate and PR and legal teams don't hold things up, the customer will approve your draft with few, if any, changes.

3.   Keep it simple and visual.

Create a case study that is easy to read and provides your audience with relevant and specific information. You have only a few moments to catch your prospective customer's attention, so the case study needs to be immediately interesting and informative with a strong benefits-oriented headline, relevant application and product imagery, a simple and clear opening and closing, content relevant to the reader, and clear calls to action.

To add further visual appeal, content elements, such as key results, customer quotes, and process diagrams, can be showcased in separate call-out boxes for quick scanning and to give prominence to important messages.

Securing approval for a case study can take time, from convincing customers to take time away from their priorities to review your content to more complicated approval processes at larger corporations, requiring involvement from PR and/or legal teams. One way content marketing teams can streamline this process is by working with sales and operations teams in advance to include a public case study in the purchase contract. When the case study and other promotional activities are contractually included in the purchase agreement, when the time is appropriate to work on the case study (i.e., when the product is implemented, and the customer is confident in success with the finished project), customers are not surprised at the request and often even look forward to sharing the success. This also unblocks any barriers created by PR or legal teams as they are contractually obligated to promote their success. A great time to consider this contractual addition is near the time of purchase when your customer may be asking for additions to the contract, such as training, discounts, or support. Decide what you're willing to give on price or margin in return for the completed case study and then write it into the contract so what both parties agreed to give the other is clearly documented.

4. **Market your case study.**

Once you have an approved case study with a strong, benefits-oriented headline; compelling images; and a simple, clear story that is targeted and easy to read, it's time to do the marketing. Showcase the customer's success on relevant web pages, such as ones in the industry your customer is working in and the related product web page; incorporate it into one of your marcom campaigns; and repurpose the case study into new content types. For instance, find out if the customer would be willing to do a webinar with a company SME and use the case study as a guide for slide creation. (See Chapter 8 for webinar development.) You can also create a short video that tells the customer's story using imagery from the case study along with footage of the product in action.

Just as with white papers, case studies are time-intensive content pieces, so take advantage of the work you've done to develop and secure an approved, published story and repurpose it into other formats to maximize the investment.

TWO REAL-WORLD EXAMPLES

As mentioned, there is no one way to create a case study. Let's look at two examples – one with more traditional storytelling and diverse use of copy, imagery, iconography, and data and another that is light on words and heavy on demonstrated ROI.

In the customer case study for JOTA Sport, one of the most experienced and successful sports car teams based in England, the CM team at Monolith aimed to celebrate success in the most competitive car race in the world, Le Mans. The team chose to focus on JOTA as it showcased the use of its AI software in the automotive market, a target segment in which the company aims to grow (Figure 10.7).

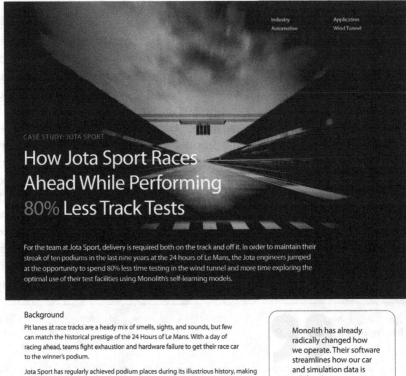

Industry
Automotive

Application
Wind Tunnel

CASE STUDY: JOTA SPORT

How Jota Sport Races Ahead While Performing 80% Less Track Tests

For the team at Jota Sport, delivery is required both on the track and off it. In order to maintain their streak of ten podiums in the last nine years at the 24 hours of Le Mans, the Jota engineers jumped at the opportunity to spend 80% less time testing in the wind tunnel and more time exploring the optimal use of their test facilities using Monolith's self-learning models.

Background

Pit lanes at race tracks are a heady mix of smells, sights, and sounds, but few can match the historical prestige of the 24 Hours of Le Mans. With a day of racing ahead, teams fight exhaustion and hardware failure to get their race car to the winner's podium.

Jota Sport has regularly achieved podium places during its illustrious history, making it one of the event's most experienced and successful sports car teams. While part of their winning streak depends on the driver, the rest relies on the ability of the team to regularly squeeze out 1/10th of a second improvements with each iteration in configuration. Until recently, this meant evaluating masses of data from the wind tunnel tests and coupling this with a healthy portion of intuition to select the right tuning choices.

But now they adopted a completely different approach using Monolith.

> Monolith has already radically changed how we operate. Their software streamlines how our car and simulation data is validated.
>
> Tomoki Takahashi
> Technical Director at Jota Sport

Read Full Case Study

TEST LESS			LEARN MORE		
Track Testing	Data Exploration	Time	Configuration	AI Recommendation	Faster
Reduced by 80%	More clarity in results	Implement changes faster	Optimal use of test facilities	Less intuition, more facts	Avoid tedious, repetitive tasks

FIGURE 10.7 In the customer case study for JOTA Sport, the CM team at Monolith celebrates the client's success in the most competitive car race in the world, Le Mans, while demonstrating how its product was successfully used in the target automotive segment. Reading the headline, the reader is immediately introduced to the hero of the story – the race car team – rather than the company's AI software product. The case study includes a variety of content elements, including three short paragraphs describing the challenge and background of the story, a quote from the customer's technical leader pulled out in a separate box, call-to-action button to read the full case study, and an offset area at the bottom with iconography and brief text, to showcase the results the customer realized.

The case study begins with a headline emphasizing the result the race team achieved, using creative wording that ties into the topic of car racing: "How Jota Sport Races Ahead While Performing 80% Less Track Tests." Reading this headline, the reader is immediately introduced to the hero of the story – the race car team – rather than the company's AI software product.

The case study includes a variety of content elements, including three short paragraphs describing the challenge and background of the story, a quote from the customer's technical leader pulled out in a separate box, a call to action to read the full case study, and an offset area at the bottom with iconography and brief text to showcase the results the customer realized.

By telling the JOTA customer story, the CM team demonstrates how the product was successfully used in a rigorous automotive application, with the aim of building trust with prospective buyers in this target segment as well as similar buyers in adjacent segments who may find the information relevant and credible.

By keeping the story brief and demonstrating success through quotes, data, and brief paragraphs, the case study gives the reader enough information to decide to click on the call-to-action button to read the full case study. When the reader clicks in to read, the CM team uses lengthier text to explain in more detail the challenges the JOTA team faced; what the impact of solving the problem meant in terms of saving track test time and cost; and ultimately how, by using the company's software, the racing team became more successful.

A second example that focuses more on demonstrated ROI is Bevel PR, one of the fastest-growing strategic communication firms in the United States, which recently expanded its global operations to London (Figures 10.8 and 10.9). Here, the case study takes a more data-driven

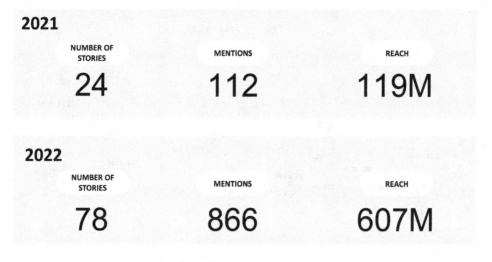

Balance Coverage Highlights

2021

NUMBER OF STORIES	MENTIONS	REACH
24	112	119M

2022

NUMBER OF STORIES	MENTIONS	REACH
78	866	607M

5 PRIVATE AND CONFIDENTIAL

beVel

FIGURE 10.8 Bevel PR case studies aim to show a tangible increase in content consumption from year to year.

approach and emphasizes the success the client had working with the firm over time. For Bevel, which provides communications services for industries including fintech, cybersecurity, and healthcare, publishing case studies of work with existing clients allows prospective buyers to get a behind-the-scenes view of the creative and research processes. More than explaining a client's problem and situation, the case study allows the company to demonstrate how its team thinks and works creatively to deliver value to clients.

Many times, a potential buyer will want to see not just one project success but a return on investment in the product or service over time. In this case, the focus on the story emphasizes the customer's longevity with the company, integrating the success of one or multiple projects to demonstrate a long-term client's success story. In this way, the case study is not about an outlier of a brand's best day on one project but a logical link between a situation with measured results and value over time.

Bevel case studies highlight year-over-year growth and also showcase key events on the brand's calendar. In Figure 10.8, for example, the case study highlights an increase in earned media for the client from 2021 to 2022 as a result of the firm's strategic communication efforts. Figure 10.9 then connects key times of the client's year with an increase in earned media coverage. By showcasing data and time comparisons, Bevel highlights the power of earned media connections in the tech and startup community, a key selling point for prospective buyers of its services.

2022: Balance's Estimated Media Reach

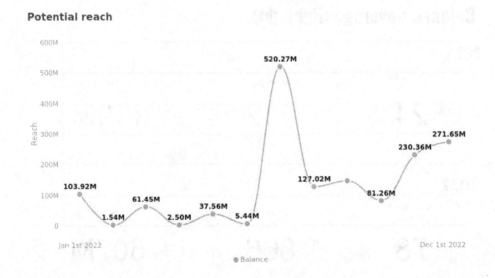

FIGURE 10.9 Bevel PR case studies often showcase key times of year and an uptick in earned media publicity resulting from the firm's work. This promotion allows case studies to appeal to people who prefer data-intensive stories.

Metrics help quantify results and are certainly critical to a successful case study, but those numbers and percentage elements are not the only way to validate a case study's success.

Case Studies and Diversity

Case studies also are valuable in showcasing diversity and localizing a brand offering to potential buyers. Ricardo Fontes and Carlos Melo (2020) discussed the importance of a "territorial brand" in making products feel local, even if they aren't. Case studies offer a chance to find local "brand ambassadors" who can validate a product to specific audiences that may otherwise be difficult if not impossible to reach.

Marketing strategies adopted in many territories do not take into consideration the intangible dimension related to local communities, their history, culture and values. By ignoring a driving force of regional identity, such strategies do not value a major source of differentiation. In fact, in a time where the immaterial and relational capital assumes a key role, locals are not only one of the most essential elements for the attractiveness of touristic destinations but also a key for their differentiation when compared to other alternatives.

CONCLUSION

Content marketing in B2B markets requires creating content to persuade a group of people at a business, each with different needs and buying criteria. Given that the B2B purchase is so complex and the role of content marketing so different, this chapter focuses on educating the CM on how to develop two of the most valued B2B content types – white papers and case studies. The primary purpose of white papers is to educate readers, build trust with potential buyers, and generate sales leads, but they can also serve as valuable resources for non-buyer stakeholders, including journalists, investors, and employees. White papers require extensive research, multiple written drafts and reviews, and collaboration with subject matter experts. Once complete and approved, white papers can be repurposed into a myriad of other content types, including blog posts, webinars, and videos, and further promoted and leveraged on social, earned, and paid channels. While the primary purpose of white papers is to educate prospective buyers and establish the company as an expert in a specific area, customer case studies' main objective is to demonstrate customer trust in the company to reduce a prospective buyer's perceived risk to purchase. To effectively educate and build trust with prospective buyers, white papers and case studies are key elements of a successful B2B content marketing plan.

CITATIONS

Beets, L.M., Handley, A., & Stahl, S., et al. "12th Annual B2B content marketing: Benchmarks, budgets and trends. 2022." *Content Marketing Institute.* 2022. Retrieved from: https://contentmarketingins titute.com/wp-content/uploads/2021/10/B2B_2022_Research.pdf

Campbell, K.S., & Naidoo, J.S. "Rhetorical move structure in high-tech marketing white papers." *Journal of Business and Technical Communication.* 2017.

Cespedes, F.V., & Narayandas, D. *Business-to-Business Marketing.* Harvard Business Publishing. December 2019.

Chevalier, S. "How many reviews do you expect when looking at a product online?" *Statistica.* May 4, 2022. Retrieved from: www.statista.com/statistics/1019495/online-shoppers-expectations-product-reviews-in-the-us/

Fontes, R., & Melo, C. "People: The most important marketing asset of territories." *Journal of Marketing Research and Case Studies.* 2020.

Geier, R. *Smart Marketing for Engineers: An Inbound Marketing Guide to Reaching Technical Audiences.* Rockbench. January 2016.

Graham, G. *White Papers for Dummies.* For Dummies. April 8, 2013.

Hammill, A. "Representing without misrepresenting: The ethics of case study writing." *Teaching Geography.* 2021.

Joseph, A.R., & Hall, J.W. "Guidelines for writing an audiology case study." *The Hearing Journal.* September 2019.

Krol, C. "2017 Content preferences survey report." *DemandGen.* 2017. Retrieved from http://e61c88871f1f-baa6388d-c1e3bb10b0333d7ff7aa972d61f8c669.r29.cf1.rackcdn.com/DGR_DG056_SURV_ContentPref_March_2017_Final.pdf

No Author. "2021 State of marketing to engineers: The COVID-19 impact." *IEEE GlobalSpec and TREW Marketing.* 2021. Retrieved from: www.trewmarketing.com/resources/2021-research-report

No Author. "2016 Content Preferences Survey Report: B2B Buyers Value Trustworthy Content with Data and Analysis." Demand Gen Report. 2016. Retrieved from: https://www.demandgenreport.com/resources/research/2016-content-preferences-survey-b2b-buyers-value-content-that-offers-data-and-analysis

No Author. "The B2B buying journey." *Gartner.* 2019. Retrieved from: www.gartner.com/en/sales/insights/b2b-buying-journey

Stelzner, M.A. "Writing white papers: How to capture readers and keep them engaged." *WhitePaperSource Publishing.* October 1, 2006.

Wall, A., & Spinuzzi, C. "The art of selling-without-selling: Understanding the genre ecologies of content marketing." *Technical Communication Quarterly.* 2018.

Wang, J., Zhang, L., Lin, K.Y., & Feng, L. "The quality of case studies on new product development: State of the art and future prospects." *Journal of Business & Industrial Marketing.* 2022.

Willerton, R. "Writing white papers in high-tech industries: Perspectives from the field." *Technical Communication.* 2007.

Willerton, R. "Proceeding with caution: A case study of engineering professionals reading white papers." *Technical Communication.* 2008.

Willerton, R. "Teaching white papers through client projects." *Business Communication Quarterly.* 2013.

Content Marketing Measurement, the Role of AI, and Career Outlook

11

Measurement and Evaluation in Content Marketing

INTRODUCTION

W. Edwards Deming, the guru of process improvement and quality management, never heard of content marketing, but one of his most famous quotes should encourage any CMs to think about their work differently.

> IN GOD WE TRUST.
> **ALL OTHERS MUST BRING DATA.**
> -W. EDWARDS DEMING

FIGURE 11.1 This famous quote from W. Edwards Deming, the guru of process improvement and quality management, should encourage CMs to think about their work differently and ensure data is a critical component of their content measurement and evaluation.

DOI: 10.4324/9781003369103-14

Maybe that's a bit intense, but there are people who view Deming's vision as business gospel. Any CMs who want to get a program off the ground, have impact, and grow their career should determine how to measure their work.

It's easy to say, but doing this is difficult, and, as a result, it's one of the weaker areas of strategic communication. CMs who do it well can write their professional ticket. Those who can't may do great work but get fired because they can't align their work and ROI with the firm's or client's goals and measurement structure.

In his book *Engage*, referring to social media, Brian Solis stated, "Engagement without analysis is akin to driving aimlessly, without direction or purpose" (Solis, 2011). A measurement journey should align with quality content marketing, but there are also added measurement elements that connect with media relations, advertising, digital strategy, and the larger business.

This chapter describes the common metrics in a content marketing measurement system that you can use to create a customized template, taking into account factors such as business maturity, size, and industry. This chapter will offer best practices and proven tactics to consider when setting up and maintaining a measurement environment. After reading this, CMs should be able to determine, with their teams and clients, what winning and losing in a content marketing program look like. This way, they create strategic alignment and accountability and are set up for success in producing on-message, high-quality content developed with clear purpose and expected outcomes in mind.

Sometimes the best place to start deciding what to do is to make clear what not to do.

WAYS NOT TO MEASURE

It takes just a few seconds of searching YouTube to find funny animal videos. When there are young kids watching, hilarity quickly reigns as a young dog discovers she has a tail. The chase is on . . . and on . . . and on . . .

Videos of animals chasing their tails are funny. For businesses and non-profits, chasing a proverbial tail because of a lack of poor alignment and measurement can lead to inefficiency, loss of revenue, and even closure. Selecting the most effective metrics to measure CM success is key to ensuring you and your team don't end up chasing your tails or simply not providing useful insight.

- **Views**: This is the total number of visits to a website. It's easy for a user to view a website and never engage with any of its elements.
- **Followers**: It's easy for any human (and many bots) to follow a brand online and never consume or engage with any content.
- **Sales**: A CM can accurately inform potential buyers, but the product may not be the right fit for a potential buyer. The product may also malfunction or not deliver as promised.
- **Sizzle**: A CM may hear people in other departments use a word like this to explain marketing measurement. Unfortunately, there's no accurate way to define what this is and how it would apply to marketing. The same holds true for terms such as *viral* and *buzz*.

Before figuring out what to measure, let's eliminate things that are impossible to measure.

Viral isn't a goal.
Sizzle isn't a goal.
Viral sizzle isn't a goal.
Sizzling viral isn't a goal.

At WEWS, the ABC affiliate in Cleveland, Digital Director Joe Donatelli teaches his team to define the goal and work backward. His guidance is rooted in a quote from K.D. Paine, who said, "The importance of social media is what happens because of it."

What a CM should know: Viral isn't a strategy.

MEASURING IMPACT VS. OUTPUT

The New York Times best-selling author Jay Baer, in his book *Hug Your Haters*, broke down measurement into two simple categories: aggregation and behavior (Baer, 2016).

You can think of aggregation as a raw, siloed number measuring the effort or output of CM (i.e., the investment). For instance:

- A CM may write 20 pieces of content. That's a raw number measuring CM output.
- A CM may get 10,000 views of those 20 content marketing pieces. That's also a raw number measuring a reader's passive viewing of a piece of content. The reader did not take any action – to this point, there is no meaningful impact from the 20 pieces of content.

Behavior is then a way to measure the impact of that effort (i.e., the return). For instance:

- Of those 10,000 views, a CM may generate ten new leads. That's behavior. A reader does not just passively view a piece of content and move on. Rather, the reader valued the content enough to engage with your brand and complete a form to access the content, and becomes a new marketing lead.
- Of the ten new leads, the sales team may further qualify those leads and eventually convert two of them into purchases (called closed-won deals). That's the ultimate behavior and a meaningful return on CM investment.

Here's where aggregation and behavior get tricky. Rarely does a potential buyer go directly from aggregation (e.g., seeing your blog post) to behavior (e.g., buying the product). There's usually a series of events that occur in between, and those events could take days, months, or longer. For this reason, CM measurement becomes a blend of aggregation and behavior. Depending on the campaign goals and the client, the same measurement tool can be viewed in two different ways.

For instance, let's go back to the CM who wrote 20 content pieces. Let's say, of those 10,000 views, 300 people clicked on a landing page link, where they have the opportunity to provide their email address to access a white paper. You could argue the 300 visits to that page are aggregation because, in and of itself, a visit to a page does not equate to a measure of return because you're not guaranteed the reader will take action and provide an email address. On the other hand, the 300 can be considered behavior because the reader took an initial action and clicked on the link to go to the landing page.

What is more important, aggregation or behavior? It's a common question with no magic answer. Here, you start to get into chasing tails. Consider this question: would you rather have 100 people read your blog or two people buy your product?

There's an argument that both are more important. Absent any context (e.g., business size, audience reach, and metric definitions), both could also be short-sighted. If the blog post previously only had five-to-ten-people liking it, then 100 readers of your blog could be meaningful. If a product costs $150,000 per unit, two new purchases could have a profound impact on the brand.

On the other hand, a company with 1 million unique monthly visitors may not see much value in 100 new people liking a post. A brand that sells products for $10 may not be enamored with just two sales.

This simple example demonstrates how challenging content marketing measurement can be. The key is to keep it as simple as possible with a mix of multiple measurement elements that transition from aggregation to behavior.

What a CM should know: Measurement is rarely an aggregation of data, measuring a direct journey from point A to point B. There's a missing contextual piece you need to consider in also analyzing behavior.

HOW TO APPROACH CONTENT MARKETING MEASUREMENT

Effective content marketing and communication are kind of like riding a city subway:

- Everyone knows where they start the journey.
- Everyone has an end destination.
- Everyone usually has stops in between.

Ideally, anyone riding public transit wants as few stops as possible in getting to the final destination. Sometimes, it's simply unavoidable to stop ten times before getting where you need to go.

The same is true with content marketing.

Jason Falls, author of *Winfluence: Reframing Influencer Marketing to Ignite Your Brand*, said every brand has the same beginning and end (Falls, 2021):

1. Do you know me?
2. Will you do what we want you to do?

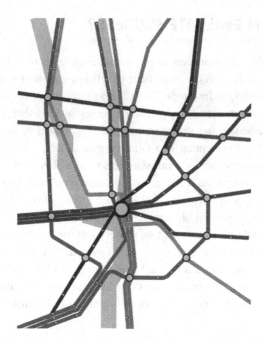

FIGURE 11.2 Successful measurement in marketing communication often resembles a subway system. Rarely does a brand go from point A to point B without a stop (or several) along the way.

In between these two major steps are the individual steps of the buyer's journey, progressing from knowing your brand to liking it and from liking it to making a purchase decision. For a CM, that journey could be one step. It could be 100.

"How many people request more information? That's a good mid-funnel number," Falls said. "Now I can see what percentage of the top goes to the middle and what percentage of the middle goes to the bottom [of the funnel]. Your job as a marketer is to affect both of those. If you can figure that out, the more successful your marketing is."

Donatelli, Baer, and Falls all bring different ideas to the content measurement discussion. When a CM combines these data ingredients, a map begins to appear:

- Start with aggregation.
- End with behavior.
- Be precise in getting from aggregation to behavior.
- Use as many steps as necessary.
- Strive for simplicity along the way.

What a CM should know: A CM should build a precise measurement system for every step of the buyer journey, funneling from aggregation to behavior. The size and depth of the funnel are always different.

HOW DOES A CM EVALUATE SUCCESS?

Ideally, a CM should evaluate success in terms that align with higher-level business goals, as discussed in Chapter 4. Return on investment (ROI) is a common way business professionals evaluate success. According to Investopedia, ROI is a performance measure used to evaluate the efficiency of an investment or to compare the efficiency of a number of different investments. To calculate ROI, the benefit (return) of an investment is divided by the cost of the investment; the result is expressed as a percentage or a ratio (Beattie, 2022).

A CM can struggle to correctly calculate this total if there's no measurement structure in place, such as agreement on what costs are considered and how return is specifically measured (e.g., a lead, an opportunity, a closed-won deal, all of these). For example, while successful content can inspire highly qualified prospective buyers to request a meeting with a salesperson, if that salesperson doesn't effectively sell, or, for whatever reason, the deal is lost, is that the fault of the CM? Under the ROI formula, if closed-won deals were included in the measure of return, it would be, and that's not fair. This is why having more benchmarks than just a simple ROI measurement can help validate the value of a CM's work and provide insights into the buyer's journey, both when the buyer makes a purchase and when they walk away.

What a CM should know: Avoid ROI as a sole source of measurement.

More than 40 years ago, George T. Doran of the Management Assistance Program coined the term *SMART goals* to help business leaders evaluate success. As described in Chapter 4, the use of SMART goals has been widely adopted in business (Doran, 1981), so a CM should feel comfortable with this language:

- Specific – target a specific area for improvement (e.g., product line)
- Measurable – quantify or at least suggest an indicator of progress (e.g., page views)
- Assignable – specify who will do it (e.g., content marketing team)
- Realistic – state what results can realistically be achieved, given available resources (e.g., increase page views by 20%)
- Time related – specify when the result(s) can be achieved (e.g., within 30 days of product launch)

There are three specific tactics a CM can use to create a more precise and protective measurement that empowers the brand, marketing team, and clients.

1. Begin every objective with the word *to*. This is an empowering and active start that gets people to think about doing something.
2. Have a specific deadline. This could be a precise date, such as June 30, 2023, or a timeframe, such as one month after the launch date.
3. Have a number. This could also be a percentage increase/decrease.

Here is a modest example of measuring effective content creation for an organization:

- To deploy a content marketing strategy for new service offering by March 1, 2023
- To receive 1,000 page views within one month of the product launch
- To increase page views 20% each subsequent month after the product launch
- To earn five byline articles within one year of the product launch
- To feature three different industries as part of a webinar series within three months of launch
- To receive 100 qualified leads from webinars through appointment scheduling link within six months of webinar series launch
- To obtain 50 qualified leads through the landing page with free white paper for those who submit their contact information
- To make 2023 the biggest sales year on record

These metrics vary from output – deploy a CM strategy by a certain date and receive 1,000 page views – to impact – receive 1,000 qualified leads from webinars and 50 from a landing page. At the end, there is a bold goal of having the biggest sales year on record. Said another way, the middle is a mix of raw numbers (pages views) that start turning into behavior (50 people filling out a form for a white paper). These goals are also specific, measurable, assignable, realistic, and time related.

What a CM should know: Every piece of content should have a quantifiable measurement journey from aggregation to behavior.

The other side of the measurement coin is the incremental approach. Lisa Gerber of Big Leap Creative struggled with clients seeking immediate success in a quick timeframe. Boosting search rankings, increasing page views, and gaining a set of new sales leads simply won't happen overnight. Gerber's approach and response appeased both mathematical minds and modern marketers:

Measure Monthly

For her clients, Gerber develops a simple metrics dashboard, which she then customizes for each client. Her team creates a baseline set of targets as a starting point. The team then begins execution and reviews the same criteria every month. In this way:

- Clients feel better seeing numbers go up gradually.
- The team feels empowered seeing certain tactics gaining traction.
- When her team members see metrics not meeting targets, they can adapt accordingly or abandon the tactic and pivot to others that perform better.
- Everyone has a mutually agreed-on map of going from aggregation to behavior.

Whether the frequency is weekly, monthly, or quarterly, what's important is to decide on the most useful timeframe for each metric and what the target should be in that timeframe and then track over time to measure progress and monitor upward or downward trends. This approach is similar to the funnel and campaign dashboard approach described in Chapter 4.

What a CM should know: When a client and CM aren't on the same page on how to measure the success of content marketing, everyone sets themselves up to fail.

MEASURING CONTENT MARKETING

Now it's time to actually start measuring. You may wonder what you can measure in content marketing. The answer: everything.

This blank canvas of measurement can be beautiful because it's so wide open. It can also be horrifying because it's so wide open.

Falls has two big-picture ideas to help with measurement:

1. You have to plan to measure.
2. It's better to own your data than to rent it.

In the rest of this section, CM metrics are described in the context of the buyer journey:

- Top of the funnel (ToF)
- Middle of the funnel (MoF)
- Bottom of the funnel (BoF)
- Beyond the funnel (BtF)

Let's start with the top.

Top of Funnel (ToF) Content Metrics

The following is a sample of several common metrics CMs use to track output along the early stages of the buyer journey. There are some items on the list that won't work for certain businesses and industries. View this list of metrics as individual tools in a toolbox that you can mix and match to find the best measurement framework for your particular team or client. CMs will most often use a tool such as Google Analytics or a content management system (CMS), such as HubSpot or WordPress, to track these metrics.

Common ToF Content Measurement Items:

- **Website traffic**: This measures traffic to a specific page or the overall website.
- **Unique monthly visitors**: This is how many different or unduplicated people visit a website during a month. Google Analytics can also break this down into specific days and weeks.
- **Total visits**: A measure of all website visits, which can include multiple visits by the same person (e.g., if one unique visitor accesses the site 25 times in a month, all 25 visits would be counted in this metric). Total visits are always higher than unique monthly visitors.
- **Persona information**: These are metrics to track activity and engagement of new contacts by persona.

Consider the user journey at this stage to clearly outline success. For example, you may be tasked with developing a content campaign for your client's expensive software service along the buyer journey. This may include ToF content, such as a flier and a blog series highlighting its unique features and benefits, as well as MoF content, such as a gated white paper educating the user about the trends in related software technologies. How many times should a prospective buyer engage with each of these pieces of content before filling out an appointment form to meet with sales? The client might think once or twice.

Under this scenario, unique monthly visitors might be more important than total visits because the buyer journey is supposed to move from reading the blog series to downloading the flier to completing a form to access a white paper to an appointment form. In reality, the journey is not this linear or predictable. This is why, as a step in the process of creating the measurement structure, a CM must research the buyer journey to understand content preferences and create relevant content the user values.

What a CM should know: Establishing content metrics is more than picking measurement items and tracking them. The most effective CMs do their research, understand the buyer journey, and select the most appropriate metrics to match the expected, and reasonable, impact.

More ToF Common Measurement Items

- **Referral traffic**: This measures website traffic that comes directly to your website from an external site, such as a search engine or social media site.
- **Exit rate**: Most commonly used to measure the performance of specific web pages on a site, this measures how often visitors exit the site from this page. The percentage is calculated by dividing the number of exits by the number of page views.
- **Bounce rate**: Most commonly used to measure the performance of a website, this measures the percentage of all sessions in which the user only visits a single page and then leaves the site. This is calculated by dividing the number of single-page sessions by the total number of sessions on the site.
- **Time on site**: This is the time (in seconds, minutes, and hours) that someone spends on a web page or website.
- **Highest trafficked content**: This ranks content according to the amount of website traffic it drove.
- **Sentiment analysis**: This determines whether people are saying nice things about the content. In a 2011 interview, Seth Grimes defined sentiment analysis as "a set of methods, typically (but not always) implemented in computer software, that detect, measure, report, and exploit attitudes, opinions, and emotions in online, social, and enterprise information sources" (Helweh, 2011)

What a CM should know: Knowing how potential buyers access, engage with, and leave the content not only helps CMs analyze metrics effectively but also helps foster further data insights or consideration of new ones. Bounce rates can be misleading. Logic would say you want a lower bounce rate (i.e., visitors staying on the website and clicking through multiple pages), but if one piece of content on a web page solves the visitor's issue, would it be bad that it counted as a bounce?

Another Type of ToF Measurement: Search Engine Optimization

If a tree falls in the forest and nobody is around, does it make a sound? If a CM makes a content marketing funnel and Google can't find it, does it have impact?

Rachel Leist of HubSpot defines search engine optimization (SEO) as:

> *"techniques that help your website rank higher in search engine results pages (SERPs). This makes your website more visible to people who are looking for solutions that your brand, product, or service can provide via search engines like Google, Yahoo!, and Bing."*

(Leist, 2022)

The following measurements help a CM know if content resonates with search formulas.

Search Engine Optimization Measurement Types

- **Domain authority**: From www.moz.com, this is "a search engine ranking score developed by Moz that predicts how likely a website is to rank in search engine result pages (SERPs)"; 100 is the highest score, and 0 is the lowest (No Author, *Moz*).
- **Page authority**: This is like domain authority but for one specific page. For instance, individual blog posts will have different page authorities. An astute CM will look at the highest page authorities on a site and mirror that SEO experience in other posts.
- **Backlinks**: These are when external sites link to a page on your site, which is a critical variable in search engine algorithm ranking. Ideally, backlinks will occur on all pages of your website, not just the home page. Not all backlinks are equal in value and SEO impact. A backlink from a friend's blog does not compare in quality to one from the website of a reputable trade journal or research institution, which will have a much greater positive impact on the visibility of your website in searches.
- **Ranking keywords:** This is how many phrases or terms a website or page ranks on the first page of a Google search.

What a CM should know: Ideally, a CM should reference the keyword strategy the SEO team has developed in creating content. In this way, both teams are aligned and working in an integrated fashion to drive traffic and engagement for the same highly ranked terms.

Middle of Funnel (MoF) Content Metrics

When interested visitors engage with your content and want to learn more, they move beyond awareness to building preference for certain brands. It is at this point that buyers move into the middle of the funnel (MoF). Measuring content at this stage includes tracking engagement and conversation with the company.

MoF Measurement Types

- **Blog comments**: These are tangible measures of engagement with a reader who feels compelled to leave a comment, positive or negative.
- **Subscriptions**: These are counted when a person signs up for one of your branded newsletters or publications, also called opting in. This demonstrates that people value your content and want to receive more from you on a consistent basis.
- **Content conversion**: This is a key metric of content performance that measures the number of individuals who provided contact information to access gated content, such as a white paper or webinar.
- **Gated content conversion rate**: This is the percentage of visitors to a web page who complete a form to access gated content.
- **Highest lead-generating content**: This ranks content according to the number of leads it converted.

What a CM should know: Aspire for subscriptions. By opting in to receive consistent communication from you, people are indicating that they are ready to buy, and your brand is top of mind and accessible in their inbox or RSS folder.

Bottom of Funnel (BoF) Content Metrics

When prospective buyers have engaged with your content and begin to form preference for certain brands, they move into the bottom of the funnel (BoF). Even though the responsibility for engaging with the person at this stage falls primarily to sales, content still plays a vital role in persuading and convincing the buyer to purchase. Here are some of the most common BoF metrics.

BoF Measurement Items

- **Conversion to MQL/SQL/opportunity/revenue**: This measures which individual piece of content or collection of content organized by campaign generated qualified conversion through the stages of the sales process, from marketing qualified lead to sales qualified lead to opportunity to closed-won revenue.
- **Appointment forms**: This measures the number of appointments or meetings scheduled with sales. Including links in content, such as www.calendly.com, makes it easy for prospective buyers to schedule meetings at their preferred time.
- **Coupon code**: This is a trackable way to reach people as they are nearing a decision. QR codes are the most common, but some brands will have special discount codes a buyer can type in during checkout. For example, Dan's podcast (referenced in Chapter 8) uses the code MPN, or strategic communicator, during commercials. This way, when a user types in the code, the advertising brand knows the person listened to the ad in Dan's podcast.
- **Phone calls**: As the label suggests, this metric tracks the number of phone calls driven by content. This may be best explained with this example from earned media content Digital Marketing Strategist Jason Falls was working with Maker's Mark bourbon and secured earned media coverage with the *Wall Street Journal*:

"When that article went live, they had to install new phone lines at their distillery," he said. "Because this one article appeared on the front page of the Wall Street Journal, all of these phone calls started to come in. They were able to sell more, and they were able to ship more. That was worth countless amounts of money to the brand."

What a CM should know: BoF measurement requires a cross-functional collaboration between sales and marketing. Sales and other units need to understand the work taking place from a content-marketing standpoint and provide feedback on the data being tracked to help optimize and improve performance over time.

Beyond the Funnel (BtF) Content Metrics

Once a customer purchases a product, content marketing does not end. In fact, in some ways, the value of content becomes even more impactful. Content beyond the funnel (BtF), often referred to as the inverted funnel, serves to support the customer's adoption of the product, reinforce brand loyalty to drive retention, influence revenue expansion of individual customers through targeted account-based marketing, and ultimately turn customers into brand advocates (Figure 11.3. The best example of brand advocacy content was discussed in the last

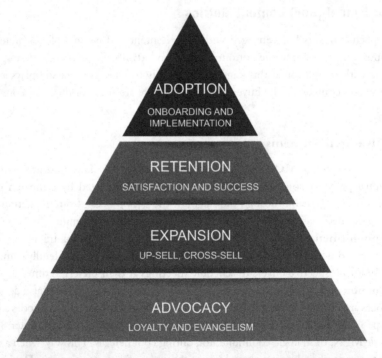

FIGURE 11.3 Once a customer purchases a product, content marketing does not end. In fact, in some ways, the value of content becomes even more impactful. Content beyond the funnel (BtF), often referred to as the inverted funnel, serves to support the customer's adoption of the product, reinforce brand loyalty to drive retention, influence revenue expansion of individual customers through targeted account-based marketing, and ultimately turn customers into brand advocates.

chapter – case studies – but it can also include interviewing customers in webinars, showcasing them in videos, and referencing their use of the product in relevant white papers, blog posts, etc. Each of these types of BtF content marketing has its own set of metrics.

BtF Measurement Items

- Tracking growth in leads at individual accounts
- New subscriptions to customer-specific newsletters
- Secured customer quotes and case studies
- Post-purchase content to encourage customers to provide reviews, such as post-purchase surveys, with links to leave a review
- Creating great backlinks with powerful websites, including Amazon, eBay, TripAdvisor, Yelp, and more

Throughout the buyer journey, content marketing plays a significant role. The CM can be overwhelmed by the many ways to measure both output and impact. In fact, this is true for most aspects of business, not just CM. To be most effective, the CM needs to understand the buyer journey and execute a content plan with agreed-upon metrics that are tracked systematically according to a consistent timeframe. With data, the CM is empowered to improve content performance along the way and celebrate the impact it's having along the entire funnel.

CONCLUSION

Good measurement empowers a CM. Access to web analytics, social media measurement tools, and real-world customer experience is essential for measuring the impact of a CM campaign.

The most successful brands proactively build a measurement map before a campaign begins and then incrementally monitor what's working and where there is room for improvement. Google Analytics and other software enable a CM to set data points that make it easy to see if content is reaching certain benchmarks with readers and potential buyers. These insights allow the marketing team to quantify and contextualize the value of a content marketing campaign through SMART goals that can be clearly and objectively measured.

Interview with the Experts: Q&A with Jason Falls, Tangible CM Measurement

Jason Falls is a leading digital strategist, author, speaker, and thinker in the digital and social media marketing industry. He is an innovator in the conversation research segment of social analytics, having published the first-ever conversation report in 2012. An award-winning strategist and widely read industry pundit, Falls has been noted as a top influencer in the social technology and marketing spaces by *Forbes*, *Entrepreneur*, *Advertising Age*, and others. A 2014 *Forbes* article named him one of ten business leaders all entrepreneurs should follow on Twitter, alongside Richard Branson, Mark Cuban, Tom Peters, and Tony Hseih. The following are excerpts from the interview.

1. ***If you were on the desert island of marketing and you could only measure three things, where do you start?***

   I would start with a set of top-of-funnel metrics to understand, for instance, how many people are aware of my product or talking about my product or company on social media. I'll measure the reach of my paid advertising and calculate how many times my brand makes an impression on an audience member.

   I'll then measure my mid-funnel to look at engagement. How many people comment on my content, call or email, or request more information? These are good mid-funnel numbers.

   My bottom-of-the-funnel metric is obviously measuring sales and what percent of impressions are actually coming through the funnel and converting.

   There are more metrics and analytics to figure out, but best to keep it simple: how many people are aware of my company; how many people are curious, asking questions and engaging; and how many people are actually buying? That's a great start.

2. ***What would you avoid measuring?***

   Earned media value. PR folks have never figured out or been given a reasonable replacement. I secured an article in the *New York Times* for my client. What is that worth? You don't really know. We know anecdotally.

   I can tell you from working years ago with Maker's Mark Bourbon, they landed in front of consumers' faces in the early 1980s when a very small article appeared about them on the front page of the *Wall Street Journal*.

   They had to install new phone lines at their distillery because this one article appeared on the front page of the *Wall Street Journal*. That was worth an amount of money to the brand. All the phone calls started to come in, and they were able to sell and ship more. That is a rare example of earned media content and placement having a direct correlation to impact on a brand. There's really no way to correlate that, and it's partially because we've never figured out a better replacement.

3. ***What about backlinks?***

   They're still important. It's low-hanging fruit, and we know, statistically speaking, from analyzing search engine optimization numbers and listening to Google all these years, that backlinks from a quality source can and do lift the visibility of your website in search.

Now, it's a moving target. SEO is something that changes every day. Google comes out with new algorithm updates that affect how all this works. Through all the years of Google algorithm updates, backlinks still count. So you need to understand what they are and how to get them.

4. *For people setting up a quality content measurement structure, what would you recommend as they establish and maintain it over time as a consistent part of their marketing process?*

The one thing that you need to remember: you have to plan to measure. Measurement is not something you do after the fact. It's not something you do reactively. It's something you do proactively. You need to track metrics along the way to be able to quantify and contextualize and understand what you're doing, not what you have done.

If you don't, when you get to the end and ask, "How did we do?" you won't know. Let's put it in the context of influence marketing. If I don't provide the influencer with a trackable link, there is zero chance that I'll know how much impact that single content creator had.

But if I set up a trackable link and I put some parameters on there, I can know "Jason Falls drove $18,469.45 in sales, and I paid him $1,500." Now you've got what you need to calculate ROI, which is what everybody wants.

Interview with the Experts: Q&A with Stu Opperman: Intangible CM Measurement

Stu Opperman, APR, is an accredited public relations professional with more than 25 years of experience in media, broadcasting, and marketing communication. He has seen and embraced the power of comprehensive communication to showcase its value beyond website traffic and earned media coverage. Opperman is president of Impact Players, a communication consulting firm that provides value and advances the agenda of clients and contacts.

Opperman and his team spent a great deal of time working with healthcare providers as they tried to navigate the COVID-19 pandemic. He's also worked with non-profits, trying to find better ways to share their stories with potential donors.

Opperman discusses his thoughts on measuring message clarity through the use of humanity and relationship building.

1. *How do you measure to make sure your story doesn't get hijacked in the press by people who might have agendas against your clients?*
   You have to set the narrative, and you have to tell the story intentionally. We're talking about telling the story that needs to be out there. Yes, some of it is reactive. But at the same time, it's important to set the narrative and move the agenda forward for my client's organization.

   Part of our job during the pandemic working with the healthcare system was getting out accurate information, telling a story, and setting the narrative.

2. *What did you do to cut through the noise with issues like COVID-19?*
   We just tried to stay with the facts and position our health experts, who have been in the field for 30, 40, 50 years. We leaned on them, put them out there to the world, and had them share information and not buy into the politics, of which we wanted no part. We just presented facts.

3. *How much of your COVID-19 communication was crafting the message compared to helping front-line healthcare workers convey your message to patients and the general public?*
   The nurse who brings you in when you walk in for a standard appointment had to make sure they felt equipped to deal with a lot of that onslaught from people who had misinformation or maybe were just scared because there was so much we didn't know.

   I consider healthcare workers, patients, and support staff all stakeholder audiences. The traditional and social media helped us communicate with all of them in a big way, but we also had to measure and gauge what the receptionists at the front door and the nurse and the doctor and the volunteers saw. Those are all audiences that have the opportunity to share a brand's narratives, facts, and story.

   I think we did a good job of putting facts and information in the hands of healthcare workers. We used many ways to arm them with messaging – sometimes it was an internal email, and other times it was a bulletin board post on the hospital intranet. Sometimes we just physically put out talking points for staff members who answer phones and respond to website requests . . . just giving them some tools to work with.

4. *Success in PR used to be "Let's get the client on TV – that will satisfy the client." Now it's a completely different landscape with earned media and content. What do you think?*
   Media is fragmented.

   I work with clients including Make-A-Wish Southern Florida to secure earned media coverage for them. I'm very proud of what we've accomplished. But we've also made it our mantra that with every story we tell, we produce our own content. For instance, when a child has their wish come true, we have a video crew that shoots the Make-A-Wish story, we take photos, we develop background information, all to provide to the TV journalist so their job [is] easier.

When a journalist says to me, "Hey, we love that story, but we don't have a crew on Saturday to shoot the video," we can send them a full content package hours after the wish takes place. It provides the journalist with everything they could ever want to tell the story. Quite frankly, when I compare the content we produce and hand to them versus the story that eventually airs on TV, it's practically the same. We're shooting it as real journalists would.

If brands create an environment where a journalist or influencer can copy, paste, and upload a story into a content management system, those brands are providing a service. Journalists will be more interested in covering future stories because the brand's story ideas have some journalistic integrity to them.

When a client dictates what a news release says and there is jargon and congratulatory mentions of everybody in the company, that's not helping the TV station or the daily newspaper. It's a waste of time.

PR teams are not great about always measuring themselves and being tangible in their benefits. However, I will tell you that, with a lot of the coverage we get with Make-A-Wish, for example, we can see directly from the results a significant amount of exposure that drives awareness. The results show in people attending their events, donating, and leaving [to] Make-A-Wish in their wills. You can't get better results than that.

5. ***What Make-A-Wish has figured out is how to showcase people who directly benefit from generous donations.***
We're very clear about going to the families and ensuring they are comfortable with any media coverage. Some families welcome it, and they think it's a wonderful part of it, and some families don't. That's fine, and we respect that.

We don't talk a lot about the health issues. We will say someone has a tumor on his brain and has had radiation, but it's general. If the family wants to share during their interview, they're welcome to.

I still think like a journalist, even though I'm not. I know somebody in PR who says that we're in the private practice of journalism. I think that's true because I think that way, I write that way, and I think it's worked.

Measuring content isn't easy, but it is necessary. A good CM may not wear a lab coat, but there is a science to the art of effective communication. Measure early. Measure often.

CITATIONS

Baer, J. *Hug your haters: How to embrace complaints and keep your customers.* Penguin Random House. 2016.

Beattie, A. "How to calculate return on investment (ROI)." August 11, 2022. Retrieved from: www. investopedia.com/terms/r/returnoninvestment.asp#axzz2AFg7t1Lc

Doran, G.T. "There's a S.M.A.R.T. way to write management's goals and objectives." *Management Review.* 1981.

Falls, J. *Winfluence: Reframing Influencer Marketing to Ignite Your Brand.* Entrepreneur Press. 2021.

Helweh, A. "The future of sentiment analysis." *Social Media Explorer.* November 2, 2011. Retrieved from: https://socialmediaexplorer.com/content-sections/news-and-noise/sentiment-analysis/

Leist, R. "The definition of SEO in 100 words or less." *HubSpot.* August 19, 2022. Retrieved from: https://blog.hubspot.com/marketing/what-is-seo

No Author. "What is domain authority and why is it important?" *Moz.* Retrieved from: https://moz.com/learn/seo/domain-authority

Solis, B. *Engage: The Complete Guide for Brands and Businesses to Build, Cultivate, and Measure Success in the New Web.* John Wiley & Sons. 2011.

The Future of Content Marketing

Wayne Gretzky is better at hockey than anyone reading this will be at content marketing. When Gretzky retired from the National Hockey League in 1999, he had 61 NHL records. He scored 92 goals in one season and had 13 straight seasons with 100 or more points. No player in NHL history has had more than ten seasons with 100 or more points. No wonder Gretzky's nickname is "The Great One."

Gretzky may not be a content marketing guru, but his most famous quote about playing hockey can certainly help any CM trying to navigate a career (Figure 12.1).

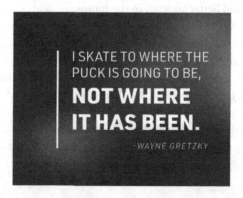

FIGURE 12.1 Wayne Gretzky's insights on hockey apply to content marketers who need to consider future trends and how those trends may impact the industry.

DOI: 10.4324/9781003369103-15

A CM may not have Gretzky's clairvoyance on the ice, but it's not a bold prediction that technology will constantly alter the marketing industry. None of us know what transformative invention is being created right now in a young scientist's basement or a Fortune 500 R&D lab that will be worth $1 billion a year from now.

What we *can* do as CMs is expect the unexpected and use the fundamentals explained in this book to adapt quickly to whatever changes occur. Here are some themes that will likely drive the CM landscape and experience over the next decade.

ARTIFICIAL INTELLIGENCE (AI) AND CONTENT MARKETING

AI is not going to take your job. However, CMs who are using AI may.

One way AI tools can help you be more effective and efficient is by taking your CM blueprint and repurposing it to other communication forms.

Paul Roetzer, founder and CEO of the Marketing AI Institute, has written two books on the role of AI in strategic communication. As he began building his highly respected PR firm, PR 20/20, which was named HubSpot's first agency partner in 2007, Roetzer saw the power that the combination of marketing automation technology from HubSpot and his team's storytelling talent could have. Four years later, he saw Watson, IBM's AI machine learning answering system, win on *Jeopardy!*.

That changed everything for him, and he began to wonder if he and his team could use AI to predict actions such as the best next tactics to use to drive client results, the optimal campaign to run, or even outcomes his team could generate.

"Can AI do that?" Roetzer wondered during a podcast interview with Dan.

As he further recounted, the answer was "Probably." Christopher Steiner's *Automate* explains how 60% of all Wall Street trades were being made by machines with no human interaction.

"The stock market has far more variables than a marketing campaign," Roetzer said. "I think a lot of marketers hesitate to pursue knowledge around AI because they think it's computer science, and that is not true at all."

For example, a CM can use an AI content tool to generate 1,000 email marketing examples. You can then tell the AI tool which examples are good, and the machine learns from this input to generate better and better versions in the future.

ChatGPT, an open AI chatbot software, is starting to create better versions of content and will continue to do so. For instance, the *New York Times* is challenging thousands of readers with its "Human or AI" writing quiz and asks readers to identify whether a piece of content was generated by a human or ChatGPT (Buchanan et al., 2022). Other AI tools, such as Jasper, Descript, MarketMuse, Wavve, and Zapier, can help CMs with keyword research, social media content creation, and multimedia support. With the onslaught of new AI tools for marketing being introduced, it's no surprise it's the industry that ranked highest in professional use of AI for its work-related tasks (Thormundsson, 2023) (Figure 12.2).

ADOPTION RATE OF GENERATIVE AI ADOPTION IN THE WORKPLACE IN THE UNITED STATES 2023, BY INDUSTRY

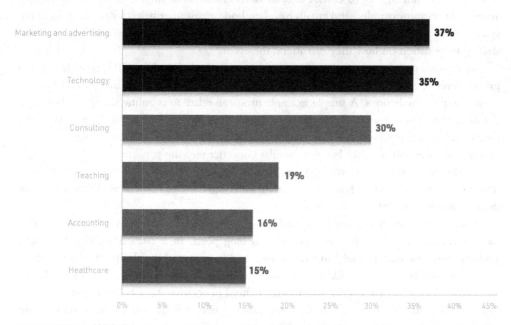

FIGURE 12.2 With the onslaught of new AI tools for marketing coming on the market, it's no surprise this industry ranked highest in professional use of AI for its work-related tasks.

So why isn't AI going to take your job?

Humans think in multiple modes (Dawes, 1979). AI thinks in one binary mode. It's zero or one. AI can be a useful tool to offload certain tactical marketing tasks that might take 20 hours to do. Roetzer told Dan humans can oversee the binary approach and gradually improve what the AI does.

"The human is still in control," Roetzer said. "But the AI will save me ten of those 20 hours. I can redistribute that time to something that machine isn't good at."

What a CM should know: Humanity can win when an effective CM uses AI to find more time for higher-value content planning, creation, and client management and service.

THE FASTEST GROWING APPLICATION IN HISTORY: CHATGPT

When ChatGPT was introduced on November 30, 2022, it changed communication forever. By January 2023, more than 100 million users had tried it. Seemingly overnight, ChatGPT became the fastest growing application in history, making AI tangible for the digital world, especially those in the communication and content marketing space. Up to this point, the primary use of intelligent tools was with marketing automation technology, which brought rules-based "if/then" intelligence to CMs. For tasks such as email marketing, CMs can use marketing automation to automatically send emails based on lead or customer behavior rules set up in the system, such as a thank-you email automatically sent to contacts who register for a webinar, sharing information on how they can attend the event.

In contrast to automation, machine learning tools, including ChatGPT, provide a much greater level of intelligence by using large quantities of data, including images and text, to make complex predictions. A simple example most can relate to is online shopping. Based on combinations of purchases made by thousands or millions of previous customers, the AI model predicts additional products you may want to purchase. Similarly, AI is used by Netflix to recommend movies you may like based on similar customer viewing patterns.

In the near term, innovative CMs are already using AI in areas such as content ideation. There is pressure on CMs to have more content ideas and increase content production, and this demand is not expected to slow down.

Meghan Keaney Anderson leads marketing for Jasper AI, a generative AI platform that helps marketing teams create content, such as blog posts. In a 2023 *Marketing Millennials* podcast interview with Daniel Murray, Keaney Anderson touted the ability of AI technology to craft meaningful content, addressing one of the most common challenges for marketers (Murray, 2023). She believes the technology behind generative AI, a type of artificial intelligence that produces various types of content, such as text or images, has improved to a point where it can solve a key pain point of CMs that she refers to as the "blinking cursor" that prompts you to begin writing.

"Everybody has gotten 90% [of the way through] their blog post and just not known how to finish it," Keaney Anderson told Murray. "And when you look at marketers, which is really our target audience for Jasper, the amount of content demands on them are just unsustainable."

ChatGPT made AI immediately real for millions who, before its launch, considered it an abstract technology that didn't apply to them in their current jobs. Overnight, millions experimented with AI to write stories or generate email subject lines or entire blog posts.

What the Future of CM May Hold With AI

Artificial intelligence has come a long way since its early use in the mid-20th century by governments looking for new military and computing solutions. From a marketing standpoint alone, in the last decade, technologies such as personalization, programmatic ad buying, and predictive modeling around customer churn, helped marketers better forecast and drive lead conversion.

AI is already being used at specific stages of the buyer journey by online retailers, such as Wayfair, which use AI to target ads to guide a prospective buyer's search (Davenport et al., 2021).

Here are a few examples of how CMs can expect to use AI to save time and improve performance in the next few years alone:

- Enhance customer relationships through personalization at scale by customizing every interaction with a known lead or customer based on previous behavior.

- Implement more intelligent, predictive lead scoring based on lead attributes and behaviors to accelerate identification of sales-ready leads.
- Further reduce time spent on repetitive, data-driven tasks, such as email subject lines, content narratives, and ROI reporting.

To this end, CMs should identify activities that involve repetitive tasks, such as producing a podcast. For instance, Roetzer advises starting with a spreadsheet that lists all the tactics it takes to publish an episode. Here is what his team has done to leverage AI tools to streamline the repetitive processes involved in producing podcast episodes:

- Roetzer said there are 17 steps in the workflow to create and publish his podcast.
- The team turns each podcast into four or five blog posts, infusing AI into 10 of the 17 steps.
- The team uses descript.com to upload and transcribe the video.
- The team uses ChatGPT to summarize the transcription.

By identifying tasks that require multiple steps, such as content production, ad creative, and social media, you can work smarter and more efficiently.

Keaney Anderson encourages brands to look at where their largest expenditures of time and money are. Teams that ask how to become more efficient in any of those ways will create the most immediate value and the highest probability of success (Figure 12.3).

WHY AI IN MARKETING?

Marketers who pilot and scale AI now have the opportunity to create a significant and sustained competitive advantage for their businesses and personal careers.

DRIVE COMPANY PROFITS UP	REDUCE TIME AND COSTS	ADVANCE YOUR CAREER
Achieve greater ROI on campaigns through unmatched consumer personalization and targeting, and more intelligent marketing.	Spend less time on repetitive, data-driven tasks so you can free up resources for more human and strategic work.	Enhance your knowledge and capabilities with AI-powered tools and partners to gain a competitive advantage as a next-gen marketer.

FIGURE 12.3 Artificial intelligence already has a foothold in many industries. Recent advances have made AI much more accessible to the general population and will likely transform content marketing as we know it.

Source: Marketing AI Institute

CMs will also need to keep an eye on the changing search engine landscape currently dominated by Google. With the launch of ChatGPT, its underlying technology is now being used by Microsoft's search engine, Bing. At its launch event, Microsoft took a bold stance, "promising a revolution in how we search" (No Author, 2023, *Forbes*).

What a CM should know: No matter how good AI gets, it will still need critical judgment from living, breathing people. A CM who can use the technology and move from writing to editing will find more results and less anxiety.

Meghan Keaney Anderson on AI's Emerging Role in Content Marketing

Meghan Keaney Anderson is head of marketing at Jasper and former vice president of marketing at HubSpot. During a 2023 *Marketing Millennials* podcast interview with Daniel Murray, she shared her thoughts, which are summarized below, on where CMs should start with AI (Murray, 2023):

- **Reimagine:** Start with a strong foundation from a messaging standpoint that's felt universally across the company – this is essential for having any sort of a brand or having any kind of recognition. With this alignment and focus in place, then reimagine how AI can save your team time to work more efficiently and strategically.
- **Reinforce and reinvest:** Our hope is that AI helps writers get off the content treadmill and into the editor's seat, making them the strategists [and] the holder[s] of quality and giving them more rhythm for original research, interviews, and story development.
- **Brainstorm:** One of my favorite use cases across my team is the person leading our SEO who is using Jasper to create the schema markup for a given post and write the meta descriptions very quickly. These need to be done for a post to rank, but they often get skipped over in the content creation process because they're just one more task to remember. So she's using Jasper to actually come up with the markup language to go alongside the post that she writes.
- **Retain and empower:** AI is a great tool for CMs to help accelerate some portions of their work, but it should never be a one-for-one replacement for a writer or a content creator. AI does not provide creative judgment, lived experience, or that sense of strategy in the writing. AI just puts words down on a page; there will always need to be a partnership between creators, marketers, and AI in order to get the best value out of it.

Let's Ask ChatGPT

We decided that ChatGPT deserved a voice in explaining the future of artificial intelligence in content marketing. On February 28, 2023, we asked it this question:

What is the future of artificial intelligence and marketing?

Here is the AI chatbot's unedited response.

AI EDUCATION PLAYBOOK

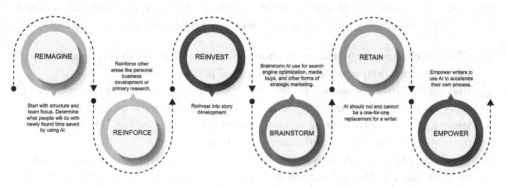

FIGURE 12.4 Even with AI, people remain a critical factor in implementing a content marketing program. Meghan Keaney Anderson advises using this AI playbook to get people thinking about the effective use of artificial intelligence in CM.

The future of artificial intelligence and marketing is very promising. AI is already transforming the marketing landscape and its impact *will only increase* in the coming years.

Here are a few ways in which AI will shape the future of marketing:

1. **Personalization**: AI-powered tools can analyze large amounts of data about consumers to create personalized marketing messages and offers. This will lead to better engagement and higher conversion rates.
2. **Automation**: AI can automate many routine marketing tasks, freeing up marketers' time to focus on more strategic activities.
3. **Predictive analytics**: AI algorithms can analyze customer behavior and predict future actions, allowing marketers to make informed decisions about their campaigns.
4. **Chatbots**: AI-powered chatbots can provide instant customer service and support, which is becoming increasingly important in today's fast-paced world.
5. **Visual search**: AI-powered visual search engines can help customers find what they're looking for more quickly and easily, which will lead to higher sales.
6. **Voice search**: As voice assistants like Alexa and Google Home become more prevalent, AI-powered marketing will become more important in order to optimize for voice search queries.

Overall, the integration of AI in marketing will lead to more efficient and effective campaigns, better customer experiences, and higher ROI for businesses. AI also has the potential to help marketers deliver more relevant and personalized experiences to customers while also improving the efficiency and effectiveness of their marketing campaigns.

Challenges of ChatGPT for CM

There are several lenses through which content marketers and strategic communicators can look at ChatGPT's answer and what it means for content marketing. Let's start with the challenges:

Citation challenges: All the information presented in ChatGPT's answer makes sense. It also likely came from secondary sources not cited in the document.

Bias and balance: Google offers ideas on its search engine optimization formula, though it doesn't give everyone its secret recipe. With ChatGPT, there is no clear sense of what information or criteria resonate best with its computer programming. This could lead to thought bias absent any counterbalance from a human.

Legal liabilities: Imagine if/when someone inputs proprietary information into software, such as ChatGPT. That information eventually will become part of the software's learning model. Medical and student information has privacy restrictions. Documents are classified. Countless items are held under virtual lock and key with nondisclosure agreements and other safeguards. People using ChatGPT must realize these dangers and ensure proper use doesn't create civil or criminal legal liability.

It can be incomplete: Important content marketing criteria, including internal links, external links, branded terms, meta descriptions, alt text, visuals, audio, and video, don't automatically appear. All those tools are key in helping a potential buyer through the purchasing journey.

Bad directions: AI needs good data inputs to do its work. As the saying goes, "Garbage in, garbage out." Incomplete data mean incomplete results. Word count specifications, tone of voice, and several other measures were not included in our question. The more precise the query, the better the likely results. ChatGPT can't magically spit out everything needed for effective content. At least not yet.

Benefits of ChatGPT for CM

On the other hand, there are several ChatGPT elements that offer content marketers the ability to do their work more effectively.

First draft support: ChatGPT developed this response in less than a minute. Is it perfect? Of course not. A CM could find and incorporate a mix of internal links, external links, branded terms, visuals, audio, and video in a short timeframe and then edit the text to match the brand voice. This should help a CM write content more quickly

Rapid repurpose: ChatGPT can quickly create 20 headline options and suggested social media content and other material that helps accentuate and promote long-form content. For a CM who writes white papers and case studies or leads webinars, ChatGPT can quickly take 30 minutes of concepts and create more digestible content. Coupling this with social media scheduling software, such as Hootsuite, a CM could automate a social media content calendar, enabling the CM to spend more time on research, strategy, and analytics.

Writing challenge: ChatGPT serves as a basic benchmark of what writing can be. Most modern marketers can create better content. This software will force writers to sharpen their writing, editing, and strategy skills.

What a CM should know: Artificial intelligence in marketing is here. The way it looks in early 2023 will be different than in late 2023 and early 2024. A CM needs to know the AI space will change rapidly and must be on top of emerging trends. A CM must then make sure there's a process in place to make sure any content put into the ChatGPT system is not proprietary or confidential. Finally, a CM must realize that AI is a tool and not the entire toolbox. There are some forms of CM in which ChatGPT could work wonders. There are other forms of CM in which it may not be the best fit.

A final reminder from Dr. Eddith Dashiell, director of journalism at the E.W. Scripps School of Journalism. In Chapter 5, we recounted her reminder to students in her Introduction to Journalism class.

> *"Storytelling should drive technology and not the other way around."*

Successful CMs will use AI to turn insights into strategy and strategy into tactical content delivery. People still need to drive that process and rely on the insights and lessons from this book and other marketing theory.

VIRTUAL REALITY AND CONTENT MARKETING

Meta, which owns and operates Facebook and Instagram, hitched much of its future business model to the metaverse with the notion it will help diverse audiences connect and share (No Author, No date).

> *"The metaverse will be built by everyone, with creative ideas and practical applications being developed every day by all sorts of imaginative people."*

Many countered with a simple and fair question: What exactly is the metaverse?

Chiradeep BasuMallick (2022) compared the metaverse to the internet of the '70s, writing that it's easy for people to talk about it but challenging to truly understand how it might function. Here is how he described it:

> *"The Metaverse is a spatial computing platform that provides digital experiences as an alternative to or a replica of the real world, along with its key civilizational aspects like social interactions, currency, trade, economy, and property ownership – founded on a bedrock of blockchain technology."*

There's more we know than don't know about the metaverse. Financially, cryptocurrency and Meta stock prices took a disproportionate beating to the rest of the stock market in 2022. They also exceeded expectations from 2019 to 2021.

What a CM should know: Anyone can write anything. VR and AR can help document the content marketing journey in a completely new way for anyone anywhere.

Companies such as Disney are investing people and profits into the metaverse as a digital storytelling device (Marr, 2022). How can virtual reality (VR) and augmented reality (AR) bring the Disney experience to people who can't visit Disney? The Disney team has already developed VR experiences, including "Tales from the Galaxy's Edge," a virtual experience based on its Star Wars properties. Marr wrote:

> *"What these technologies offer Disney and other entertainment and media conglomerates is a whole new range of tools for building new audience experiences. Disney has traditionally always been for-ward-looking and was quick to jump the arrival of previous game-changing breakthroughs such as the arrival of television, computer-generated animation, video games, and the internet, so there's no reason it will treat the arrival of the age of VR and the metaverse any differently."*

In 2022, Disney applied for and received a patent for a virtual world simulator that will allow it to simulate augmented digital worlds without the need for users to wear headsets or glasses (Martin, 2022). *Los Angeles Times* reporter Hugo Martin wrote:

> *"Visitors could be tracked through their smartphones or other devices they are carrying so that the track-ing information could be relayed to a computer connected to projection devices located throughout the theme parks. After locating the visitors, the "Virtual World Simulator" could project an image of a Dis-ney character in front of the guests, with hidden speakers providing voices for an immersive experience."*

Media empires will follow Disney's lead in trying to answer similar questions. Eventu-ally, smaller businesses and non-profits will travel down this road. Storytelling is the pave-ment that allows this journey to occur.

Think of what a CM could do with a virtual experience:

- Document a pain point that prompts a potential customer to learn about potential products
- Showcase how a product specifically addresses concerns or opportunities at hand
- Formulate ways to see how a product could work for a potential buyer or customer persona

Anyone can write anything. VR and AR can help document the content marketing journey in a completely new way for anyone anywhere.

CAREER OUTLOOK FOR CONTENT MARKETERS

For the last half century, IBISWorld has gathered one of the world's best teams to offer research in thousands of industries. In January 2023, Jared Ristoff offered a rosy outlook on the entire marketing industry.

"In December 2022, consumers' assessment of current business conditions improved. The share of consumers who said business conditions were 'good' increased 1.2% to 19.0%; the share of consumers who said business conditions were 'bad' fell 3.5%."

Ristoff's report found that an increased need for digital communication was driving the growth of the entire marketing industry. The report cited an expanded use of consumer tech-nology that will need to be matched by marketing consultants.

"Marketing consultants will be called upon to provide technical advice and strategies for rolling out new products and services," he wrote. "Customers will engage with companies and purchase products and services using an ever-expanding number of new devices."

The industry analysis also cited the importance of good project management skills as a key to future success, highlighting the importance of managing people and processes to meet deadlines and fully understand customer and client needs.

Expected Growth in Content Marketing

Technavio published a 2022 study (No Author, 2022, *Technavio*) that found content marketing will grow into a $487 billion industry by 2027, growing at an average annual rate of 15.8%. It named the United States, China, Japan, India, and Germany as top content marketing global markets and highlighted low barriers of entry into the marketplace as a key reason for continued success. The report connected rising social media use, a growing demand for digital content, and the increased access of mobile computing as key drivers for content.

Let's compare content marketing with digital advertising. The digital ad space saw substantial growth from 2017 to 2022, with a 15.5% average increase. That number will decline to 2.7% through 2027.

Authentic stories matter.

They're also more cost effective. DemandMetric, a marketing advisory firm, found that content marketing was 62% less expensive than traditional marketing and three times better at generating sales leads (No Author, 2022, *DemandMetric*).

Content Marketing Salary Overview

What is a fair starting salary and career overview for a CM?

Clearscope's 2022 content marketing salary report surveyed more than 300 CMs globally and found the average content marketer earned $95,379, a nearly 20% increase from 2020. The median salary was $83,750. The largest group of respondents earned between $60,000 and $80,000 annually (Daly, 2023).

B2B content marketers earn more than those in B2C, with the average B2B content marketing salary topping $97,000.

For people with three years' experience or less, the average salary was just more than $67,000. There's also a $15,000 spike when someone goes from a CM writer to a CM manager.

 $95,379 / YEAR

THE AVERAGE CONTENT MARKETER EARNS OVER $95,000 ANNUALLY

 **90% REMOTE**

NEARLY 90% OF THOSE SURVEYED WORK REMOTELY MOST OF THE TIME

 **CAREER GROWTH**

CMS HAVE THE OPPORTUNITY TO PROGRESS FROM INDIVIDUAL CONTRIBUTOR ROLES TO DIRECTOR AND EVENTUALLY V.P. AFTER THE 10-YEAR MARK

FIGURE 12.5 Salaries and benefits continue to increase for people entering the content marketing profession.

Source: Daly, 2023.

In general (and this is different at every organization), most CMs begin their careers as writers or coordinators. In one to three years, they move into a manager role. Within three to five years, they will likely become a director. At the ten-year mark, there's an opportunity to be a vice president. As you progress through your career from entry- to mid- and senior-level roles, the skills you're expected to possess expand. They start with content tasks, such as the creation of social media posts. As you progress into mid-level roles, you're expected to work on search engine optimization and write prospect- and customer-facing content, such as for email marketing. Finally, in senior level roles, you work cross-functionally, managing teams and leading strategic thought leadership content (described in Chapter 6) (No Author, 2019, *Fractl*).

Salary increases aren't the only industry perk (Daly, 2023). Nearly 90% of those surveyed work remotely most of the time. More than 85% report insurance benefits, and more than half get stipends for home office supplies and professional development.

CONCLUSION

Growing industry
Growing opportunity
Growing salary
Growing impact

The future is bright for content marketing and those who practice the craft. The technology driving CM is changing, and those working in the field will need to remain lifelong learners and stay constantly abreast of fast-moving changes being driven by transformational drivers such as artificial intelligence. General-purpose applications, such as Chat-GPT, as well as marketing-specific tools, can benefit CM with improved efficiency when applied thoughtfully to perform repetitive tasks or help with content ideation. As the number of tools being introduced to CMs continues to grow, so do the expected salaries and career growth. In 2022, the average content marketer earned $95,379, a nearly 20% increase from 2020, and CMs have the opportunity to progress from individual contributor roles as writers or coordinators to managers, directors, and eventually vice presidents after the ten-year mark.

From this book, you've learned about the CM journey and how to navigate a brand into the hearts and minds of potential customers. You've also seen how storytelling and research can come together to create powerful opportunities. And you've discovered dozens of different ways to tell meaningful stories that empower brands, businesses, and non-profits of any shape and size.

It's a big world out there. Effective content marketing helps brands make the most of it. Now it's time for you to share your story with the world and enjoy a fruitful career in the process.

Interview with the Experts: Paul Roetzer, Founder and CEO of Marketing AI Institute

Paul Roetzer, author of *Marketing Artificial Intelligence: AI, Marketing, and the Future of Business*, is the founder and CEO of Marketing AI Institute. His professional passion is helping marketing professionals increase their ethical understanding of AI use in marketing and strategic communication.

1. ***When did AI become this focal point of your professional world?***
   I came out of Ohio University School of Journalism, so I had a major in public relations and a specialization in business. I started a marketing agency and became HubSpot's first partner in 2007, which sort of threw us into the marketing automation, social media, and content marketing space. In 2011, I wrote my first book, *The Marketing Agency Blueprint*, about how to build a modern marketing agency; Brian Halligan, the former CEO of HubSpot, wrote the foreword.

   People would come to our agency and say, "We want to grow. We want to generate 500 leads next year. We want to grow revenue by $200,000. We want to launch this new product. How do we do it?"

   What I had come to believe was that humans were incapable of doing that optimally. When I graduated in 2000, there were 500 ways we could spend our client's marketing budget. Now there are 5,000. My theory was "What if IBM's Watson – whatever the AI behind it – can make predictions about what I should do for clients, what strategies to follow, what campaigns to run, what outcomes we can generate?"

   That was really the origin of it. A few years went by, and my second book, *The Marketing Performance Blueprint*, was the first time we publicly talked about AI. It was really just a research project to share what we were learning and what we think could happen to the industry if AI becomes a thing.

   Then that became the only thing marketers wanted me to discuss. So I started traveling the world talking about artificial intelligence in marketing and sales. We eventually launched the Marketing Artificial Intelligence Institute.

2. ***What is the biggest misconception of AI and marketing?***
   It is that AI is abstract and like sci-fi robots, the things we see in movies. I think a lot of marketers hesitate to pursue knowledge around it because they think it's computer science. That is not true at all.

3. ***What is step one to understanding AI?***
   You have to find an approachable way to understand the topic in a very practical way. As a marketer, you have to go experience it. That's what we're trying to teach people. What is AI? How does it work? What are some sample use cases?

4. ***Some brands are very good at collecting data. Some aren't. How do you get brands to harness their data or get it from somewhere else?***

Data is another area where I think brands may shy away from AI because they think they have to understand how data is structured and how to collect it. Data is core to parts of AI, like doing personalization at scale, for example. Brands need their CRM to be clean, and the data that's coming in has to be structured properly.

But if a brand wants to use a copywriting tool to help write blogs, social media posts, or ads, they don't need data. Just use your brand website – that's your data. The input is the text from the page.

I feel like marketers get thrown off when we start talking about data. In many use cases, it is not some complex thing where marketers need to go get data scientists to build data lakes.

5. ***What's next with AI that has you excited?***
In the near future, there are three kinds of businesses:

1. There's AI native.
   An entrepreneur looks at an industry and says, "I can build a smarter version of that. I know what AI is capable of. I can find inefficiencies across how they do their job, how they do marketing, sales, service communications; I'm just going to build a smarter version of it. We'll start a new company. We'll build a smarter version."
2. There's AI emerging.
   AI emergent companies see an opportunity to build smarter companies - and evolve. We've been doing this for 15 years and are pretty good at it. AI can create efficiencies that let us take our current staff and redistribute some of their time to do things we weren't even investing in before.
3. There's AI obsolete.
   These groups don't figure this stuff out and sit back and wait for it all to get done by everybody else. Over time, they will become less relevant because it will be too late – you can't flip a switch.

We're going to see a lot of innovation. Some of it is good; some is bad. Change is happening, and it's going to affect a lot of people.

CITATIONS

BasuMallick, C. "What is the metaverse? Meaning, features, and importance." *Spiceworks*. October 10, 2022. Retrieved from: www.spiceworks.com/tech/artificial-intelligence/articles/what-is-metaverse/

Buchanan, L., Cain Miller, C., Krolik, A., & Playford, A., "Did a fourth grader write this? Or the new chatbot?" *New York Times*. December 26, 2022.

Daly, J. "The content marketing salary report." *Superpath*. January 3, 2023. Retrieved from: www.super path.co/blog/content-marketing-salary-report

Davenport, T.H., Guha, A., & Grewal, D. "How to design an IA marketing strategy." *Harvard Business Review*. July 2021.

Dawes, R.M. "The robust beauty of improper linear models in decision making." *American Psychologist*. 1979.

Marr, B. "Disney: The metaverse, digital transformation, and the future of storytelling." *Forbes*. October 7, 2022.

Martin, H. "A glimpse into Disneyland's future? Disney may one day project 3-D images for individual guests." *Los Angeles Times*. January 7, 2022.

Murray, D. "139: How to use AI as a marketer, with Meghan Keaney Anderson." *The Marketing Millennials Podcast*. February 16, 2023. Retrieved from: https://open.spotify.com/episode/2BZrymih3iFwmRG TvkOHyH?si=7606057a304443ea

No Author. "A guide to marketing genius: Content marketing." *Demand Metric*. No date. Retrieved from: www.demandmetric.com/content/content-marketing-infographic

No Author. "Content marketing market by objective, platform, and geography – forecast and analysis 2023–2027." *Technavio*. December 2022. Retrieved from: www.technavio.com/report/content-marketing-market-size-industry-analysis

No Author. "Here comes the Bing Chatbot – Microsoft's ChatGPT for search has arrived, forcing Google's hand." *Forbes*. February 9, 2023.

No Author. "The metaverse is the future of digital connection." No date. Retrieved from: https://about. meta.com/metaverse/

No Author. "The most desirable content marketing job skills to get you hired in 2019." *Fractl*. 2019. Retrieved from: www.frac.tl/work/marketing-research/content-marketing-job-skills/

Ristoff, J. "Marketing consultants in the US." *IBISWorld*. January 2023.

Thormundsson, B. "Global Total Corporate Artificial Intelligence (AI) Investment from 2015 to 2021," June 23, 2022. Retrieved from https://www.statista.com/statistics/941137/ai-investment-and-funding-worldwide/

Index

product benefits: buyer education 36; example 174; home page element 123; introduction 182; product collateral type 173–174

product brochure 180–186; content, flows *188–189*; elements 180, 182, 185; example (Keysight) *181*; information, inclusion 185; interior pages 182; interior pages, example *184–185*; last page/back cover 182, 185; last page/back cover, example *186*; opening pages, example *183*; storytelling, inclusion 185

product collateral 68, 171; CM knowledge 174; elements 172–175; format, product brochure 180–186; format, product flier 187–188; format, product web page 175–179; images/links (web page element) 176

product description: clarity 173; example 174; product collateral type 173–174; web page element 176

product features 176; change 19; home page element 123; product collateral type 174–175

product flier 187–188; content, flows *188–189*; elements 187; front page/back page 187–188; secondary content 187

product positioning 15, 22–29; initiation 15–16; Who, Where, Why, What (four Ws) 16, 24–26

Product, Price, Place, Promotion (4Ps) 53

product web page 175–179; call to action, white paper involvement 215; information supply, CM knowledge 179

"*Professional Development Map*" 81

professional videographers/photographers, storage need 27

project: description process 217; kickoff meeting, core elements (development) 213

prospective buyers: advocacy 176; anonymous prospective buyers, content attraction 65; attraction/interest 66, 187; content choices 4–5; content engagement 235; conversion 66; differentiation 173; education 64, 180, 190; fear/hesitation, reduction 216; inspiring 232; needs, meeting 58; purchase process 190; reaching 121; selling point 223; trust, building 221; webinar registration 161; work/appeal 1

prospectors (new product development strategy) 16

protagonist (success), action (impact) 147

provider selection drivers 41

pseudo-events 86

public relations (PR): earned media, comparison 96–97; success, discussion 243; teams, self-measurement 243; teams, usage 96; usage 9

Pulizzi, Joe 10, 63, 121, 133

purchasing decision: criteria (TrustRadius study) 172; involvement, identification 25

QR codes, usage 238

qualified leads, receiving 233

questions and answers (webinars) 164–165

quotes: home page element 124; news release element 98

Rackspace, customized solutions 17

reason to believe (RTB) 74

referral traffic, ToF measurement item 235

repurposing: content, repurposing 69, 171; genres, repurposing 58; importance 53; rapidity (ChatGPT benefits) 252; tactics 193; white papers, repurposing 215

research and development (R&D): departments, technical personnel responsibility 18; product management/planning, interactions 30; prototype 19; schedule 19; teams, assistance 214; usage 31

researching, process *64*

resolution (three-act play component) 78, 79–80

return on investment (ROI): CM avoidance 232; display 168; earning 8; elevation 251; performance measure 232; reporting (reduction), AI (usage) 249

Revella, Adele 25–26, 36; interview 48–52

Ries, Al 23

Ristoff, Jared 254

Rockefeller, John D. 95

Roetzer, Paul 246–247, 249; interview 256–258

Rose, Robert 1, 86–87, 88; storytelling Q&A 88–90

RSS folder, usage 237

rundown (webinars) 162, *163*

Rust, Scott 30

salary, overview/comparison 255–256

sales (CM success metric) 229

sales enablement 32; content 19

Sales Hub (platform offering) 178, *178*

sales qualified leads (SQLs) 61

Says Who? test 74

Schultz, Don 90

Printed in the United States
by Baker & Taylor Publisher Services